The World of Small States

Volume 7

Series Editors

More information about this series at http://www.springer.com/series/15142

Anne-Marie Brady • Baldur Thorhallsson
Editors

Small States and the New Security Environment

Springer

Editors
Anne-Marie Brady
Department of Political Sciences and International Relations
University of Canterbury
Christchurch, New Zealand

Baldur Thorhallsson
Faculty of Political Science and the Centre for Small State Studies
University of Iceland
Reykjavik, Iceland

ISSN 2627-5996 ISSN 2627-6003 (electronic)
The World of Small States
ISBN 978-3-030-51528-7 ISBN 978-3-030-51529-4 (eBook)
https://doi.org/10.1007/978-3-030-51529-4

This Springer imprint is published by the registered company Springer Nature Switzerland AG.
The registered company address is: Gewerbestrasse 11, 6330 Cham, Switzerland

Contents

Chapter 1
Small States and the Turning Point in Global Politics

Anne-Marie Brady and Baldur Thorhallsson

A series of events has put massive pressure on the previously stable international order and the rule-based multilateral global system of governance in the last few years—to name just a few: Putin government's disruptive foreign policy, the disastrous impact of Brexit on the economy and politics of both the UK and the EU, President Trump's iconoclastic foreign and trade policy that alienates allies as much as it affects strategic competitors, Xi Jinping's promotion of a new China-centred bloc, the Belt and Road Initiative and the pressure on countries to accept Huawei for 5G, China's deepening security partnership with Russia, and the global impact of the devastating Covid-19 pandemic; meanwhile, smaller Middle Eastern powers are also caught in a two-way regional Cold War (Iran versus Saudi Arabia; Saudi, United Arab Emirates, and Egypt versus Turkey, Qatar, and the Muslim Brotherhood), plus another set of tensions that emerge from an actual hot war, the Syrian civil war, a war that has been inflamed by the failing global order and return of great power and regional power competition. In recent years, all states, large and small, have further been challenged by the spread of radical terrorist acts on a global scale, the refugee crisis, greater trade protectionism, and the ever-worsening effects of climate change.

The formerly stable post-World War II international order is coming to an end, but the new global order is as yet unclear. Earlier expectations about a multipolar order emerging, characterised by cooperation among the great powers, has failed to

---

A.-M. Brady
Department of Political Sciences and International Relations, University of Canterbury, Christchurch, New Zealand
e-mail: anne-marie.brady@canterbury.ac.nz

B. Thorhallsson (✉)
Faculty of Political Science and the Centre for Small State Studies, University of Iceland, Reykjavik, Iceland
e-mail: baldurt@hi.is

A.-M. Brady, B. Thorhallsson (eds.), *Small States and the New Security Environment*, The World of Small States 7,
https://doi.org/10.1007/978-3-030-51529-4_1

come to fruition.[1] The world is now seeing a return of both "might is right" politics and the reassertion of spheres of influence.

The very nature of conflict and how we define it is shifting too as foreign political interference, terrorism, and cyberattacks are on the increase. The boundaries between domestic and foreign policy are becoming less and less distinct. Porous borders, whether climactic, cyber, or physical, make it impossible for even small island nations such as Iceland and New Zealand, the home nations of the two editors of this book, to remain remote from the changing global order.

The new security environment is especially challenging for small states. Time and again, at great turning points in history, small states have been the pawns of great power competition. Small states are heavily affected by global shifts in power, and they must rely on the rule-based international order to protect their rights. Small-state security depends on stability, predictability, and cooperative solutions to global problems.

Small states are generally defined as those nations that are small in landmass, population, economy, and military capacity. Yet in the era of hybrid warfare, the old concepts of size of territory as a measure of relative power may no longer be as significant as the size of a nation's maritime or space boundaries—or cyber defence, national resilience, and unity, plus digital diplomacy capacity.[2]

Henderson defined the characteristics of small states as follows: 1) low participation in international affairs due to limited resources; 2) narrow scope, as limited resources lead to the limiting of foreign policy interests and the small size of the state's foreign affairs bureaucracy restricts its ability to have a broad international role; 3) economic focus, a tendency to focus foreign affairs interests on economic issues and trade; 4) internationalism, as small states tend to rely heavily on multilateralism, international organisations, agreements, and alliances to protect national interests; 5) moral emphasis, as small states tend to be moralistic but have no resources to back up their rhetoric; and 6) tendency to be risk avoidant and fearful of alienating powerful states, though occasionally they can be risk takers.[3]

Small states make up half of the membership of the United Nations. Our three-year research project "Small States and the New Security Environment" (SSANSE) has assessed the defence and foreign policy choices and challenges of small states in the North Atlantic Treaty Organization (NATO) such Albania, Denmark, Estonia, Iceland, Latvia, Lithuania, and Norway; NATO partner states like Armenia, Bahrain, Finland, Georgia, New Zealand, Qatar, and United Arab Emirates; as well as the situation in small island developing states (including overseas territories of NATO member France) in Oceania. All of these states must face up to the new security

[1]Chris Seed, Secretary of Foreign Affairs and Trade, New Zealand, "Opening Remarks to Foreign Affairs, Defence and Trade Select Committee," New Zealand Parliament, December 12, 2020, https://www.parliament.nz/resource/en-NZ/52SCFD_EVI_92819_FD3013/51eea4ab1967c2ba7bdddb9d7d6824f0f8ba2e6e.

[2]See Chaban et al. (2019).

[3]Henderson (1991).

environment and develop a nimble and proactive strategy to deal with it. Yet one of the characteristic weak points of small states is that they tend to be deficit in the dedicated think tanks and research institutes that provide governments with the deep policy analysis and contestable policy advice they need in a changing, challenging, geostrategic situation.

The SSANSE project is a preparedness initiative, examining the current defence and foreign policy choices and challenges of small states. The SSANSE project contributes new thinking on how small states can respond to the "new normal" in international security. We asked researchers to examine a series of questions, including the following:

- How can small states survive and prosper in the current unpredictable and hostile security environment?
- How can small states best deal with new challenges, such as cyberattacks, political interference, and climate change?
- How can small states compensate for their structural weaknesses?
- Should small states work more to partner with other like-minded small and medium power governments and give up the notion that they need to seek shelter with one or other of the great powers?
- Is neutrality or pacifism the ultimate goal of an independent foreign policy path?
- How can small states make themselves more resilient in the new security environment?
- For this book in particular, we looked at how the small states of NATO and partners are adjusting to the new geopolitical, geo-economic, security environment. Do they need political, economic and societal shelter provided by larger states and international organizations?
- Do NATO small states manage the tension between alliance commitment and economics differently from non-NATO small states?
- What are the core strategic interests of the small states we studied, and how can they be strengthened?
- How can NATO better work with its partner small states in future?

The SSANSE research team organised several conferences and workshops in New Zealand, Iceland, and the USA to develop the ideas of the project. We also provided many open and closed-door policy briefings to policymakers as our analysis had a strong policy focus. The SSANSE Project leaders, Anne-Marie Brady and Baldur Thorhallsson, and co-directors, Margarita Šešelgytė and Alan Tidwell, led a team of international emerging, as well as senior, researchers to create a series of written projects responding to the parameters of investigation. The result of all this work was two edited books,[4] including this one; doctoral and masters' theses; op eds aimed at the wider public; and a series of policy briefs targeted at

[4]Brady (2019).

policymakers.[5] Our project has helped train a cohort of international young researchers on small state studies. We hope they will use this knowledge and training as a stepping stone to careers in diplomacy, defence, and academia.

There is an extensive body of research on small state theory upon which the SSANSE project was built, which exceeds what can be summarised or addressed here.[6] The University of Iceland's Centre for Small State Studies has fostered a number of research teams on small state studies resulting in influential publications such as Archer, Bailes, and Wivel's study of small states and international security; Ingebritsen, Neumann, Gstöhl, and Beyer's study on small states and international relations; and Bailes, Herolf, and Sundelius's study on Nordic states as small states.[7] Efraim Karsh has analysed the question of small states and neutrality.[8] Jeanne A. K. Hey has provided a useful overview of small state theory,[9] as did the work of Henderson, Jackson, and Kennaway in their studies on New Zealand as a small state.[10] Larsen has discussed the need for new thinking on NATO strategic policy and the need to work more closely with NATO partner states in order to respond to the "new normal" in security.[11]

Overall, the majority of scholarly studies on small states have tended to focus on the small states of Europe. There has never before been a study specifically focusing on the foreign policies of the small states of NATO or the small states of Eastern Europe, Middle East and North Africa (MENA), or those of Oceania. Nor has any study evaluated small states from the perspective of NATO's strategic priorities, particularly in the light of the current global strategic environment.

Much of the small state theoretical literature is on the experiences of and outcomes for specific small states. We found that there is a scarcity in approaches and theories that draw lessons about small states in general. This is problematic since

---

[5]SSANSE Pop Up think tank at University of Canterbury: https://canterbury.ac.nz/arts/research/ssanse/pop-up-think-tank/.

[6]Alcala and Ciccone (2004), pp. 613–646; Alesina and Spolaore (2003); Archer and Nugent (2002), pp. 1–10; Archer et al. (2014); Bailes et al. (2013); Bailes et al. (2006); Bailes et al. (2016), pp. 9–26; Baker (1959); Barston (1973); Brady (2019); Carvalho and Neumann (2015); Cooper and Shaw (2009); Corbett and Connell (2015), pp. 435–459; Deudney (2007); Easterly and Kraay (2000), pp. 2013–2027; Finnemore and Sikkink (2001), pp. 391–416; Frankel and Romer (1999), pp. 379–399; Henderson et al. (1980); Hey (2003); Ingebritsen et al. (2006); Karsh (2010); Kattel and Thorhallsson (2013); Katzenstein (1984); Katzenstein (1985); Mathisen (1971); Neumann and Sieglinde Gstöhl (2006); Olafsson (1998); Rokkann and Urwin (1983); Steinmetz and Wivel (2010); Thorhallsson (2012); Thorhallsson (2010); Thorhallsson (2011), pp. 324–336; Thorhallsson (2019); Thorhallsson and Steinsson (2017); Vital (1967); Wohlforth et al. (2017), pp. 526–546.

[7]Archer et al. (2014), Bailes et al. (2013) and Bailes et al. (2006).

[8]Karsh (2010).

[9]Hey (2003).

[10]Henderson et al. (1980) and Henderson and Kennaway (1991).

[11]Jeffrey A. Larsen, "Time to Face Reality: Priorities for NATO's 2016 Warsaw Summit," Research Paper 126, NATO Defense College, 15 January 2016.

scholars of small states emphasise that small and large states are vastly different in terms of needs and challenges, and this ought to lead to different logics of behaviour.

The lack of theorising about small states means that there is a dearth of simple abstract frameworks for thinking intelligently about small states. In a sense, theories are like maps. They are intended to simplify the world by removing unnecessary details in an attempt to make it easier for us to navigate it. Unfortunately, there are few maps to guide our thinking about small states. This means that scholars of small states often have to rely on realist, liberal, and constructivist theories as they think about small states.

A common complaint is that both realist and liberal approaches are too imprecise for analysing small states' foreign policy. Realist theories are primarily concerned with large states and are derived from studies of great power politics. Critics of constructivism claim that it is not a comprehensive theory about international politics but rather a framework for thinking about social facts. This means that there are no consistent lessons that can be drawn from constructivism about small states, unless care is taken to craft specific theories about small states rooted in constructivist theory.

To fill the theoretical gap, a framework referred to as shelter theory has been developed over the last decade by scholars at the Centre for Small State Studies in Iceland.[12] This theoretical framework hopes to guide scholars, students, and policymakers to better evaluate the options and policies of small states, as well as forecast outcomes for small states.

Of course, like any other theory or framework, it is an un-nuanced depiction. It may tell us a lot about the challenges and opportunities facing small states, and their general patterns of behaviour, but it cannot perfectly explain every single action that a small state takes. The shelter theory framework is derived from the challenges and needs that the literature documents as unique to small states, as well as a large literature on the actions that small states have tended to take to alleviate the burdens and satisfy the needs that come with smallness.

Shelter theory holds that small states need to seek political, economic, and societal shelter. What this means is that there are certain inherent political, economic, and societal problems that small states face (or problems that small states need shelter from) and certain actions that small states take to alleviate these problems (what the framework refers to as "shelter-seeking").[13]

Small states need political, economic, and societal shelter provided by larger states and international organisations in order to thrive and cope with crises. Political shelter takes the form of direct and visible diplomatic or military backing and other strategic coverage at any given time of need provided by another state or an international organisation, as well as the protection provided by international rules and norms.

---

[12] Thorhallsson (2010, 2011, 2019).

[13] Thorhallsson (2019).

Small states are militarily weak as they have fewer resources, including human resources, which can be put towards military use. They lack the economies of scale needed for a strong military with diverse capabilities. Historically, small states' vulnerability to conquest and coercion was seen as their main vulnerability. Small states lack the resources to support a large diplomatic force, and they are unable to keep diplomatic missions in every corner of the world. Small state external affairs representatives often have to be generalists, as opposed to issue experts, which risks undercutting the knowledge and deliberation behind small state foreign policies and negotiations.

Due to the aforementioned disadvantages, whether explicitly or not, small states rely on the security assurances and military assistance of larger states or alliances. Small states also need diplomatic backing or assistance from other states. Shifting negotiations from bilateral to multilateral venues is favourable for small states as the norms and rules of international organisations can constrain the brute power of large states and reduce the power asymmetry between the large and the small states.[14]

Economic shelter can take the form of direct economic assistance, a currency union, help from an external financial authority, beneficial loans, favourable market access, or a common market; it could even include access to strategic goods such as medical equipment, as was shown during the Covid-19 pandemic. Economic shelter can be provided by a more powerful country or by an international organisation.[15] Small states have small domestic markets, which means that their economies are more reliant on foreign trade, tourism, and foreign direct investment than those of large states. This dependence on external markets exposes small states to the instability of global markets and can lead to more volatility in the economies of small states. Small state economies rely on an open and stable world economy where they can trade freely.

Small state economies also tend to lack sectoral diversity. So unlike large and diverse economies, small state economic growth may fluctuate wildly depending on what occurs within a single sector. This means that small states frequently experience more booms and busts. When a crisis occurs, small state governments may lack the means to lift themselves up on their own. In contrast, medium and large powers have greater ability to redistribute resources from one sector or from one affected region to another and are thus able to dampen the blow of a temporary crisis. Yet in crisis situations—like Covid-19—the smallness of the small state economy can be an advantage, allowing small state governments greater agility to make policy adjustments.

Small states need to position themselves in a way where they access economic assistance in times of crisis. Small state governments do this by joining and supporting international organisations, such as the International Monetary Fund, or

[14]Thorhallsson (2019).

[15]Thorhallsson (2010, 2011).

by developing strong ties to larger states. Economic shelter enables small states to reduce the frequency and severity of economic crises and to achieve greater prosperity.

Societal shelter refers to the importance of cultural transactions, the transfer of new ideas, norms, lifestyles, ideologies, myths, and ritual systems in order for small states to compensate for the lack of expertise in their small communities.[16] Traditional international relations theory tends to focus on the pursuit of security and prosperity, which are indeed important. However, shelter theory also holds that small states require societal shelter and that this need can account for some of the behaviour of small states. The extent of societal shelter that a small state has may also account for the quality of life within the small state. Small states' pursuit of societal shelter is potentially as important as the pursuit for political and economic shelter. This is one way that shelter theory clearly distinguishes itself from other alliance theories.

In the societal realm, small states may be at a disadvantage relative to larger societies. Some small states have homogenous populations, so there is a greater risk that these states may experience social stagnation, as there are potentially fewer unorthodox and influential innovators, artists, entrepreneurs, and leaders from which to draw on. Much more so than larger states, small states rely on interactions with other cultures, ideas, and ideologies to ensure that there is a healthy marketplace of ideas. Many small states take active measures to avoid isolation by importing innovation and ideas from other cultures. It is through constant interaction with other cultures, ideas, and ideologies that a society evolves and moves forward.

Shelter theory addresses three interrelated issues of common concerns to small states: the reduction of risk before a possible crisis event, assistance in absorbing shocks in times of crises, and help in recovering after such an event. In short, shelter theory posits that small states will need some form of external shelter in order to survive and prosper. They are dependent on the economic, political, and societal shelter provided by larger states, as well as regional and international organisations.[17] It should be noted that for many small and medium-sized countries, shelter is quite complicated. As the case studies in our book richly illustrate, small states may seek security shelter from traditional friends, diplomatic shelter from those same partners, while leaning heavily in to the multilateral system, and they seek economic shelter from a range of countries, not necessarily the same as those powers that provide them political, societal, and security shelter.

Shelter relations can have costs for the beneficiary. For instance, the post-2008 global financial crisis European Union-International Monetary Fund (EU-IMF) rescue packages were provided with strict conditions regarding states' domestic policies. NATO and EU shelter may carry considerable financial as well as political

---

[16]Thorhallsson (2019); Thorhallsson, "The Icelandic Collapse." For a historical account on the importance of political, economic, and cultural features in centre-periphery relations see Rokkan and Unwin (1983).

[17]Thorhallsson (2019).

costs for small states.[18] The shelter provider tends to expect the protected state to follow its foreign policy preferences, and this may have a negative impact on small state domestic policies and domestic public opinion.[19] Seeking shelter can potentially cause rifts within small societies, which can be seen in the deep divisions in Iceland and New Zealand in relation to these two countries' special relationship with the US during the Cold War,[20] and up to the present day, and controversy over present-day relations with China.

The pursuit of shelter, its costs, benefits, or lack thereof, should be carefully examined by small state policymakers. Shelter theory could help shed light on a small state's bilateral political, economic, and societal relations with larger powers such as China, Russia, and the USA. It may also help to evaluate the cost-benefit balance of multilateral cooperation. The choice of a shelter provider will always depend on the proportion of benefits to cost.

Our book *Small States and the New Security Environment* uses the theory of shelter to examine how some representative small states in NATO, MENA, and Oceania are responding to new and old security threats in the new security environment. One third of the membership of the North Atlantic Treaty Organization (NATO) are small states, and most of NATO's partners are small states too. All the major NATO powers have strategic interests in the regions of their partner states—so any security challenges or new developments there are of direct interest to NATO priorities. NATO is at a pivotal point as it responds to the complex new security environment. The Alliance is reassessing these threats and planning how to respond. The new security environment is forcing NATO to consider re-conceptualising its Strategic Concept, set at the 2010 Lisbon Summit, which is currently defined as collective defence, crisis management, and cooperative security.

The small states of NATO such as Albania, Iceland, Latvia, Lithuania, Latvia, and Norway and NATO partner or neighbouring small states such as Armenia, Bahrain, Kuwait, New Zealand, Qatar, and United Arab Emirates are on the front lines of the challenges in the new security environment. The global great powers of China, Russia, and the USA are once again jostling for dominance. Each small state has finite resources to protect itself, so each must find their own way to manage relations between the dominant powers while protecting their national interests.

Small States and the New Security Environment extends theoretical debates on the role of small states in the changing international system, as well as on the issue of how states manage their relations between the major powers in the new security environment. We examine how two representative small states, Norway and New Zealand, engage in policymaking, lobbying, and maintaining shelter in the changing politics of Washington, DC. We look at small states' risks and opportunities related to the global proliferation of armed drones and the challenge hybrid warfare poses for traditional defence mechanisms. We discuss a case study of shelter

---

[18] Bailes and Thorhallsson (2013) and Katzenstein (1998).

[19] Thorhallsson and Gunnarsson (2017).

[20] Thorhallsson and Steinsson (2017).

balancing in action, examining how tiny Albania manages political interference attempts by China while developing economic links at the same time as maintaining strong political links with the USA while leaning in close to NATO and working hard to get into the EU. We look at how small states like Denmark have responded to Russia's pressure in the North Atlantic by building a NATO West Nordic Security Zone. We look at the New Slovak Security Strategy in the context of V4 and Euro-Atlantic security environment, with a specific focus on Visegrad security and defence cooperation and their contribution to NATO. We analyse how the Baltic states have engaged in close regional defence cooperation and societal resilience strategies in order to respond to increased Russian aggression in Eastern Europe.

We also look at small European neutrals such as Ireland and Malta and examine their relations with NATO. We found they have extensive cooperation with NATO and use their neutrality to gain greater status and influence in their relations with NATO. Finally, we analyse the foreign and security policy dilemmas of Armenia, Qatar, Bahrain, Kuwait, and United Arab Emirates (four out of six members of the Gulf Cooperation Council (GCC)), all of which cooperate with NATO within NATO's Istanbul Cooperation Initiative.

We could not have achieved all of this research without the support of NATO Science for Peace and Security (NATO-SPS), which provided student scholarships for the emerging scholars of our project, travel support for our workshops, and funding for the project administration at the Centre for Small States Studies in Iceland. We also benefited from crucial conference funding and additional graduate assistance funding provided by the University of Canterbury in Christchurch, New Zealand; the New Zealand Political Studies Association; the Amiya Foundation; the Wigram Foundation; and the Woodrow Wilson International Center for Scholars.

The editors are grateful for the support of their families throughout the life of this project and for the hard work of all the researchers who tried out the project ideas within the various activities we all organised. With finite resources, our project has demonstrated the capacity within small states to pool resources and expertise to come up with proactive policy choices.

We dedicate this book, with admiration and respect, to Alyson J. K. Bailes (1949–2016), diplomat, scholar and polyglot, and friend to so many, whose ideas helped to shape thinking in the project.

The current global operating environment is unpredictable and unstable. States face a long transition towards a new global order. Small state governments must be adaptable, resilient, and entrepreneurial in their response to the new security environment. Small states can compensate for their inbuilt vulnerability by adopting strengthening measures such as digital diplomacy, cyber defence, and foreign interference public awareness campaigns. They can partner with other like-minded small and medium states and work to reinforce shared global norms. The new security environment requires governments to be proactive rather than reactive.

Small can be huge. We are indeed at a turning point in global affairs. But with careful actions and proactive thinking, small states can secure their future and strengthen national security and independence.

References

Alcala F, Ciccone A (2004) Trade and productivity. Q J Econ 119:613–646
Alesina A, Spolaore E (2003) The size of nations. MIT Press, London and Cambridge
Archer C, Nugent N (2002) Introduction: small states and EU. Curr Polit Econ Europe 11(1):1–10
Archer C, Bailes AJK, Wivel A (eds) (2014) Small states and international security: Europe and beyond. Routledge, Abingdon
Bailes AJK, Thorhallsson B (2013) Instrumentalizing the European Union in small state strategies. Eur Integr 35(2)
Bailes AJK, Herolf G, Sundelius B (eds) (2006) The Nordic countries and the European security and defence policy. SIPRI–Oxford University Press, Oxford
Bailes AJK, Johnstone RL, Thorhallsson B (2013) Scotland as an independent small state: where would it seek shelter? Sjórnmál og stjórnsýsla 9(1)
Bailes AJK, Thorhallsson B, Thayer BA (2016) Alliance theory and small state alliance 'shelter': the complexities of small state alliance behaviour. Third World Thematics 1(1):9–26
Baker FA (1959) The power of small states: diplomacy in World War II. University of Chicago Press, Chicago
Barston RP (1973) The other powers: studies in the foreign policy of small states. Allen and Unwin, London
Brady A-M (ed) (2019) Small states and the changing global order: New Zealand faces the future. Springer, Basel
Carvalho B, Neumann I (2015) Small states and status seeking: Norway's quest for higher standing, 1st edn. Routledge, Oxford
Chaban N, Kelly S, Brady A-M (2019) Small states and new era of public diplomacy: New Zealand and digital diplomacy. In: Brady A-M (ed) Small states and the changing global order: New Zealand faces the future. Springer, Basel
Cooper AF, Shaw T (eds) (2009) The diplomacies of small states: between vulnerability and resilience. Palgrave MacMillian, London
Corbett J, Connell J (2015) All the world is a stage: global governance, human resources, and the 'problem' of smallness. Pac Rev 28(3):435–459
Deudney D (2007) Bounding power: republican security theory from the Polis to the global village. Princeton University Press, Princeton
Easterly W, Kraay A (2000) Small states, small problems? Income, growth, and volatility in small states. World Dev 28(11):2013–2027
Finnemore M, Sikkink K (2001) Taking stock: the constructivist research program in international relations and comparative politics. Annu Rev Polit Sci 4:391–416
Frankel JA, Romer D (1999) Does trade cause growth? Am Econ Rev 89(3):379–399
Henderson J (1991) New Zealand and the foreign policy of small states. In: Henderson J, Kennaway R (eds) Beyond New Zealand II. Longman Paul, Auckland
Henderson J, Kennaway R (eds) (1991) Beyond New Zealand II: foreign policy in the 1990s. Longman Paul, Auckland
Henderson J, Jackson K, Kennaway R (eds) (1980) Beyond New Zealand: the foreign policy of a small state. Methuen, Auckland
Hey JAK (ed) (2003) Small states in world politics: explaining foreign policy behavior. Lynne Rienner, Boulder/London
Ingebritsen C, Neumann I, Gstöhl S, Beyer J (eds) (2006) Small states in international relations. University of Washington Press/University of Icelandic Press, Seattle/Seattle and Reykjavík
Karsh E (2010) Neutrality and small states. Routledge, Abingdon
Kattel R, Thorhallsson B (2013) Neo-liberal small states and economic crisis: lessons for democratic corporatism. J Baltic Stud 44(1)
Katzenstein P (1984) Corporatism and change: Austria, Switzerland, and the politics of industry. Cornell University Press, Ithaca and London

Katzenstein P (1985) Small states in world markets: industrial policy in Europe. Cornell University Press, Ithaca and London
Katzenstein P (ed) (1998) Tamed power: Germany in Europe. Cornell University Press, Ithaca
Mathisen T (1971) The functions of small states in the strategies of the great powers. Universitetsforlaget, Oslo
Neumann IB, Sieglinde Gstöhl S (2006) Introduction. In: Ingebritsen C, Neumann I, Gstöhl S, Beyer J (eds) Small states in international relations. University of Washington Press, Seattle
Olafsson BG (1998) Small states and the global system: analysis and illustrations from the case of Iceland. Ashgate, Aldershot
Rokkan S, Unwin DW (1983) Economy, territory, identity: politics of west European peripheries. Sage, London
Rokkann S, Urwin DW (eds) (1983) Economy, territory, identity: politics of west European peripheries. Sage Publications, London; USA, New Delhi
Steinmetz R, Wivel A (eds) (2010) Small states in Europe: challenges and opportunities. Ashgate Publishing, Aldershot
Thorhallsson B (2010) The Icelandic crash and its consequences: a small state without economic and political shelter. In: Steinmetz R, Wivel A (eds) Small states in Europe: challenges and opportunities. Ashgate Publishing
Thorhallsson B (2011) Domestic buffer versus external shelter: viability of small states in the new globalised economy. European Political Science Symposium. Eur Consortium Polit Res 10:324–336
Thorhallsson B (2012) Small states in the UN Security Council: means of influence? Hague J Diplomacy 7
Thorhallsson B (ed) (2019) Small states and shelter theory, Iceland's external affairs, 1st edn. Routledge, New York
Thorhallsson B, Gunnarsson P (2017) Iceland's relations with its regional powers: alignment with the EU-US sanctions on Russia. NUPI Working Paper 874. Norwegian Institute of International Affairs, Oslo
Thorhallsson B, Steinsson S (2017) Small state foreign policy. Oxford Research Encyclopaedia of Politics. http://oxfordre.com/politics/view/10.1093/acrefore/9780190228637.001.0001/acrefore-9780190228637-e-484
Vital D (1967) The inequality of states: a study of the small power in international relations. Clarendon Press, Oxford
Wohlforth W, de Carvalho B, Leira H, Neumann I (2017) Moral authority and status in international relations: good states and the social dimension of status seeking. Rev Int Stud 44(3):526–546

Anne-Marie Brady is the NATO partner project director (PPD) of the Small States and the New Security Environment (SSANSE) Project, funded by NATO-SPS from 2017 to 2020. She is an expert on Chinese politics, polar politics, Pacific politics, and New Zealand foreign policy. Professor Brady is a Global Fellow at the Woodrow Wilson Centre in Washington, DC. In 2014, she was appointed to a two-year term on the World Economic Forum's Global Action Council on the Arctic.

Baldur Thorhallsson is a Professor of Political Science and founder of the Centre for Small State Studies at the University of Iceland and NATO Project Director (NPD) of the SSANSE Project. His research focus has primarily been on small state studies, European integration, and Iceland's domestic and foreign policy. His latest book is titled "Small States and Shelter Theory: Iceland's External Affairs". He has been a visiting fellow and taught on small states and European integration at several universities, such as the Queen Mary University of London, the Military Academy of Lithuania, and Williams College (MA, USA).

Chapter 2
Building Shelter in Washington: The Politics of Small State Engagement

Alan C. Tidwell

2.1 Introduction

Small states seeking shelter with the United States face the daunting challenge of ensuring that both their economic and security relationships are durable. Building shelter requires both establishing a standing functional relationship with both the executive and legislative branches of the US government and creating a platform for the advocacy of critical interests. The specific nature of these relationships and political operations necessary to create and sustain them varies substantially. With this in mind, the three case studies below illustrate the diversity of engagement options available to shelter-seeking states according to their position relative to the great power.

Israel presents a unique case study insofar as its politics reflects its singular position in the international arena. The lessons of the Israeli case, however, can have broad applicability inasmuch as they demonstrate the range and depth of options available to states with substantial interests in US politics. The Norwegian case frames a structure for long-term engagement exemplary of a small state with a broad array of interests that are not limited exclusively to one area, such as defence. Finally, the case of New Zealand reflects the advantages and drawbacks of a shelter-seeking strategy defined by a small number of key critical interests focusing on free trade.

The overlap and contrast of the three cases tell a story of shelter seeking that is instructive of how small states engage with the US government and the challenges they face with respect to managing the politics of shelter with the US. Many small

A. C. Tidwell (✉)
SSANSE, Georgetown University, Washington, DC, USA
e-mail: act35@georgetown.edu

A.-M. Brady, B. Thorhallsson (eds.), *Small States and the New Security Environment*, The World of Small States 7,
https://doi.org/10.1007/978-3-030-51529-4_2

states seeking shelter vie for political attention and access. Similarly, decision-makers in Washington must manage numerous small states as they seek attention.

2.2 The Politics of Shelter

The quality of shelter varies depending upon the relationship between the sheltering and sheltered states. Shelter's contractual nature means that not all shelter relationships are the same. Moldova's shelter relationship with the US compares poorly with Denmark's. Numerous factors account for the variance in shelter relationships. Some of the variance arises from factors that cannot be changed, such as geography, whereas some variance comes from the behaviour of states. Writing about alliance relationships with the US, Fruhling observes that treaties create "… both expectations and obligations of support…" for the parties. The signatories "… must decide how much emphasis they will place on either aspect when they decide how to…" implement their agreement. The manner in which such agreements are implemented is "…inherently political".[1] While small states may well have a broad panoply of foreign policy settings with the US, how and whether they are honoured is ultimately political. The politics of shelter focuses more on how states engage rather than on what issues they pursue. Hardly passive when facing these political decisions, states will seek to influence the outcome in their favour. Larger states, such as the UK or Japan, do not merely wait for Washington to decide the fate of their relationships. Instead, London and Tokyo actively pursue their preferred outcomes. The same can be said of many small states seeking shelter in Washington. Even those small states that do not have a formal treaty with the US must contend with the political nature of their relationship. Like their larger cousins, some small states manage the sheltering relationships better than others.

Many states seek shelter with the US, and this fact alone makes the politics in Washington challenging. The nature of decision-making in Washington also creates difficulties for small states, which must contend with the divided nature of the US government. Finally, recent shifts in the American political landscape have forced some small states to reconsider the way in which they engage with Washington. For many small states, their sheltering relationship with Washington is weak, if not non-existent. Fiji, Mauritius and Guinea-Bissau, for example, have similar relationships with the US. Their visibility in Washington is minimal, as is their capacity to influence US decision-making. The shifting American political landscape also leaves them largely unnoticed. On the other hand, Israel remains the pre-eminent sheltering small state, although Israel's unique relationship with the US makes it difficult for other states to replicate. Norway serves an interesting example of a sheltering relationship because of its diverse policy agenda. Finally, New Zealand's sheltering relationship has been buffeted when the *niche* policy settings pursued by Wellington

[1] Frühling (2016), p. 13.

ran afoul of changes in Washington. Each of these three states has fully developed foreign policies with the US, but the pursuit of those foreign goals concerns politics. Taken together, these three states illustrate the many political challenges that small states encounter when seeking shelter.

Before considering the politics of shelter encountered by Israel, Norway and New Zealand, it will be useful to highlight some relevant aspects of politics of advocacy and decision-making in Washington. Ben Rhodes, deputy national security adviser and speech writer in the Obama administration, coined the colorful term "the blob" to refer to the foreign policy establishment.[2] While reflecting the amorphous nature of the foreign policy community in Washington, "the blob" needs some exploration. The executive branch dominates foreign affairs. Within the executive branch are a diverse range of agencies and departments, many of which contend with one another for influence. Take for instance competition between the state and defence departments, where the former lays claim to leadership on foreign policy whereas the former has a far greater budget and more extensive presence overseas. While the executive branch has primary responsibility for foreign affairs, it does not have a monopoly. The co-equal legislative branch also shares a significant interest and controls the purse strings that enable the executive branch's actions. Both branches operate within an advocacy environment in which interests—corporate and social—advocate for policy preferences.

Advocacy and lobbying emerge from freedom of speech and representative government and has grown into big business, although precisely judging its size proves difficult. One way of determining the number of lobbyists is to use the 1995 Lobbying Disclosure Act, which requires all lobbying on behalf of clients to be reported. According to the Center for Responsive Politics, some 11,502 lobbyists worked in 2018 and are generating US$3.36 billion in spending.[3] The reported spending may actually exceed US$6 billion because of lobbying carried out through think tanks and consulting.[4] Poor compliance with the requirements outlined in the Lobbying Disclosure Act leaves the total number of lobbyists and money spent somewhat speculative.[5]

Lobbying relies on the provision of information and maintaining relationships.[6] Providing information helps to develop relationships with the executive branch and members of Congress and their staff. Both the executive and legislative branches swim in a sea of contending interests. The 535 voting members of Congress, for example, have at least three groups when it comes to foreign affairs. Local

[2]D. Samuels, "The Aspiring Novelist Who Became Obama's Foreign-Policy Guru," *New York Times*, 5 May 2016.

[3]Center for Responsive Politics, *Lobbying Database*, https://www.opensecrets.org/lobby/. Accessed 30 June 2018.

[4]T. LaPira, "How Much Lobbying Is There in Washington? It's DOUBLE What You Think," *Sunlight Foundation*, http://sunlightfoundation.com/blog/2013/11/25/how-muchlobbying-is-there-in-washington-its-double-what-you-think/. 2013.

[5]Newhouse (2009), pp. 73–92.

[6]Nownes (2006).

constituents come first, then a broader domestic business and social interests with embassies trailing at a distant third. Effective lobbying of congressional offices requires personal contact,[7] a difficult goal to meet. The best way for lobbyists to build relationships revolves around "providing credible, reliable information".[8]

Washington's crowded foreign policy environment often requires more than diplomats to represent on behalf of their country. More seasoned advocacy may be required to deliver the desired shelter results for small states. Lobbying on behalf of a foreign entity, such as a government or business, requires compliance with the Foreign Agents Registration Act. For example, the Embassy of Vietnam hired three firms in 2006 concerning their efforts to secure congressional approval of Permanent Normal Trade Relations status for Vietnam.[9] As of 17 January 2019, 430 active registrants representing some 650 foreign entities appear in the Foreign Agents Registration Act database. The Fratelli Group, for example, works as an agent representing countries including Colombia, Japan, New Zealand, Singapore, South Korea and Taiwan.[10]

Beyond lobbying, small states may promote their foreign policy interests through organisations such as the Center for Strategic and International Studies (CSIS), the Brookings Institution or the Wilson Center.[11] These "think tanks" often do less conceptual policy work and frequently act as venues and conveners promoting ideas. The United Arab Emirates, for example, has donated more than $500,000 in support of CSIS programming.[12] Countries such as the UAE can then rely on CSIS to promote ideas in line with their foreign policy goals. These sorts of contributions, to think tanks, universities and other similar organisations, do not get reported as "lobbying" under US legislation. They also become an input in the foreign policy process; they become part of the blob.

In most instances, small states engage directly with the administration in pursuit of shelter. After all, the executive branch is home to the departments of defence, treasury and commerce. The US President is the commander-in-chief of the military and ambassadors represent the President. In some instances, effective shelter requires not only concurrence of the administration but also funding from Congress. Usually, the executive branch can advocate successfully for their own policy outcomes. Sometimes, however, additional advocacy is required to get congressional

---

[7]Baumgartner (2009).

[8]D. Rehr, "Congressional Communications Report," Washington, DC, 2018, http://www.congressionalcommunicationsreport.com/.

[9]US Department of Justice, *FARA Database*, https://www.fara.gov/docs/5611-Exhibit-AB-20060522-3.pdf. Accessed 15 May 2006.

[10]US Department of Justice, *FARA Database*, https://efile.fara.gov/pls/apex/f?p=181:200:12190325063119::NO:RP,200:P200_REG_NUMBER:5867. Accessed 17 January 2019.

[11]E. Lipton, B. Williams and N. Confessore, "Foreign Powers Buy Influence at Think Tanks," *New York Times*, September 7, 2014.

[12]Center for Strategic and International Studies. *Government Donors* [WWW Document],], https://www.csis.org/support-csis/our-donors/government-donors, 2019. Accessed 7 January.

agreement. At other times, small states may not think their interests are adequately served by the administration and may engage with the legislative branch to manage risk and further those interests against unwanted executive action. This *beltway hedging* requires skill and experience in the politics of Washington. (The phrase *beltway hedging* is used to avoid confusion with hedging in international relations literature.) Israel uses *beltway hedging* with considerable skill. Another strategy for managing political risk in Washington is *diversification*, where states seek to have multiple policy interests that span the political divide. The essence of *diversification* revolves around the idea of having interests that appeal to a wide audience in Washington. Norway's use of *diversification strategy* in Washington reflects its broad foreign policy interests. A *niche strategy* offers an interesting counterpoint to the previous strategies. As small states have limited resources, the *niche strategy* is one that can be developed into a specialty, drawing on expertise of a given country. That expertise can then be used to give voice to the small state that wields it in Washington. New Zealand's expertise in economic diplomacy and emphasis on free trade inform its *niche strategy* in Washington.

2.3 Israel

Since its founding, Israel has been building shelter with Washington. The nature and quality of that shelter have varied over the years, and Israeli leadership has taken steps to enhance the quality of shelter over the years. Unlike some small states, however, Israel has had some domestic US strengths as it has built shelter in Washington. Israel's shelter rests on two historical strengths. The first concerns the civil society voice of the Jewish American community. Years before the founding of Israel, synagogues throughout the US advocated on behalf of their congregants. In addition, civil society groups, such as the B'nai B'rith, helped give further voice to Jewish Americans. Together groups such as these not only formed a coalition in support of the founding of Israel but also contributed to the knowledge of how to work in Washington. This deep understanding of how policy is made in Washington helped lay the foundation of the *beltway hedging* strategy, where support in one branch of the government can be used to offset inaction or opposition in another branch. The second strength concerns the very establishment of Israel, which came with bipartisan support in the US Congress.[13] US political support for Israel has waxed and waned over the years as both Democrats and Republicans balance a diverse range of US foreign policy interests. Three examples illustrate how Israel uses *beltway hedging* in managing the politics of shelter in Washington.

On 3 March 2015, Israeli Prime Minister Benjamin Netanyahu stood before a joint sitting of the US House of Representatives and Senate urging members to reject the Iran nuclear agreement. Not in attendance, however, were many representatives

[13]Cavari and Nyer (2016).

from the executive branch. Netanyahu had been invited to speak by the then Speaker of the House John Boehner, with the active assistance of US-born Israeli Ambassador Ron Dermer. This rankled the Obama White House. Critics of Netanyahu "… called it an unprecedented violation of diplomatic protocol and an affront to the presidency".[14] At the time, the prime minister did not succeed in squelching the Iran nuclear deal, but his speech underscored Israel's use of Congress as a hedge against unwanted executive branch action.

Netanyahu's address to Congress resulted from years of Israeli diplomacy on Capitol Hill. When Yitzhak Rabin became Israel's fourth ambassador to the US in 1968, he complained that Israeli foreign policy had no clear objectives for its diplomatic mission in Washington.[15] In response, he outlined a menu of goals, including a "...plan for maintaining Israeli's leverage with the American administration and Congress…".[16] Israel appointed its first congressional liaison officer (CLO) in the summer of 1973, shortly before the Yom Kippur War.[17] By the early 1980s, Israel's strengthened outreach to Congress was in full swing. Moshe Arens, the Israeli ambassador to the US from 1982 to 1983, recounts in his memoirs his almost daily regimen of meeting with members of Congress.[18] During that time, he had the task of representing the Israeli point of view on their role in the Lebanon War. In 1982, to advance Arens' work, Prime Minister Menachem Begin made a visit to Washington, which included briefing a group of mostly unhappy US senators. Senator James Abdnor (Republican—South Dakota), a Lebanese American, expressed his concern for the safety of his aunt living in Lebanon. Ambassador Arens obtained details of Abdnor's aunt's home address in Lebanon, and within hours the Israeli Defence Force (IDF) was looking for her. Shortly afterwards, the IDF found her, put her on a plane and flew her to Washington, DC. The surprised Senator was happy to know she was safe. The Abdnor story underscores the importance that Israel's government places on maintaining strong relations in Congress. It also illustrates the ways in which Israel's government works to strengthen shelter. Most recently, the Trump administration's decision to recognise Jerusalem as Israel's capital tested the strength of that shelter.

The background to the Trump administration's decision stretches at least back to the passage of the 1995 Jerusalem Embassy Act, which passed the House of Representatives 374-37 and the Senate 93-5.[19] The act mandates that the US embassy be moved from Tel Aviv to Jerusalem by 1999. Also provided for in the act is the possibility that the President issue 6-month waivers in moving the embassy in to protect US national security interests. Waivers have been issued by presidents

---

[14]Marshall (2015), pp. 8–10.

[15]Rabin (1996), p. 124.

[16]Ibid.

[17]*Zvi Rafiah oral history*, Stephen F. Austin State University, 2012. http://www.sfasu.edu/heritagecenter/5381.asp.

[18]Arens (2018).

[19]Jerusalem Embassy Act of 1995, Washington, D.C: (U.S. Government Printing Office), 1995.

Clinton, Bush, Obama and Trump, until December 2017. Then on December 6, the President announced plans to officially move the US embassy from Tel Aviv to Jerusalem.

A CBS News poll found that 41% of US respondents approved of Trump's actions, while 43% disapproved.[20] Furthermore, a poll conducted by the American Jewish Committee found that 47% of responding Jewish Americans disagreed with the Trump administration's moves.[21] On the other hand, the Trump administration's actions were overwhelming in line with the views of self-described evangelical Americans.[22] Taken together, the poll data suggest that the management of shelter requires ongoing attention by Israel's government.

Israel has at times taken positions or actions that put it in conflict with elements of either the US government or the public. The invasion of Lebanon, opposition to the Iran nuclear deal and moving the capital to Jerusalem are three examples in which elements of the US government and/or public have disagreed. The tension caused by that disagreement has buffeted Israel's shelter. A central challenge for Israel, then, concerns the management of those tensions, often by employing *beltway hedging* through the US Congress or various elements of the American public.

2.4 Norway

In recent years, few states have done a better job of managing the politics of shelter than Norway. Where Israel has used *beltway hedging* as a way of managing risks in the sheltering relationship, Norway has managed risk by a *diversification strategy*. Not unlike an investment fund, Norway distributes risks to shelter by diversifying its policy settings. Those settings include the following:

1) Having a formal alliance with the US through the North Atlantic Treaty Organization (NATO)
2) Signaling a willingness to be proactive on defence and defence spending
3) Advocating and enacting international norms broadly appealing to the US
4) Engaging in peacemaking activities in numerous areas relevant to US interests
5) Creating links with US domestic politics and
6) Energising the Norwegian-American diaspora.

[20] J. De Pinto, "Americans split on Trump's handling of relations with Israel--CBS News poll," *CBS News*, https://www.cbsnews.com/news/poll-americans-split-on-trumps-handling-of-relations-with-israel-cbs-news-poll/. 2018.

[21] American Jewish Committee, "AJC 2018 Survey of American Jewish Opinion," https://www.ajc.org/news/survey2018. Accessed 23 January 2019.

[22] P. Bump, "Half of evangelicals support Israel because they believe it is important for fulfilling end-times prophecy," *The Washington Post*, 14 May 2018.

These policy settings did not come about in order that a diversification strategy be developed, but Oslo manages its presentation in Washington, cutting across party lines and ideological settings.

Norway as a founding member of NATO secured its most vital alliance relationship. As a long-standing member, Norway has deeply integrated into NATO's architecture and has developed the habit of interacting with NATO counterparts. Allied to NATO membership, Norway has long had strong investments in defence, relative to many other NATO countries. It withstands the accusation of freeriding better than most other small states with a defence budget that nears 1.6% of gross domestic product (GDP) in 2018 (Norway's defence spending would likely be higher without NATO). Norway's acquisitions include several major US weapon platforms such as the P-8 Poseidon and F-35 Joint Strike Fighter. In addition, the development of the Joint Strike Missile by Kongsberg and Raytheon complements and deepens Norwegian/US defence links. Oslo has used its NATO membership to promote its defence relationship with the US through, for example, a series of ongoing bilateral working groups (i.e. US-Norwegian Study Group) connecting Norwegian and US defence personnel on topics of particular pertinence to the US. These workshops help deepen the relationship by creating institutional and interpersonal links, as well as provide useful information on relevant topics.

Unusual for many smaller powers, Norway has used its soft power to advance international norms of international poverty alleviation and peacemaking. Support of international peacemaking has been linked to mediation and peacemaking efforts in places often closely associated with US interests. Norway has led peacemaking efforts in Israel/Palestine, Guatemala, Haiti, Colombia, and the southern Philippines. Even when peacemaking occurs outside the areas of traditional US interests, such as Sri Lanka, it proved valuable to Oslo. Secretary of State Condoleezza Rice often sought out Norwegian counterparts during their trips to Washington; she typically requested briefings on the current state of Sri Lankan peace talks. Such frequent one-on-one contact with the US Secretary of State gave Norwegian leaders unusual access in which a broad range of security and non-security matters could be raised.

In addition to these international links, Norway has succeeded in gaining a domestic US constituency to advocate on its behalf. Some of the roughly 4.5 million Norwegian Americans, many in Minnesota and North Dakota, maintain an interest in Norway. The Norwegian ambassador spends most of his time, when traveling in the US, in these heavily Norwegian northern states. In fact, starting in 1974, the longest running country-to-country military exchange runs between the Minnesota National Guard and Norway. The result of these connections means that Norway can count on the congressional delegations of Minnesota and North Dakota to be broadly informed and supportive of their issues.

Norway's congressional support stretches beyond Minnesota and North Dakota. In 2009, the Congressional Friends of Norway caucus was created, bringing together both Republicans and Democrats friendly to Oslo. Then on 2 March 2017, Republican Rep. Martha McSally from Arizona, along with Norwegian Foreign Minister Brende, launched *Norway Creates Jobs in the United States: Norway's Impact on the American Economy* (Aas, 2017). The report, produced by the Embassy of

Norway in Washington, emphasised the role of Norwegian investments in the US and its impact on employment and productivity.

Where does this *diversification strategy* leave Norway today? Its policy settings mean that it has not burned its bridges. The Trump administration may not be interested in the environment and climate and may be cool on NATO, but Norway is a consumer of US defence equipment and an avid supporter of the US. At the end of the day, *diversification* delivers effective shelter for Norway.

2.5 New Zealand

New Zealand's shelter with the US has varied since the end of World War II. In 1951, New Zealand, along with Australia and the US, signed the Australia, New Zealand, United States Security Treaty (ANZUS). This tripartite agreement served as the basis for shelter. In 1986, the US suspended obligations under the ANZUS agreement in reaction to New Zealand's embrace of a nuclear-free stance. Passage in the New Zealand parliament of the Nuclear Free Zone, Disarmament, and Arms Control Act 1987 ended any thought of reversing the tide and marked a new phase in New Zealand-US relations. In the years immediately following the passage of the legislation, New Zealand's political engagement with Washington sought to repair relations with the US while not giving ground on the fundamentals of the nuclear question. By necessity, New Zealand's political engagement with Washington focused on what New Zealand ambassador to the US John Wood termed restoring "contact and dialogue".[23] Today, the US and New Zealand have ended their security alliance, although ANZUS still binds Australia to both New Zealand and the US. While the US and New Zealand might not be formal allies, they both still participate in the intelligence-sharing agreement United Kingdom-United States of America Agreement (UKUSA), or Five Eyes.

New Zealand adapted to the change in relationships and sought to deepen shelter by building contact and dialogue through a *niche strategy* focusing on trade. During the 1980s, New Zealand, along with the US-business-backed *Committee to Assure the Availability of Casein*, lobbied for the importation of casein (aka milk protein) into the US. Later, near the turn of the century, the US began negotiating bilateral free trade agreements (FTAs), including an FTA between the US and Australia. New Zealand saw an opportunity to deepen its relationship with Washington. The opportunity—pursuit of an FTA—was not without risks. While the former security relationship proved domestically difficult in New Zealand, an FTA would be contentious with some domestic US sectors, such as dairy producers. Wellington began its free trade campaign in earnest in 2000. In 2002, New Zealand was buoyed when it became clear that Australia and the US would start negotiations for an FTA. In a statement outlining prospects for an Australia-US FTA, the US trade

[23]Wood (2010).

representative hinted that the administration would ask for the views of Congress on an FTA with New Zealand. Congressional views were mixed.

Recognising the centrality of Congress to the FTA, the New Zealand embassy allocated a staff member to coordinate their congressional outreach, which included the creation of the Friends of New Zealand congressional caucus in 2005. The *New Zealand Herald* reported on 18 February 2005 that the 54-member bipartisan caucus would try and nudge the Bush administration towards an FTA.[24] Ultimately, New Zealand failed to persuade the administration on the worth of an FTA with New Zealand. The cause of the stillborn FTA stemmed from the strength of the New Zealand agricultural and dairy sectors, a difficult topic in any discussion about trade with the US, as well as a lingering aftertaste of the New Zealand nuclear policy.[25] New Zealand Prime Minister Helen Clark's observation that had Vice President Gore won in 2000 the Iraq War would not have happened did not help matters. The *Christchurch Press* reported the annoyance that her comments provoked in US senators visiting Wellington.[26]

Failure to achieve an FTA with the US did not dissuade New Zealand from pursuing free trade in other ways. New Zealand's *niche* diplomacy had room for a bigger and more complex agreement—the Trans Pacific Partnership (TPP). Representatives from 12 countries met on 5 February 2016 to sign the TPP agreement, which started in 2005 as an effort by four small Asia-Pacific Economic Cooperation (APEC) economies (Brunei, Chile, New Zealand and Singapore) to pursue economic liberalisation.[27] The US joined negotiations in 2008. US accession to the TPP necessitated both executive and congressional agreement. First, Congress had to give the US administration trade promotion authority, meaning that whatever the executive brought to Congress would receive an either up or down vote. Both trade promotion authority and final vote on TPP were important to New Zealand. In pursuit of TPP's passage, Wellington appointed former New Zealand Prime Minister and Secretary-General of the World Trade Organization Mike Moore as ambassador to Washington. As a strong advocate of the trade deal, Moore oversaw spending at least $549,825 on lobbying Capitol Hill.[28] Supporters of the TPP agreement delivered trade promotion authority in Congress, but the vote on the agreement itself never happened. Neither presidential candidate, Hillary Clinton nor Donald Trump, supported TPP. One of President Trump's first acts was to sign an executive order withdrawing the US from the agreement. Once again, New Zealand's *niche strategy* pursuing free trade came up short.

[24]C. Espiner, "Getting 54 members of the United States House of Representatives to join a. . . ." *New Zealand Herald*, 18 February 2005.

[25]Elms (2016), pp. 1017–1039.

[26]C. Espiner, "PM's Remarks Not Forgotten," *The Christchurch Press*, 13 January 2004.

[27]Elms (2016), pp. 1017–1039.

[28]U. S. Department of Justice, Foreign Agents Registration Act database, efile.fara.gov. Accessed 29 February 2020.

At this writing, it appears as if New Zealand will shift the subject of its *niche strategy* away from trade to Pacific security. This reflects Wellington's Pacific reset, which includes, in the words of Winston Peters, a "focus on building deeper, more mature political partnerships with Pacific Island countries, and supporting their independence and sustainable social and economic resilience".[29] Foreign Minister Peters explains the import this has for New Zealand-US relations. He said:

> We are saying today to the United States that we welcome your involvement but ask you to join us in doing more because nations with common interests and common causes can achieve more together than any of us can manage on our own.[30]

A *niche strategy* built around Pacific security will not likely antagonise domestic US interests in the way that trade has. Unlike free trade, the Pacific security strategy cannot be stymied by a single bill or agreement. Instead, Pacific security will likely encompass an array of things and will not be measured by a single agreement or piece of legislation.

2.6 Conclusions

The ways in which small states seek shelter in Washington vary. Israel, Norway and New Zealand each have different approaches to managing the politics of shelter. Israel has hardly shied away from controversy. It can withstand the executive branch's ire or counter the policy settings of the administration by offsetting that risk through links with Congress. This *beltway hedging strategy* does not come without costs. Developing and maintaining links with congressional allies and energising domestic support consume time and money. The approach becomes more complex when considering that part of Congress turns over every 2 years.

Norway's *diversified strategy* has much to recommend it. That strategy comes about, however, after decades of work. Consider Norway's embrace of sustainable development as an international norm. In 1987, former Norwegian Prime Minister Brundtland, then chair of the World Commission on Environment and Development, gave her name to the Brundtland Report, which promoted sustainable development. The elements to building a diversified strategy for managing shelter require years of work by policymakers.

---

[29]W. Peters, "Pacific Partnerships," *Georgetown Address in partnership with the Center for Australia, New Zealand, and Pacific Studies - Georgetown University and the NZ Embassy*, http://www.scoop.co.nz/stories/PA1812/S00195/speech-peters-pacific-partnerships-georgetown.htm. 2018.

[30]W. Peters, "Pacific Partnerships." *Georgetown Address in partnership with the Center for Australia, New Zealand, and Pacific Studies - Georgetown University and the NZ Embassy*, http://www.scoop.co.nz/stories/PA1812/S00195/speech-peters-pacific-partnerships-georgetown.htm. 2018.

New Zealand's *niche strategy* makes sense in terms of why Wellington pursued it. As a country deeply dependent upon international trade and with a long-running commitment to free trade, its embrace seems entirely reasonable. The break with the US helped to de-emphasise security as well. *Niche strategies* make sense in terms of being good at one thing provided that one good thing does not get rejected, as happened with New Zealand's and the TPP in 2017. Trump's ascendency essentially shut down New Zealand diplomacy in Washington. The Pacific reset may well reinvigorate New Zealand's shelter in Washington, but it is too early to tell at this writing. New Zealand could shift its strategy of shelter, adopting, for example, a *diversified strategy* or *beltway hedging*, both of which consume time and money.

Global insecurity created by America First and the Trump administration, the rise of the revisionist powers Russia and China, and continued instability in the Middle East all underscore the importance of shelter for smaller powers. Many smaller powers find themselves stuck with Trump's America, for better or worse. The calculus of managing the politics of shelter has not appreciably changed even with the rise of Trump—there is no great power alternative to the US. Looking to those states that have demonstrated the highest capacity to manage the politics of shelter serves as a roadmap. Equally, the hiccup in relations experienced by New Zealand shows the importance of finely tuning one's political management to meet the situation.

States that face a change in the shelter environment in Washington may well wish to re-evaluate their shelter strategy with Washington. While the Trump administration and the US Congress both present a comparatively more chaotic face than in previous years, steps can still be taken to help maintain or even deepen shelter. The list below includes some steps small states seeking shelter could do in the face of a changing environment in Washington:

- *Focus on uncontroversial linkages* to raise the profile both in the executive and legislative branches in Washington. Norway linked with the Minnesota National Guard, creating meaningful, stable and safe links.
- *Avoid being pigeonholed. Diversify foreign policy settings.* Over-reliance on one issue alone limits outreach. In Washington, if policymakers believe Lithuania is only concerned about Russia, then those policymakers may not engage on other issues. Even pursuing a *niche strategy*, it is important to have views on a range of issues.
- Related to the previous point, *undertake an inventory* of already established links with Washington. Some interactions with Washington may lend themselves to updating or reinforcing, the net result of which would be to bolster the politics of shelter.
- *Identify areas where a smaller state has expertise needed elsewhere.* Norway has done this with its deep interests in the Arctic. New Zealand could, for example, lead a working group on the Antarctic, land rights and conflict, governance in the South Pacific or protection of fishing rights in exclusive economic zones (EEZs).
- *Identify domestic US interests* that share yours. Israel does this linking with supportive Jewish American and evangelical Christians. Similarly, Norway

embraced the diaspora Norwegian American community. New Zealand has done this linking with friendly elements of the American dairy sector. Numerous other examples can be found, but this requires keeping up to date with an ever-changing landscape.

- Continue to *work on supporting and creating international norms*. Norway built an international constituency around peacemaking and sustainable development. Other small states could follow suit and see where they can develop international projects that both promote an international good as well as promote visibility and access in Washington.

The ways in which small states manage the politics of shelter in Washington vary between states and over time. Israel's approach to managing the politics of shelter through *beltway hedging* has only deepened with time. Likewise, Norway has developed and used its diverse foreign policy interests as a way of insulating it from political change in Washington and thereby reducing the level of risk. The diversification strategy has delivered positive results for Norway. New Zealand, on the other hand, has sought to manage the politics of risk through the lens of a *niche strategy* built on the back of trade. This, it turns out, was a reasonably high-risk strategy inasmuch as the politics of trade intersects with strong US economic interests. While not abandoning a *niche strategy*, New Zealand has opted to shift from trade to Pacific security as a somewhat safer bet on which to build shelter in Washington.

References

Arens M (2018) In defense of Israel: a memoir of a political life. Brookings Institution Press, Washington DC

Baumgartner F (2009) Lobbying and policy change: who wins, who loses, and why. University of Chicago Press, Chicago

Cavari A, Nyer E (2016) Trends in US congressional support for Israel. The Begin-Sadat Center for Strategic Studies, Ramat Gan

Elms D (2016) The origins and evolution of the trans-pacific partnership trade negotiations. Asian Surv 56(6):1017–1039

Frühling S (2016) Wrestling with commitment: geography, alliance institutions and the ANZUS treaty. In: Australia's American Alliance. Melbourne University Press, Melbourne, p 13

Marshall R (2015) Netanyahu's speech to congress causes tremors in the "unshakable" alliance. Wash Rep Middle East Aff 34(3):8–10

Newhouse J (2009) Diplomacy, Inc. Foreign Aff 88(3):73–92

Nownes A (2006) Total lobbying: what lobbyists want (and how they try to get it). Cambridge University Press, Cambridge

Rabin Y (1996) The Rabin memoirs. University of California Press, Berkeley, p 124

Wood J (2010) Negotiating within Washington: thrown in at the deep end—a New Zealand diplomat looks back. In: American negotiating behavior: wheeler-dealers, legal eagles, bullies, and preachers. U.S. Institute of Peace Press, Washington

Alan C. Tidwell Professor of the practice, is the director of the Center for Australian, New Zealand and Pacific Studies at the Edmund A. Walsh School of Foreign Service at Georgetown University and co-director of the SSANSE Project. His area of specialisation includes work on conflict in the Australasian region. Tidwell served for several years as director (1995–1997) and deputy director (1992–1994) of the Centre for Conflict Resolution at Macquarie University and as acting executive director and research director (1994–1995) of the Australian Centre for American Studies at Sydney University. From 2001 through 2004, he was a programme officer with the United States Institute of Peace, where he focused on conflict resolution and education.

Chapter 3
The Hybrid Challenge and Small States

Caroline Kennedy-Pipe and Iftikhar Zaidi

3.1 Introduction

Hybrid warfare is a currently fashionable term used to describe a type of military and political conduct featuring simultaneity in the use of conventional and unconventional tactics with features of regular and irregular war and supported or led by the application of other elements of national power.[1] While that combination is not entirely new,[2] we now witness the potent addition of cyberattacks, fake news, electoral intervention in the affairs of other states and the widespread utilisation of local groups (some of which may be terrorist) to instigate disharmony and confusion in the target country or warzone. Insurgency, in its evolved form, is now a potent mix

[1]National power is defined as the combination of Diplomatic, Informational, Military and Economic (DIME) Power of a state. Used originally in the US military, the UK's Royal College of Defence Studies has also embraced this typology. It is this definition to which we refer. We include 'Culture' as a separate and influential component of National Power which in the UK and US constructs is not treated separately. See RCDS (2017).

[2]The concept of Total war appeared in the nineteenth century and involved a blurring of lines between combatants and civil targets and the application of a nation's total might e.g. diplomatic, informational, military, economic, moral and social resources against the elements of national power of the enemy including its entire population. See Ludendorff (1935); Martin Shaw, "Dialectics of War: An Essay in the Social Theory of Total War and Peace," https://doi.org/10.2139/ssrn.2718985 and SSRN: https://ssrn.com/abstract=2718985; Chickering and Förster (2003).

C. Kennedy-Pipe (✉)
Loughborough University, Leicestershire, UK
e-mail: c.m.kennedy-pipe@lboro.ac.uk

I. Zaidi
Cranfield University, Bedford, UK

A.-M. Brady, B. Thorhallsson (eds.), *Small States and the New Security Environment*, The World of Small States 7,
https://doi.org/10.1007/978-3-030-51529-4_3

of old and new means. Some commentators have traced the lineage of such hybrid/mixed behaviour back to the ancient world.[3]

One key enabler of this form of warfare is the new technologies developing around the Internet. Foremost among these are communication strategies to rapidly promote a political agenda and incite public disruption. In short, the 'people' are targeted not only in a conventional sense by warfare but also through the delivery of emotional and personal messages directed to individuals and repeatedly reinforced, perhaps even via their mobile phones.

A hybrid war has three distinct arenas: first, utilisation or posturing for a conventional battlefield; second, provoking unrest, confusion and paralysis among communities through careful use of information and events; and, third, a variety of actions on the diplomatic, political and economic stages of international politics. This third arena is one in which states might engage with allies to persuade international and regional organisations to act in concert against a threat or, alternatively, one that may take the form of disruption and physical revision of international norms, as was seen with regard to Russian actions in Ukraine and Crimea. Diplomacy and winning a battle of persuasion are no mean feat in an era where truth is elusive and contested and propaganda is eminently powerful. To defend effectively against such tripartite warfare or insurgency is, to say the least, difficult. It requires any state or alliance to maintain a determined counter-strategy across all three arenas, enacted over a sustained period. Defence against hybrid war presents a particular challenge for small states, especially those that must nestle in the shadow of a great power.

In this chapter, we examine the recent history of hybrid warfare during the 1990s following the collapse of the bipolar world. This collapse permitted shifts and changes in war that enabled a wide range of actors to take advantage of ideological voids and political instability. We identify some crucial and new elements in the character of hybrid wars and the nature of hybrid threats. We argue that while the breadth and scope of hybrid threats ought to make these a cross-government and societal concern, ownership and response are difficult to articulate when smaller states necessarily must continue to live on good terms with their larger neighbours. We look at the particular implications for small states such as Finland in terms of the threat from Russia, and we utilise 'sheltering' theory as developed by Baldur Thorhallsson[4] in order to examine a possible set of responses for small states to hybrid challenges, arguing that classical alliance theory cannot explain the behaviour of small states in the current environment of hybrid warfare.

Alliance theory[5] evolved to describe a particular dynamic in international relations that became increasingly apparent in the polarisation of power after 1945. The theory explained great power behaviour and that of powers aligned with them. One of the earliest challenges that alliance theory had to withstand was that it emerged in

---

[3]Williamson and Mansoor (2011).

[4]See Thorhallsson (2011), pp. 324–336.

[5]Lisaka (1962). See also Osgood (1966).

the backdrop of a particular departure from the wisdom of balance of power and in a world with atomic weapons, polarisation and non-alignment. Three main alliances emerged, the two ideologically aligned blocks and the so-called nonaligned movement pioneered by Tito's Yugoslavia. Polar dialectic often served to ease, incentivise, coerce or compel such states to their respective folds. However, at the same time, even for the so-called non-aligned states, there was always some sort of 'alliance of convenience' as states driven by core interests, economics, leadership and politics, and/or cost-benefit calculations aligned selectively with either of the poles. Cuba is an example, with its switch from a de facto US ally to a Marxist-Leninist ideology and natural alignment with the Soviet camp.[6] Alliance theory struggled to explain small state behaviour and still struggles to account for the current dilemmas of how small states such as Finland can 'shelter' under alliances such as the North Atlantic Treaty Organization (NATO) in an age of hybrid warfare.

3.2 History and Evolution

After the end of the Cold War, contradictory trends in warfare were apparent. For many scholars during the 1990s, the Soviet collapse brought about a new world order in which international politics had taken on a more optimistic shape. Scholars expressed the sentiment that war itself had been unlearnt and had been consigned to historical memory, along with other arcane practices such as duelling and slavery.[7] In short, hard military power had been replaced by 'soft' power.[8] However, any idea that war had gone away is simply incorrect. Throughout the 1990s, civil wars and proxy wars, as well as terrorist threats, proliferated across the globe. Robert Keohane and Joseph Nye were prescient in predicting how important 'soft' power would become. It most certainly is a feature of hybrid warfare, thus leading us to the somewhat simplistic—but nevertheless accurate—claim that hybrid war consists of a mix of hard and soft power. Cultural power, too, is important in that it allows many (or indeed all) protagonists to claim that they are the custodians of religious sentiment and ethnic and historical traditions and are also keepers of sacred sites and artefacts.[9]

Much of this complexity was not recognised. Perhaps in the afterglow of 'winning' the Cold War, Western military dominance seemed assured. The Bosnian War had been eventually resolved, and NATO prided itself on the defeat of Serbia. The Kosovo War did not result in a single combat fatality on the Western side. This mode of winning from the air with so-called precision bombing led to the concept of a

[6] Allison and Zelikow (1999).

[7] Mueller (1995).

[8] Keohane and Nye (1998).

[9] Hassner (2009).

'Virtual War'.[10] The Revolution in Military Affairs (RMA) seemed to have brought about an age of accurate targeting and fewer civilian casualties. Liberal states could, it seemed, wage war at a distance with few sacrifices from their troops and little disruption to domestic politics. There were unintended casualties on the other side, with some caused directly by the NATO bombing campaign. But, at least for Western states, future war was to be short, sharp and waged at a distance.

The events of 9/11 transformed international politics. With the wars in Afghanistan (2001) and Iraq (2003), a traditional type of warfare returned—that of conventional 'boots on the ground'. Yet the opening episodes in these wars appeared to confirm earlier trends for distance in that the initial Afghan campaign was in many ways similar to the Kosovo War, fought initially largely from the air with the added involvement of special operation teams to hunt down al-Qaeda. While Iraq involved a larger military deployment, airpower remained crucial too. However, the '9/11 wars' did not prove easy. Victory cannot be considered complete until the enemy's will to continue fighting has been sufficiently eroded. In a conventional war, this usually occurs when the counteroffensive is defeated. But in both of these conflicts, the counteroffensive was delivered in a different mode from that of the offensive and through enemies who had morphed within civil society. Opposition came in the shape of a complex and multifaceted insurgency.[11]

The insurgents transformed these wars into a quagmire in which Western troops were forced to encounter the brutality of insurgency and endemic violence waged by a variety of sub-state actors, some of whom were proxy forces, some of whom were fighting civil wars and all of whom had their own locally based agendas. The eventual disintegration of Iraq created the breeding ground for al-Qaeda to evolve and adapt and for the Islamic State of Iraq and Syria (ISIS) to emerge. The advent of multiple militias—some of which were controlled and sustained by external actors—and the operations of various criminal gangs fed off the area's human and material resources for their own political and economic gain. Refugees and those fleeing the region's war zones were exploited for political as well as financial capital. The so-called weaponisation of the migrant issue in politicised hybrid warfare continues to be a subject of considerable importance since homeless and dispossessed persons remain vulnerable to recruitment for the purposes of predatory groups and states.

In 2011, the 'Arab Spring' reinforced the United States' stance against committing manpower directly into theatres of war. The response in Western circles to the uprisings across the Arab world against brutal rulers—such as the Qaddafi regime in Libya—was characterised by a desire to 'encourage' the overthrow of unsavoury regimes but to do so using small special operation teams rather than significant numbers of troops. The character of the conflict in Syria since 2011 has also been determined by American reluctance to commit ordinary troops on the ground. Instead, we have seen the deployment of bombing campaigns coupled with overt encouragement of rebel and militia groups.

[10] Ignatieff (2001).

[11] Zaidi (2009).

Western states continue to demonstrate preference for technology and surrogate forces through their persistent use of armed drones in Afghanistan, Pakistan, Yemen and Syria, as well as by their reliance on local forces and private security contractors. One important consequence is that 'opponents'—whether terrorists or other criminals—adapt their behaviour by refusing to stay 'in theatre' to be hunted down and potentially killed. Insurgents and terrorists have become increasingly mobile, often crossing borders into complex urban environments and sometimes staging terrorist atrocities to provoke and unsettle. Army Public School and College (APSC) Peshawar (2014), Mumbai (2008) and Paris (2015) attacks and the numerous attacks in London are examples of this agility and adaptability. While individuals or groups may perpetrate such acts to serve a personal agenda, at the same time they are consciously or unconsciously supporting or exploiting the designs of external powers. A counter-hybrid war strategy may thus have to engage with such groups as an auxiliary line of action. Mercenaries and groups with no obvious political or criminal agenda can become an instrument deployed in the third arena of hybrid warfare, working for a state or indeed under the control of a non-state actor. Malign states engaging with such groups ostensibly keep their hands clean and avoid attribution yet retain a high degree of control. In this sense, as was witnessed during the 1970s, terrorists, or what are identified as terrorist groups, may be part of an agenda motivated and funded, if not always totally controlled, by an external power.

3.3 Hybrid Wars?

In the UK, the contemporary outbreak of terrorist attacks, which began with the London suicide bombings of 2005, has been widely linked to the influence exerted by websites that highlight Western abuse of Muslim populations in war zones. Radicalised men—and some women—have travelled from the UK to fight in Iraq or Syria or have chosen to perpetrate terrorist attacks on UK soil. All the post-9/11 battlespaces have witnessed such opponents utilising a wide range of tactics to disrupt superior state forces even as they are embroiled in asymmetric but difficult struggles at home and also in conflicts abroad. This context has given rise to acts by random and apparently isolated individuals or by small teams that do not seem connected to or commanded by other entities. Rather, they seem to be self-motivated, even when facilitated by external entities.[12] It also provides opportunities for covert state organisations to cultivate, motivate and even create radicalised cells and/or individuals and use them to commit sensational acts. Such individuals or groups never know for sure who may be helping and/or facilitating them.

[12]For further discussion on generational shift in how insurgencies operate and what their future direction may be, see Ifti Zaidi, "Insurgencies: The Third Generation," Conference paper presented at the AOC Crows, Edinburgh, Online: https://www.eweurope.com/Content/14th-15th-May-Main-Conference-Programme/6_12/.

In short, what is now labelled hybrid warfare has been utilised by a range of groups, proxies and terrorists over many years. However, it was the Russian intervention in Ukraine (following on from the invasion of Georgia in 2008) and Russian actions in Syria that have stimulated much of the contemporary debate about the meaning, use and effectiveness of hybrid warfare. The Ukraine conflict is considered by many analysts in the West to be a 'model' for hybrid war and one that has implications for other small states such as Finland in its relations with Moscow.

From a conventional Western perspective, Russia has, since the turn of the century, behaved like a revisionist power. Arguably, this has been provoked by NATO's deliberate expansion to the East and by that alliance's incorporation of states such as the Baltic republics. Russian analysts and spokespersons cite as antagonistic the ambition of Ukraine and countries such as Georgia to acquire membership in Western organisations. They also object to the European Union extending its influence and association agreements, such as was done for Ukraine. Russia felt threatened by an eastward tide of NATO and EU influence. Hence, Ukraine became a crucial testing ground for Moscow. The geostrategic and historic importance of Crimea to Russia and its Black Sea fleet arguably left Moscow with little choice but to act in defence of its longer term strategic interests.

Russia's 2008 intervention in Georgia was about securing territory and influence as well as protecting ethnic Russians. However, the war in Georgia was but a prelude to the annexation of Crimea and the bloody and ongoing war in Ukraine from February and March 2014, a conflict that renewed interest in the character of hybrid warfare.

Military action in eastern Ukraine and Crimea was preceded by the disruption of Russian-speaking peoples in the region, using a potent propaganda campaign that cited historical examples of supposed injustice and grievances, as well as the appearance of so-called little green men, unbadged and technically unrecognised in the escalating conflict. But, as Andrew Monaghan has pointed out, there was a powerful conventional warfare element.[13] Some 40,000 Russian troops were massed on the border while the battles at Donbas Airport involved high-intensity conflict, including the deployment of armour, artillery and multiple launch rocket systems, as well as drones and electronic warfare. Keir Giles from Chatham House in London has added a critical voice to the speculation that Russian operations in eastern Ukraine somehow constituted irregular warfare.[14] He pointed out that the Russian incursion into Ukraine was ultimately a large-scale conventional military cross-border intervention undertaken in August 2014. Russian troops and transport, although badged by the Russian authorities as primarily present to deliver and organise humanitarian aid, proved to be militarily decisive.[15]

[13]Monaghan (2015).

[14]Ibid.

[15]Giles (2016).

Most analysis of the current mode of Russian hybrid war has centred around an understanding of the so-called Gerasimov doctrine, as developed by Valery Gerasimov, Russian chief of the General Staff.[16] In 2013, in a much-read essay, Gerasimov wrote of blurring lines between states of war and peace. He went on to describe 'long distance' and 'contactless' actions against the enemy as the primary means of achieving combat and operational goals. Some Western scholarly and military communities cite his essay as evidence of an innovative, far-sighted and novel approach to war, essentially a new Russian military doctrine. This 'new' approach is additionally perceived as facilitating and underpinning an expansive and aggressive foreign policy agenda. Consternation and controversy have been stirred up by a combination of the Gerasimov doctrine, modernisation of the Russian Armed Forces, energy 'blackmail' and the annexation of Crimea, as well as by the success of Russian policy in Syria in neutralising Western action to remove Syrian leader Bashar al-Assad. In response, Western policy in Syria has signally failed to remove the government, to control territory or to stem human rights abuses. The retaking of the ancient city of Palmyra from ISIS by Russian-backed forces, widely reported and applauded in the Russian media, highlighted the Kremlin's ability to celebrate and promote the prowess of Russian military might despite coinciding with openly circulating reports of Russian complicity with members of ISIS.[17]

Russia and its official media outlets deny that a 'hybrid' doctrine, as described in the West, is applied by the Russian Armed Forces. Some sources even deny the existence of any such doctrine. Indeed, in the specific case of Ukraine, the weakness of the Ukrainian Army, the presence and embrace of the 'polite people' in the East (not the more sinister 'little green men', as described in the West) and the overwhelming support of the Russian people for the Crimea intervention (and Parliament in March 2014) have all been emphasised. This was a unique confluence of factors that, according to some analysts, it would be impossible to replicate it elsewhere, such as in the US mid-west or in Poland.[18]

But does that also hold true for Finland or the Baltic states? There are historical, cultural and ethnic claims made by Russia on these states, while the Russian-speaking population in Finland has been 'targeted' by Moscow-inspired propaganda. The Crimea War and its justification by the Kremlin reminded Finns that Moscow has at times viewed their state as part of the greater Russian homeland. Thousands of Finns have dual Russian citizenship, and some commentators fear that Moscow has planted agents among them who could infiltrate social and military institutions. In this context, Finland's defence minister recommended that Finns with dual Russian citizenship should not hold positions that could allow them access to state security apparatus. In the wake of the Ukraine crisis, such fears were heightened when Johan

---

[16] McDermott (2015).

[17] Ari Heistein and Vera S. Michlin, "Russia's Hybrid-Warfare Victory in Syria," *The National Interest*, 19 May 2016, https://nationalinterest.org/feature/russias-hybrid-warfare-victory-syria-16273.

[18] McDermott (2015).

Backman, a Finnish pro-Russian activist, opened a so-called representative office in Helsinki for the Donetsk's People's Republic—the breakaway Ukrainian territory.

Finland, which is vulnerable to its large neighbour, has taken robust measures to fend off 'hybrid' or mixed activities. Helsinki has cooperated with NATO but stopped short of seeking admittance to full membership and remains keenly aware of the so-called Finlandisation of the country during the Cold War and alert to the 833-mile border it shares with Russia. A delicate but sophisticated balancing act means good relations with Moscow even while Finland, as an EU member state, has backed economic sanctions against Russia over Crimea.

As well as being subjected to airspace incursions by Russian aircraft, recently Finns have been bombarded with fake news and the output of troll farms, which attempt to create conflict and disruption in online communities by posting deliberately inflammatory or provocative comments. Propaganda hostile to the Finnish government has taken a variety of forms, not the least of which are claims from Moscow that Russian speakers in Finland face routine discrimination over property rights. In response, Helsinki has set up a public diplomacy programme to train government officials about disinformation and increased the emphasis on media 'literacy' in schools.

Latvia, Estonia, Lithuania, Sweden and Norway are also wary of hybrid warfare from the East. Russia has allegedly used its shared border with Norway to 'mischief make' by allowing refugees fleeing the Middle East to make their way across the border on bicycles! This reinforces the view that part of Russia's hybrid war strategy is the 'weaponisation' of migrants, including the exploitation of the migrant/refugee crisis to further divide politicians and peoples throughout Europe who disagree (sometimes violently) about migrant and/or refugee policies.

A contrary thesis is presented by Andrew Korybko, whose 2015 study of hybrid wars claimed that the US was the only country then engaged in hybrid war. He argued that it was 'counterproductive for any of the Eurasian Powers to attempt it in their region' due to proximity issues and the unintended consequences or spillover from what he calls the resulting 'black holes' on their own borders. He predicted that the 'US will exercise a full monopoly on Hybrid War for at least the next decade, if not in perpetuity owing to the unique international circumstances in which it is waged'. He has further argued that 'Hybrid War is the new horizon for US regime change strategy'.[19] This mixture of regular and irregular warfare will, he says, be the future for US interventions in pursuit of its foreign policy interests, particularly in an era of fake news.

It is now clear that this adaptive form of warfare is successful, whatever is the outcome of debates about the essence of Russian military doctrine and whatever claims may be made about future US strategies. Western responses to Russian provocations—or, for that matter, Russian responses to US hybrid warfare—appear to be predicated on avoiding direct military conflict. In this sense, the Russian 'gains' in Ukraine and Crimea have extended Moscow's grip on the region. Despite

[19]Korybko (2015), pp. 1574–1586.

sanctions, diplomacy and some military posturing (the latter limited to NATO reinforcing its strategic presence in both Norway and Estonia), Russian tactical and strategic 'gains' remain intact.

A cleverly articulated hybrid war strategy implemented by revisionist and ambitious power(s) does indeed produce confusion, discord and disharmony in the targeted state or region. There may be confusion as to the overall objectives (or even whether any intentional design exists at all) and what may contribute to achieving those intentions. Even more elusive and difficult to identify with clarity are the possible linkages between apparently disparate actions spread over a long period. How does communal disruption in one village link to the appearance of protestors in another city or to the circulation of rumours on the Internet? How can these different events be put together? Uncertainty tends to generate dissonant views, often reinforced by elite political or financial interests. The nature of the threat, its aim and its provenance are variously disputed, resulting in an often disjointed and ambiguous counter-strategy. This makes it difficult to determine whether thresholds for retaliation may have been crossed.

3.4 Conclusions: Does Sheltering Work?

Of the three arenas of hybrid war discussed earlier—first, utilisation or posturing for a conventional battlefield; second, provoking unrest, confusion and paralysis among communities through careful use of information and events; and, third, a variety of actions on the diplomatic, political and economic stage of international politics—actions relating to the first are the easiest to decipher. Even the best guarded strategy or strategic intent may be discerned from an analysis of hostile power interests, force and infrastructural development, training and alliances—in short, a military equivalent of what Henry Mintzberg describes as a 'pattern in a stream of actions'.[20] The second and the third arenas, however, require a more critical analysis as it is here that strategic lines are often hard to discern. Furthermore, the experiential lens[21] for strategic analysis—the bedrock of conventional military planning and system thinking—is not terribly useful in a mixed conventional/insurgent scenario. Unless the targeted state can process national security as a broad, interrelated and mutually informing system, it is unlikely that it could make the connections necessary to construct a comprehensive response.

The Finnish Army may be better prepared to tackle hybrid threats in the first arena than many of its European counterparts because, according to the Swedish Defence Agency, since 2014 the Finns have created a system of rapid reaction forces and swift mobilisation units throughout its 280,000 military personnel. Lessons have been learnt from Russian actions in Crimea, where it took special forces and

[20]Mintzberg (2007).

[21]Johnson et al. (2017).

paramilitary forces only a few days to seize the territory. Finnish 'readiness' units are designed to allow conscripts to be led by professional soldiers, having received advanced training on weapon systems as well as being integrated with local authorities, the police and the Finnish Border Guard (FBG) national security agency.

Finland has also sought 'shelter' under the NATO alliance and took part in Trident Juncture 18, NATO's biggest military exercise since the Cold War in October and November 2018. The exercise was a rehearsal (or preparation) for how the US-led alliance would respond to the invasion of an ally. All NATO members, plus Sweden and Finland, participated in the exercise, which took place only a few hundred miles from Norway's border with Russia. Finland claims that it was punished for its participation by a disruption of its Global Positioning System (GPS) signal, alleging that Russia had in fact 'jammed' the system. This suggests intimidation of this small state with a view to discouraging any ambition it may have to join the NATO alliance. The Finnish leadership, in line with its policy of 'balancing' between the East and West, summoned the Russian ambassador to explain the mysterious GPS jamming and also clarified that it would not be seeking full membership in NATO. The wider debate in Finland speculates about who Russia may be targeting. Is it seeking to stir up the Russian-speaking population, or should Russian actions be seen as a response and a rebuke to NATO? Hence, the disruption in Finland during the Trident Juncture exercise may be read not only as intimidatory for Helsinki but also as a warning to NATO.

As we have shown, the second arena of hybrid war—provoking, exploiting and supporting unrest and dissension among peoples through the careful use of information and other forms of national power—is nothing new. In fact, Sun Tzu[22] talks about hollowing out one's enemy from the inside and absorbing the whole without fighting in his famous treatise on *The Art of War*. War among people or violent social movements are what Heifetz describes as adaptive problems.[23] Such 'adaptive problems' do not follow the rules of systems and are, therefore, not easy to deal with. Conflicts may be deeply rooted in history, ideology, religion and culture or in general deprivation. Solutions and responses that are unsympathetic to differing perspectives and deal only with the present or the near future must be inadequate because they treat the problem not for what it actually is but as how it has been constructed to be, that is, as a tame[24] or a critical[25] problem that does follow rules.

Prescriptions for fighting hybrid threats abound. An extensive literature seeks to categorise and classify social movements and conflicts. This remains important because, as seen in the Iraq War after 2003, the widespread misunderstanding of the 'people' by invading forces and their politicians meant an inevitable failure to understand the complexities of local politics. That failure allowed other external actors to fill the voids created by poor security planning and policing and the

[22]Tzu (2000).

[23]Heifetz et al. (2009).

[24]Rittel and Webber (1973), pp. 155–169.

[25]Grint (2010), pp. 169–186.

misunderstanding of Sunni/Shia relations, plus a fateful ignorance of the motivations of external actors.

Finland is an advanced democracy but is nevertheless vulnerable to the 'mischief' of suspicions being articulated about the 'loyalty' of those citizens holding dual Russian citizenship. That a senior government minister suggested dual citizenship may prohibit recruitment to certain sensitive positions illustrates how easy it is to stir up questions about which citizens are 'trusted' and who may be provoked as apparent victims of discrimination.

A third arena of hybrid war concerns diplomatic, political and economic initiatives on the international stage. Sun Tzu recognised the power of indirect warfare. To take the enemy without fighting, and in the process conserve vital resources, mandates the avoidance of direct confrontation. Long-term social and political effects come as a consequence of sustaining an attack on the enemy on different fronts while keeping the scale and tempo of the 'offensive' within limits tolerable to the political elite and above the threshold of survivability for the masses. The dilution of economic, social and human capital in disparate directions generates a defensive mindset, making the target state further vulnerable to other forms of attack. This style of warfare circumvents constraints such as alliances and military parity and avoids direct conflict.[26]

Interference in elections through cyberattacks is an issue that dogged the US presidential election and the UK's Brexit vote. Finland, too, has a deeply rooted fear of cyberwarfare emanating from the East. Helsinki called for the creation of an international alliance to combat the growing threat and, in 2018, to become the base for a cyber-defence initiative for the West through the establishment of the NATO-backed European Centre for Excellence. Funding comes from the US, the UK, France and the Nordic states, thus extending cooperation into cyberspace. This dimension gives the act of sheltering practical as well as symbolic and deterrence application. By this means, alliance support is extended into a domain in which the 'fight' against states with different 'values' may become 'unseen' even while it remains crucial to democracy, as Antti Häkkänen, Finland's Justice Minister, has noted.

Concern about the possible penetration of the electoral system is such that plans for electronic voting have been abandoned. What may prove to be an advantage for small states is their population size. Manual voting remains feasible for a smaller populace, whereas in larger states such as the US or even the UK the electoral process becomes too time-consuming. Additionally, electronic methods to encourage and attract voters are being considered as a way to revive voter turnout. In this respect, larger states may be more vulnerable to hybrid attacks. There are more 'entry' points for attack, and there is certainly more contestation of the national narrative than in a small state such as Finland.

Hybrid war exhibits a non-kinetic extension of Ludendorff's concept of a total war with a covert twist. In the last decade, we have witnessed hostile cyberattacks on

---

[26]Korybko (2015), op. cit.

banking, elections, security infrastructure, individuals and groups. As society becomes increasingly dependent on technology with everything from our daily lives, social interactions, homes and work exposed, the scope for malicious access has grown manifold. Stirring political, class, clan, tribe and gender relations, perhaps even to make parts of the target state ungovernable and easy to penetrate by a host of external and hostile actors, has never been easier.

Arguably, the more populous and complex a state is, the more vulnerable it may be to the provocation of dissension and discord. Hybrid war can be waged at long distance; a contagious border provides a particularly dangerous blend of possibilities. The current and vivid examples of this are Russia and Ukraine, and India and Pakistan. Finland and the Baltic states find themselves particularly vulnerable on both accounts, proximity and complexity.

Acknowledgements We would like to acknowledge the help of Dr Duncan Depledge of Loughborough University, UK.

References

Allison GT, Zelikow P (1999) Essence of decision: explaining the Cuban missile crisis. Longman, New York

Chickering R, Förster S (eds) (2003) The shadows of total war: Europe, East Asia, and the United States, 1919–1939. Cambridge University Press, New York

Giles K (2016) Russia's 'New' tools for confronting the West: continuity and innovation in Moscow's exercise of power, Research Paper, Russia and Eurasia Programme. Chatham House, London

Grint K (2010) Wicked problems and clumsy solutions: the role of leadership. In: Brookes S, Grint K (eds) The new public leadership challenge. Palgrave Macmillan, Basingstoke, pp 169–186

Hassner RE (2009) War on sacred grounds. Cornell University Press, New York

Heifetz RA, Linsky M, Grashow A (2009) The practice of adaptive leadership: tools and tactics for changing your organisation and the world. Harvard Business School, Boston

Ignatieff M (2001) Virtual war: Kosovo and beyond. Picador, New York

Johnson G et al (2017) Exploring strategy: text and cases, 11th edn. Pearson, London

Keohane RO, Nye JS (1998) Power and interdependence in the information age. Foreign Aff 77 (5):81. https://doi.org/10.2307/20049052

Korybko A (2015) Hybrid wars: the indirect adaptive approach to regime change. Kindle Edition, Moscow, pp 1574–1586

Lisaka G (1962) Nations in alliance: the limits of interdependence. Johns Hopkins University Press, Baltimore

Ludendorff E (1935) Der Totale Krieg. English edition:The Nation at War (trans: Rappoport AS). Hutchinson, London

McDermott R (2015) Does Russia's hybrid war really exist. Eurasia Daily Monitor 12:103

Mintzberg H (2007) Tracking strategies: towards a general theory. Oxford University Press, Oxford

Monaghan A (2015) Putin's way of war: the 'war' in Russia's hybrid warfare. Parameters 45 (940):2015–2016

Mueller J (1995) Quiet cataclysm: reflections on the recent transformation of world politics. Harper Collins, London

Osgood RE (1966) NATO: the entangling alliance. University of Chicago Press, Chicago

RCDS (2017) Getting strategy right enough. RCDS, London

Rittel HWJ, Webber MM (1973) Dilemmas in a general theory of planning. Policy Sci 4 (2):155–169

Thorhallsson B (2011) Domestic buffer versus external shelter: viability of small states in the new globalised economy. Eur Polit Sci 10:324–336. Symposium, European Consortium for Political Research

Tzu S (2000) The art of war (A modern Chinese interpretation) Tao Hanzhang and Youan Shibing (trs). Sterling Publishing Company, New York

Williamson M, Mansoor PR (eds) (2011) Hybrid warfare fighting complex opponents from the ancient world to the present. Cambridge University Press, Cambridge

Zaidi MI (2009) The conduct of war and the notion of victory. PhD diss., Cranfield University

Caroline Kennedy-Pipe is Professor of International Security and International Relations at the University of Loughborough. She was visiting fellow at the Rothermere Institute at the University of Oxford in the summer of 2018.

Iftikhar Zaidi is a Senior Lecturer in Leadership and Strategy at Cranfield University. He retired from the Pakistan Army in 2011 and has been a directing staff at the Pakistan Military Academy, Kakul; the Command and Staff College, Quetta; and the National Defence University, Islamabad.

Chapter 4
How to Give China Face Yet Not Bow to Pressure: Albania's Delicate Balancing Act with China

Anne-Marie Brady and Hiromichi Higashi

4.1 Introduction

Albania is one of the founding members of the 17+1 grouping, which has an essential role in China's ambitious Belt and Road Initiative (BRI). Albania's economic and political relations with China have quickly gathered momentum since 2012. China and tiny Albania (population: 2.8 million) waged a war of words after the 1977 ideological split between Enver Hoxha's Party of Labour of Albania (PLA) and the Chinese Communist Party (CCP). Yet in 2016, the Chinese ambassador to Albania characterised relations between China and the Republic of Albania as a "traditional friendship bearing new fruits".[1] Is Albania repeating its history and leaning to one side?

This chapter examines contemporary Albania-China relations through the lens of CCP political interference activities, what the CCP government calls "united front work", assessing both China's intentions and Albania's response. The chapter uses Brady's "Magic Weapons" template on CCP united front work in the Xi era to assess

An earlier version of this paper was published at Sinopsis, republished with permission: https://sinopsis.cz/en/are-we-real-friends-albania-china-relations-in-the-xi-era/.

[1]Secretariat for Cooperation between China and Central and Eastern European Countries, "Albania-China Traditional Friendship Bearing New Fruits: Interview of the Ambassador of China Mrs. Jiang Yu with Albanian Daily News," December 30, 2016, http://www.china-ceec.org/eng/sbhz_1/t1427655.htm.

A.-M. Brady (✉) · H. Higashi
University of Canterbury, Christchurch, New Zealand
e-mail: anne-marie.brady@canterbury.ac.nz

A.-M. Brady, B. Thorhallsson (eds.), *Small States and the New Security Environment*, The World of Small States 7,
https://doi.org/10.1007/978-3-030-51529-4_4

the situation in Albania.[2] Under CCP General Secretary Xi Jinping, united front work has an important role in China's increasingly assertive foreign policy, which follows a three-pronged approach: (1) state-to-state interactions, (2) employment of military force and (3) covert operations via international united front work activities. United front work is the task of all party members and party-state-military agencies. Our chapter also provides a unique perspective on how a small state can achieve political, economic and societal shelter[3] via adroit juggling of relationships with various great powers, as well as multilateral arrangements.

4.2 Why China Is Interested in Albania

During the Cold War years, Albania was a symbol of the global power struggle between the Soviet Union and the People's Republic of China (PRC).[4] Albania was originally in the Soviet-led Eastern Bloc. But in the 1960s, as the Sino-Soviet split deepened, Albania was at odds with both the Soviet Union and Yugoslavia. Albania turned to China for protection and received many millions of dollars in economic aid and military equipment, as well as 7000 Chinese advisers.[5] By 1966, 70% of Albanian trade was with the PRC.[6] Premier Zhou Enlai visited Albania three times; Albania's senior leaders also visited China frequently.[7] In 1967, the CCP praised the relationship between the two nations as an "unbreakable militant friendship".[8]

Yet within 10 years, the "unbreakable militant friendship" had splintered over ideological differences. By the late 1970s, Enver Hoxha was openly critical of the CCP's expanding relations with the United States (US) and other Western nations. The CCP government punished Albania by cutting economic and military assistance and withdrawing its experts. The China-Albania militant friendship bolstered

[2]Anne-Marie Brady, "Magic Weapons: China's Political Influence Activities under Xi Jinping," https://www.wilsoncenter.org/article/magic-weapons-chinas-political-influence-activities-under-xi-jinping.

[3]See Anne-Marie Brady and Baldur Thorhallsson, "Small States and the Turning Point in Global Politics," in this volume.

[4]Marku (2017).

[5]Michael Dobbs, "Tiny Albania Kicks Out Chinese," *The Washington Post*, July 26, 1997, https://www.washingtonpost.com/archive/politics/1977/07/26/tiny-albania-kicks-out-chinese/4402c514-f86a-4af5-b0ed-92369e3cbe53/?noredirect=on.

[6]Steinberg and Paxton (2016), p. 726.

[7]Ye Hao, "The Development of China-Albania Relations and Its Lessons," CIIS, November 20, 2014, http://www.ciis.org.cn/gyzz/2014-11/20/content_7385229.htm.

[8]"Tirana's Art Troupe Held Closing Performance in Shanghai During the Closing Performance of the Arab People, the Albanian People Fight Forever Together," *People's Daily*, December 7, 1967, https://rmrb.online/simple/?t372353.html.

Hoxha's draconian rule, but by the end of the Cold War, Albania was one of the poorest and most isolated of the former Eastern Bloc states.

With all this history, it is remarkable that Albania and China now appear to be developing a strong political, economic and strategic connection again. Relations took a long time to repair. In 1989, the PRC and Albania moved to a pragmatic relationship when the two countries signed an agreement on economic and technological cooperation. Albania's interactions with China remained at a low ebb for years. But Albania's NATO, EU, Taiwan and Muslim connections, as well as the country's strategic resources and geopolitical significance, are among the reasons China restored its relations with Albania to a deeper level.

In 1990, the communist era came to a peaceful end in Albania. Democratic elections were held in 1991. Successive Albanian governments focused on integrating their economy with Europe and seeking the political shelter of membership in the North American Treaty Organization (NATO). In 1992, Albania joined the North Atlantic Cooperation Council, and then in 1994, it entered NATO's Partnership for Peace.

Albania also began to develop relations with the Republic of China (ROC, Taiwan). Parliamentarians established an Association of Friendship between Albania and Taiwan.[9] In 1999, Taiwanese diplomats offered Albania US$1 billion in aid over 10 years to switch recognition to the ROC from the PRC.[10] At the same time, the Albanian government was also in talks to receive loans from the PRC.[11] The pro-Taiwan parliamentary group was closed in 1999, after the Albanian government's policy on China changed.[12] In a joint communiqué with the PRC in 2000, the Albanian government reiterated its support for the "One China" policy and stated that the "Republic of Albania will not establish official ties or conduct official contacts with Taiwan in any form".[13]

Albania is a Muslim-majority nation and has had many connections to international efforts to combat Islamic terrorism, some of which link to China's interests. After the end of the communist era, Muslim charities flocked to help rebuild Albania. Many of Albania's new democratic leaders were Muslim. In 1994, Osama bin Laden established a base in Albania via a Saudi charitable organisation.[14] In 1997, the

[9]Catherine Sung and Arsim Zekolli, "Association Says Albania in Tug-of-War over Taiwan," *Taipei Times*, December 13, 1999, http://www.taipeitimes.com/News/local/archives/1999/12/13/0000014715.

[10]Tubilewicz (2007), p. 145.

[11]Ministry of Foreign Affairs of the People's Republic of China (FMPRC), "Joint Communique between the People's Republic of China and the Republic of Albania," December 7, 2000, https://www.fmprc.gov.cn/mfa_eng/wjdt_665385/2649_665393/t15781.shtml.

[12]Sung and Zekolli. "Association Says Albania in Tug-of-War over Taiwan."

[13]FMPRC, "Joint Communique between the People's Republic of China and the Republic of Albania."

[14]Stratfor Worldview, "Part 3: Albanian Unrest Presents Opportunity for Bin Laden," *Stratfor*, January 24, 2001, https://worldview.stratfor.com/article/part-3-albanian-unrest-presents-opportunity-bin-laden.

Central Intelligence Agency (CIA) helped to reform and retrain the Albanian security agency SHIK (Shërbimi Informativ Kombëtar) after SHIK's director and deputy director were forced to resign due to their links to radical Islam.[15] In 1998, SHIK and the CIA conducted a joint operation against bin Laden's group in Tirana.[16] The Albanian government worked with US intelligence to detain and expel foreigners using Albania as a hub for terrorist activities in Europe.[17] During the 1999 Kosovo War, when more than half a million Kosovar Albanians were forced out of their homeland, the PRC sided with Serbia and vehemently protested against NATO intervention. The Albanian government allowed the US to use its territory and airspace to attack Serbia during the war. In 2004 and 2005, the CIA used Albania as a transit point for "renditions" of suspected terrorists.[18] Then in 2006, the Albanian government agreed to provide refuge to five Uighur men who had been wrongfully detained by the US government and held in Guantanamo prison. The US government allowed PRC Ministry of State Security officials to interrogate the men in Guantanamo.[19] All five men were cleared by the US of involvement in any terrorist activities. They were sent to Albania as no other state would take them, and they feared returning to China. The CCP government pressured the Albanian government to hand them over, but Albania held firm.[20]

Albania's participation in NATO and EU candidacy are frequently highlighted in Chinese government materials.[21] In April 2009, Albania became a full member of NATO.[22] In the same year, Albania joined the European Free Trade Association and applied to join the European Union; in 2020, Albania began formal accession talks to join the EU. Albania is the first country in the West Balkans to host a NATO airbase.

---

[15]Chris Deliso, "Spy Book Reveals Operational Details of 1998 CIA Balkan Counter-Terrorism Operation," Balkanalysis.com, accessed March 26, 2020, http://www.balkanalysis.com/albania/2011/02/04/spy-book-reveals-operational-details-of-1998-cia-balkan-counter-terrorism-operation/.

[16]R. Jeffery Smith, "U.S. Probes Blasts' Possible Mideast Ties," *The Washington Post*, August 12, 1998, https://www.washingtonpost.com/wp-srv/inatl/longterm/eafricabombing/stories/albania081298.htm.

[17]International Crisis Group (2001), https://www1.essex.ac.uk/armedcon/world/europe/south_east_europe/macedonia/MacedoniaBinLadenandtheBalkans.pdf.

[18]Fred Abrahams, "Albania Must Come Clean on Torture Claims," *Balkan Insight*, December 12, 2014, https://balkaninsight.com/2014/12/12/albania-must-come-clean-on-torture-claims/.

[19]Tim Golden, "Chinese Leave Guantánamo for Albanian Limbo," *The New York Times*, June 10, 2007, https://www.nytimes.com/2007/06/10/world/europe/10resettle.html.

[20]Bruce Konvisor, "A Strange Kind of Freedom - Albania Wants to Expel Uighurs Sent There by U. S.," The Uyghur American Association, June 13, 2016, https://uyghuramerican.org/article/strange-kind-freedom-albania-wants-expel-uighurs-sent-there-us.html.

[21]This link has now been removed from the website https://www.yidaiyilu.gov.cn/wcm.files/upload/CMSydylgw/201902/201902010410054.pdf.

[22]North Atlantic Treaty Organization, "NATO Secretary General Welcomes Albania and Croatia as NATO Members," April 1, 2009, https://www.nato.int/cps/en/natolive/news_52342.htm.

It was also in April 2009 that Chinese leaders praised Albania as a "traditional cooperative partner".[23] This special terminology signifies that China hopes that its present-day relations with Albania will be a model to other small states. Year 2009 marked the 60th anniversary of the establishment of diplomatic relations between the PRC and Albania. In that year, Albania and China signed an agreement to take relations to a new level, prioritising economic cooperation.[24] But it was not until 2012 that Sino-Albania relations really took off. In 2012, Albania joined the China-CEEC group, a China-centered strategic bloc of states in Central and Eastern Europe. In 2017, Albania also signed an agreement to participate in the Belt and Road Initiative.

During the Mao years, the CCP's main interest in Albania was winning the ideological and strategic war against the Soviet Union. But in the Xi era, Albania is of interest to China as a source of natural resources and because of Albania's strategic location strategic. Albania is also interesting to China because it is geopolitically important to the US, Russia, and other states.

4.3 Albania and the Belt and Road Initiative

In 2014, the Xi government launched the Belt and Road Initiative (BRI), a global political, economic and strategic bloc. PLA spokesperson Peng Guangqian boasts that the BRI will reshape the global order.[25] BRI builds on the Jiang Zemin era "going out" policy, which aimed to stimulate the Chinese economy by acquiring privileged access to global natural resources and gaining contracts for international infrastructure projects.

BRI has created a China-centered network of roads, railways and ports, as well as a "Digital Silk Road", which will connect China's BRI partners to China's own information communication systems such as Huawei and the BeiDou Global Navigation Satellite System (GNSS). If China can persuade BRI partner states to host BeiDou ground stations and incorporate BeiDou navigation systems into local mobile phone networks, it will greatly enhance China's military capabilities.[26] Global navigation systems are a critical enabler for military operations. They provide missile positioning and timing and access to fleet-based broadband for unclassified

---

[23] "Wen Jiabao Makes Four Suggestions During Talks with Albanian Prime Minister Berisha," www.gov.cn, April 21, 2009, http://www.gov.cn/ldhd/2009-04/21/content_1291992.htm; Chen Xiaochen, "Elaborate on China's Foreign Partnership: Strategic Collaboration at the Highest Level," *Sina Finance*, November 24, 2014, https://finance.sina.com.cn/china/20141124/024420898324.shtml.

[24] "Wen Jiabao Makes Four Suggestions During Talks with Albanian Prime Minister Berisha," April 21, 2009, http://www.gov.cn/ldhd/2009-04/21/content_1291992.htm.

[25] This link has been removed from the website http://www.taiwan.cn/xwzx/gj/201501/t20150109_8645599.htm.

[26] Brady (2017).

and classified systems, and they enable environmental situational awareness. The US invented the Global Positioning System (GPS) for military operations, and the whole world now depends on it. But by 2020, the US may have lost its technological advantage in GPS over strategic rivals Russia and China, which are developing their own rival global navigation systems, Global Navigation Satellite System (GLONASS) and BeiDou.

The six tasks of BRI are as follows:[27]

1) Using economic ties with foreign countries to support China's food security
2) Supporting Chinese industry to engage in economic stimulation activities
3) Preventing a debt crisis in China by balancing regional development in China
4) Improving the standard of living in China
5) Expanding China's external transport routes
6) Reducing the impact of chokepoints such as the Malacca Straits

The BRI "five connections" are the following:[28]

1) Policy coordination
2) Transportation links
3) Trade links
4) Currency swaps
5) Information and communication technology links[29]

Albania signed a Memorandum of Understanding (MOU) with China on BRI in April 2017. But it was already linked to BRI through China-CEEC (China-Central and Eastern European Countries), which was merged into BRI in 2016. Albania was one of the founding members of the China-CEEC politico-economic bloc, which aligns China with 17 European countries: Albania, Bosnia and Herzegovina, Bulgaria, Croatia, Czechia, Estonia, Greece, Hungary, Latvia, Lithuania, Macedonia, Montenegro, Poland, Romania, Serbia, Slovakia and Slovenia. China-CEEC was set up in 2012. Until Greece joined in 2019, the grouping was also known as "16 +1".

Albania's touted role within the BRI strategy is as a source of strategic natural resources for China. Mineral products and metals made up 31% of Albania's exports in 2016, including chromium, copper, nickel and crude oil.[30] In March 2016, a Canadian company, Banker's Petroleum, sold its Albanian oil exploration and production rights to Geo-Jade Petroleum, a Chinese company whose main

[27]This link has been removed from the website http://news.xinhuanet.com/fortune/2013-12/14/c_125858096.htm.

[28]Belt and Road, "'Belt and Road' Basics," accessed March 26, 2020, https://beltandroad.hktdc.com/tc/belt-and-road-basics.

[29]Belt and Road, "Country Profiles," https://beltandroad.hktdc.com/tc/country-profiles.

[30]The Observatory of Economic Complexity, "Albania," https://oec.world/en/profile/country/alb/.

businesses are located in Kazakhstan.[31] Bankers Petroleum was forced to sell its Albanian investments after the Albanian government accused it of money laundering, tax fraud and polluting the environment.[32] Geo-Jade has full rights to develop the Patos-Marinza oilfield, Europe's largest onshore oil reserve, and a 100% interest in the Kucova oilfield, Albania's second largest oilfield. Beijing-based mining and metal company Sinomine Resource Exploration also has a subsidiary in Albania to conduct mining site construction, and it is doing surveying with a local geological institute.[33] China is also investing in Albania's agricultural sector.[34]

Another potential role for Albania within BRI is as a transport hub. In November 2015, Albania, Montenegro and the company Pacific Chinese signed a trilateral Memorandum of Understanding on plans to construct the Adriatic-Ionian Highway.[35] This coastal highway will run from Trieste to Kalamata and will link Italy, Slovenia, Croatia, Bosnia and Herzegovina, Montenegro, Albania and Greece. The highway could help Albania become a hub for maritime transport. However, the project has been fraught with controversy over allegations of money laundering and corruption.[36] Following massive student protests in late 2018, the Albanian government cancelled plans for the development of the Thumanë-Kashar section of the highway in 2019.[37]

BRI strategic documents recommend setting up trade zones. In 2015, Albania announced plans to establish three economic and technological development zones: Spitalla Free Economic Zone, Koplik Free Economic Zone and Vlorë Free

---

[31]Fatjona Mejdini, "Chinese Buy Rights to Oil Fields in Albania," *BalkanInsight*, March 21, 2016, https://balkaninsight.com/2016/03/21/chinese-company-to-take-over-oil-fields-of-albania-03-21-2016/; Geo-Jade Petroleum Corporation, "Oil and Gas Exploration and Development," http://www.geojade.com/html/en/business/index.html#page1.

[32]Adriatilk Llalla, *Letter to Bujar Nishani and Ilir Meta*, http://www.pp.gov.al/web/Information_on_US_visa_s_revocation_for_prosecutors_1043_2.php#.XnvY-YgzY2y.

[33]This link has been removed from the website http://www.nfmec.com/index.php?c=article&id=423.

[34]Embassy of Albania, "Ambassador Jiang Yu Meets with Algerian Minister of Agriculture and Rural Development," Ministry of Foreign Affairs of the People's Republic of China, November 15, 2017, https://www.fmprc.gov.cn/web/wjdt_674879/zwbd_674895/t1510542.shtml.

[35]"Albania, Montenegro and Pacific Company Sign MoU for Blue Corridor Project," November 25, 2015, https://invest-in-albania.org/albania-montenegro-and-pacific-company-sign-mou-for-blue-corridor-project/; "China to Invest in Albania in Infrastructure, Agriculture and Tourism," November 27, 2015, https://invest-in-albania.org/china-to-invest-in-albania-in-infrastructure-agriculture-and-tourism/.

[36]Gjergj Erebara, "Albania Arrests Ex-Officials Over Unbuilt Road," *BalkanInsight*, February 2, 2018, https://balkaninsight.com/2018/02/02/albania-former-officials-of-road-authority-arrested-for-abuse-of-power-02-02-2018-1/.

[37]Vincent W.J. van Gerven Oei, "Only Public Universities Late with Applying for Accreditation," *Exit News*, August 7, 2019, https://exit.al/en/2019/08/07/only-public-universities-late-with-applying-for-accreditation/; "Feasibility Study Finds the Albanian Government Doubled Highway Cost," *Exit News*, August 8, 2019, https://exit.al/en/2019/08/08/feasibility-study-finds-the-albanian-government-doubled-highway-cost/.

Economic Zone.[38] China's deputy Premier, Zhang Gaoli, said that China would expand its investment in Albania and specifically mentioned investment the free trade zones, as well as transport infrastructure and energy projects.[39] Skeptics say Albania has previously promoted multiple free trade zones, which have received little interest from foreign investors, deterred by problems relating to land ownership in Albania, the lack of infrastructure and problems as basic as reliable electricity, ongoing political instability and endemic corruption.[40]

In 2016, China's Everbright Group bought Tirana's Nënë Tereza International Airport Company, and it has a concession on the airport until 2027.[41] The aim is to set up a logistics centre to transport Chinese goods into Europe and to promote tourism in Albania, especially tourists from China.[42] Albania is a crucial link in the Trans Adriatic Pipeline, which connects the oilfields of Shanghai Cooperation member Azerbaijan with the markets of Europe.

Albania is also connected to China's Digital Silk Road. China's global navigation system, BeiDou, is now in use in Albanian mobile networks.[43] China's controversial telecom company Huawei has an Albanian-registered company, Huawei Technologies Albania SH.P.K. Huawei contributes to Albania's 4G network, and Huawei phones are common in Albania.[44] However in 2019, the Albanian government signed an MOU with the US government affirming that Huawei would not be involved in the 4G upgrade or in 5G in Albania, and there are no signs of a BeiDou ground station on Albanian soil.

---

[38]"Albania Plans International Tender for Developers in Three Economic and Technological Development Zones," Ministry of Commerce of the People's Republic of China, April 29, 2015, http://www.mofcom.gov.cn/article/i/jshz/zn/201505/20150500963294.shtml.

[39]This link has been removed from the website http://paper.people.com.cn/rmrb/html/2017-04/18/nw.D110000renmrb_20170418_4-03.htm.

[40]Edison Kurani, "Albania Announces Free Zones with Reduced Tax on Profits. Will Investors Be Encouraged?" *Independent Balkan News Agency*, May 25, 2015, https://balkaneu.com/albania-announces-free-zones-reduced-tax-profits-investors-encouraged/.

[41]"China Everbright Group Buys Albanian Airport Operator," *Reuters*, October 8, 2016, https://www.reuters.com/article/us-china-albania-everbright/china-everbright-group-buys-albanian-airport-operator-idUSKCN1271ZE.

[42]Edison Kurani, "China Is Ready to Invest in Albania: Charter Flights from Beijing to Tirana," Confindustria Est Europa, May 6, 2016, http://www.confindustriaest.eu/en/cina-investimenti-albania-voli-charter/.

[43]"Director Wang Li of Beidou Navigation System: What New Changes and New Conveniences Will Beidou System Bring to Enterprises?" *SOHU*, April 18, 2019, https://www.sohu.com/a/302848155_339728.

[44]Alice Elizabeth Taylor, "Huawei Director Arrested for Spying in Poland," *Exit News*, January 12, 2019, https://exit.al/en/2019/01/12/huawei-director-arrested-for-spying-in-poland/; Huawei, "Albania Upgrades Electrical Grid in the Balkans," accessed March 26, 2020, https://e.huawei.com/sg/publications/global/ict_insights/201802151130/industry-variations/201806011609.

4.4 China's Efforts to Influence Albanian Political and Economic Elites

CCP united front efforts in Albania follow a predictable pattern: a focus on political parties, the local government, the business sector, the youth and intellectuals. Because a generation of Albanian elites had many interactions with China in the Mao-Hoxha years, CCP united front efforts can draw on a pool of older generation Albanian "friends of China" to help push forward cooperation.[45] However, none of these individuals are currently in a position to influence contemporary political decisions. The post-1991 elite received their training in Albania or the West and, regardless of their politics, tend to be more at home in Europe or the USA than Xi's parallel universe.

The CCP is trying to foster a new generation of Albanian "Friends of China" with offers of generous scholarships and trips to China. Chinese ambassador Jiang Yu describes Albanian students learning Chinese as "missionaries for China-Albanian friendship".[46] Albania has one Confucius Institute at the University of Tirana, which is partnered with Beijing Foreign Studies University.[47] It opened in May 2013, and Confucius classrooms were set up in several high schools in Tirana in the same year.[48] The PRC Tirana embassy has gifted teaching materials to assist with Chinese-language classes.[49] The Albanian PRC embassy and Huawei's Albanian subsidiary sponsor Chinese culture competitions.[50] Huawei also sponsors the "One Thousand Dreams" programme in Albania.[51] This programme will train 1000 information technology (IT) talents for Huawei, donate 1000 books to university libraries and give 1000 toys to children's hospitals. Twenty-nine Albanian government officials and scholars have been sent to China on short-term trips to study China's agricultural techniques.[52] In 2016, the Chinese embassy in Albania hosted

---

[45]Cooperation between China and Central and Eastern European Countries, "Diplomats in the Embassy in Afghanistan Hold Talks with Representatives from All Walks of Life," January 12, 2018, http://www.china-ceec.org/chn/hzjl/glyhz/hdxw/t1525298.htm.

[46]"Tirana: Chinese Ambassador Visits Elementary and High Schools," *CRI Online*, September 24, 2015, http://albanian.cri.cn/321/2015/09/24/182s145535.htm.

[47]This link has been removed from the website http://www.hanban.org/article/2015-10/26/content_619994.htm.

[48]"Albania Sets off 'Chinese Learning Fever'," June 4, 2013, http://www.china-ceec.com/aebny/2013/0604/4771.html.

[49]"Hanban presents Chinese textbooks to Albania," January 29, 2013, http://www.china-ceec.com/aebny/2013/0129/2303.html.

[50]"The First Chinese Culture Competition Was Held in Tirana," June 9, 2016, https://www.fmprc.gov.cn/web/zwbd_673032/gzhd_673042/t1370862.shtml.

[51]"Huawei Launches the One Thousand Dreams Program to Improve ICT Education for the Youth and Provide Care for Children in Central and Eastern Europe," April 12, 2019, https://www.huawei.com/en/press-events/news/2019/4/huawei-ict-one-thousand-dreams-program-europe.

[52]"Sino-Albania Agricultural Human Resources Development Cooperation Project Launched," August 30, 2017, https://www.fmprc.gov.cn/web/zwbd_673032/gzhd_673042/t1488512.shtml;

the Sino-Albanian College Students Belt and Road Friendship Activity.[53] Chinese companies Hong Kong Ta Kung Wen Wei Media Group and China Everbright Limited funded the event. At the 2019 China-CEEC meeting, the Albanian government agreed to host a China-CEEC Youth Development Center.[54]

The PRC embassy supports the Sino-Albanian Youth Friendship Association,[55] the Albania-China Cultural Association, the Albania-China Friendship Association and the Albania-China Parliamentary Group of Friendship.[56] The Albania China Friendship Association was re-established in 1991.[57] An earlier group closed down after the ideological split between the two countries. The Friendship Association promotes Albania's participation in BRI and works closely with the Tirana PRC embassy.[58] In 2017, the head of the Friendship Association, Iljaz Spahiu, was awarded the CCP Central Propaganda Department funded Special Book Award of China.[59]

Cultural links are a traditional channel for united front work. The PRC's Chinese Disabled People's Art Troupe, the Beijing Song and Dance Troupe, the Nanjing Folk Orchestra and a Chinese martial arts group have all toured Albania in recent years, and Chinese art exhibitions have also visited.

Party-to-party links are an important channel for CCP united front work. The CCP utilises senior current and former politicians as bridges to their governments and, in exchange, offers them status, free trips to China and BRI events, and access to the CCP leadership for business opportunities. The Albania-China Parliamentary Group of Friendship is led by Vasilika Hysi, deputy speaker of the Parliament and senior MP in the Socialist Party led government.[60] The Socialist Party of Albania, the Democratic Party of Albania and the Socialist Movement for Integration have all participated in the CCP's "China-Europe High-level Political Parties Forum"

Liu Wei, "The Ancient Capitals of the Six Dynasties Witness China-Albania Friendship," September 25, 2017, http://cohd.cau.edu.cn/art/2017/9/25/art_8576_532319.html.

[53]This link has been removed from the website http://www.hanban.org/article/2016-12/26/content_669716.htm.

[54]Ministry of Foreign Affairs of the People's Republic of China, "The Dubrovnik Guidelines for Cooperation between China and Central and Eastern European Countries," April 17, 2019, https://webcache.googleusercontent.com/search?q=cache:7WJWQvmxFhEJ:https://www.fmprc.gov.cn/mfa_eng/wjdt_665385/2649_665393/t1655224.shtml&cd=3&hl=en&ct=clnk&gl=nz.

[55]"China-Arab Youth Friendship Association," November 21, 2017, http://al.china-embassy.org/chn/zagx/zajw/t1512462.htm.

[56]"Albanian President Meets with Delegation of China's Political Advisors," *Xinhua*, April 18, 2019, http://www.xinhuanet.com/english/2019-04/18/c_137985748.htm.

[57]"Albania-Chinese Friendship Association and Albania-Chinese Friendship Group," November 24, 2004, https://www.fmprc.gov.cn/web/gjhdq_676201/gj_676203/oz_678770/1206_678772/1206x2_678792/t171793.shtml.

[58]"Zhou Ding, Ambassador to Albania Meets with President of the China-Albania Friendship Association," January 26, 2019, http://al.chineseembassy.org/chn/zagx/zajw/t1632624.htm.

[59]Li Huiru, "Good Literary Works Should Value Reality: Special Book Award Winners." China.org, August 24, 2017, http://www.china.org.cn/arts/2017-08/24/content_41468831.htm.

[60]"Albanian President Meets with Delegation of China's Political Advisors."

inter-party meetings from 2010 to 2016, as well as China-CEEC Young Leaders Forums.[61] Luan Rama, vice chair of the Socialist Movement for Integration, participated in the 2017 "CCP in Dialogue with World Political Parties High-Level Meeting", which launched the CCP's direct participation role in Chinese foreign policy.[62] Former Albanian President Rexhep Meidani has participated in China-CEEC public diplomacy events and is a vocal supporter of Albania's participation in the BRI.[63] In 2018, a delegation from the CCP International Liaison Department visited Albania.[64] Xinhua claimed that Albanian politicians were "willing to learn" from the CCP's experience in "governing the Party and governing the State".[65]

As of 2019, China is Albania's third-largest export market and third-largest import source.[66] However, Italy is still overwhelmingly Albania's biggest export market with 72% share compared to China's mere 3.5%, while Italy is also Albania's biggest source of imports with 31% share compared to China's 6.7%. In 2018, CGTN, the PRC's foreign-language television network, claimed that "China is the single largest investor in the Albanian economy".[67] Yet according to Albanian government statistics, the Netherlands is actually Albania's largest investor, while China still only ranks ninth.[68]

Albania has taken up a relatively small amount of loans from China in the current period, and despite a lot of publicity about potential funding of projects, very little of them have come to fruition. Albania has a very high level of public debt, 68.8% of gross domestic product (GDP) in 2019. But Albania's public debt is mostly held with the International Monetary Fund (IMF), World Bank, German Development Bank and EU, though China has loaned money to Albania in the past.[69]

In December 2000, on the same day that Albania signed a communiqué renouncing all diplomatic contact with Taiwan, China announced that it was loaning Albania US$100 million to finance the construction of the Bushat Hydropower Station.[70] The loan ballooned to US$150 million and was paid off over 12 years at 3.5% interest,

[61]"High-Level Political Parties Forum Boosts China-Europe Cooperation," August 2, 2016, http://www.scio.gov.cn/32618/Document/1486302/1486302.htm.

[62]"SMI, Luan Rama: Political Parties, Role in Society's Emancipation," *Albanian Daily News*, December 1, 2017, https://www.albaniandailynews.com/index.php?idm=17005&mod=2.

[63]Yu et al. (2018), p. 196.

[64]"Chinese Delegation Visits Albania," *Xinhua*, June 13, 2018, http://www.xinhuanet.com/politics/2018-06/13/c_1122981971.htm.

[65]Ibid.

[66]"Albania Major Trade Partners," November 1, 2019, https://www.countryaah.com/albania-major-trade-partners/.

[67]"Oil Sector: AMI China Invest in Albania Oil Industry," *CGTN*, August 9, 2018, https://news.cgtn.com/news/794d444d35454464776c6d636a4e6e62684a4856/share_p.html.

[68]"Who Were the Largest Foreign Investors in Albania in Q1?" June 25, 2019, https://invest-in-albania.org/who-were-the-largest-foreign-investors-in-albania-in-q1/.

[69]Edison Kurani, "Albania's External Debt Increases, the Government is Responsible for Most of It," *Independent Balkan News Agency*, January 7, 2019, https://balkaneu.com/albanias-external-debt-increases-the-government-is-responsible-for-most-of-it/.

[70]Dreher et al. (2017), https://china.aiddata.org/projects/42265.

adding more than US$60 million to the cost.[71] In 2013, the Albanian government announced that it was in negotiation with China Communications Construction Company to develop Shëngjin Port at a cost of 2.2 billion euros.[72] But the port development plans did not progress.[73] In 2014, China's Exim Bank offered Albania 250 million euro to build the Arbër Highway in northern Albania and offered another large block of funding for roading and irrigation projects.[74] The Arbër Highway contract was given to China State Construction Engineering Corporation (CSCE), with a plan to use Chinese labour, despite high unemployment in Albania. But in 2016, the Albanian media reported that Chinese diplomats were conducting an investigation into the project due to corruption allegations.[75] In 2017, CSCE withdrew from the contract, and the contract was taken over by an Albanian firm, Gjoka Construction.[76] The road is now being financed through a public-private financing scheme between Gjoka and the Albanian state. In 2017, China granted a relatively modest 10 million yuan (1.5 million euro) to the Albanian government to modernise the agricultural sector.[77] The Bank of China is one of the funders of the 3.2-billion-euro Trans Adriatic Pipeline, which will cross Albania.[78] Most of the Adriatic-Ionian Highway will be debt financed by China's Exim Bank.[79] However, the Albanian Thumanë-Kashar section of the highway, which was to be financed by the EU through the Berlin Initiative, has not gone ahead.[80] Thus, despite all the big talks about BRI infrastructure projects that Albania could be involved in, according to an

---

[71] Kircher and Matthews (2018).

[72] Edison Kurani, "China is Offered the Strategic Port of Shengjin in Albania, After Roads in FYROM and Montenegro," *Independent Balkan News Agency*, November 27, 2013, https://balkaneu.com/china-offered-strategic-port-shengjin-albania-roads-fyrom-montenegro/.

[73] "Europort Shëngjin, a Pharaonic Project Rewarded with a Nice Obelisk (and No Investment)," *Ship2Shore*, March 14, 2016, http://www.ship2shore.it/en/ports/europort-shngjin-a-pharaonic-project-rewarded-with-a-nice-obelisk-and-no-investment_60589.htm.

[74] Edison Kurani, "Albanian Government Gives Way to a 250 Million Euro Investment for the Construction of the Road of Arber," *Independent Balkan News Agency*, April 12, 2017, https://balkaneu.com/albanian-government-gives-way-to-a-250-million-euro-investment-for-the-construction-of-the-road-of-arber/.

[75] "Kina nis Hetime për Qeverinë Shqiptare, Dyshime për Korrupsion me Rrugën e Arbrit [China Launches Investigation on Albanian Government, Corruption Allegations on Arber Road]," *KOHA*, March 10, 2016, https://archive.koha.net/?id=27&l=102460.

[76] "Govt Accepts €250mln for Arberi Road Construction," April 13, 2017, https://invest-in-albania.org/govt-accepts-e250mln-arberi-road-construction/.

[77] Marina Mikhaylova, "China Backs Albania's Farming Sector with 10 Mln Yuan (1.3 Mln Euro) Grant," *SeeNews*, June 6, 2016, https://seenews.com/news/china-backs-albanias-farming-sector-with-10-mln-yuan-13-mln-euro-grant-527742.

[78] "TAP Completes Successful Euros 3.9 Billion Project Financing," January 11, 2019, https://www.tap-ag.com/news-and-events/2019/01/11/tap-completes-successful-euros-39-billion-project-financing.

[79] Bieber and Tzifakis (2019), http://biepag.eu/wp-content/uploads/2019/08/The_Western_Balkans_as_a_Geopolitical_Chessboard.pdf.

[80] "Real Cost of Thumane-Kashar, EUR 169 Mln," *Albanian Daily News*, August 8, 2019, https://www.albaniandailynews.com/index.php?idm=34385&mod=2.

assessment in the 2019 Munich Security Report, Albania is the only West Balkan state not receiving any loans from the BRI project.[81]

The CCP government is trying to encourage more Chinese tourists to visit Albania.[82] In 2016, Albanian Foreign Minister Ditmir Bushati signed a Memorandum of Understanding to simplify visa application procedures for citizens of Albania and China.[83] As of 2018, Chinese citizens no longer need a visa to visit Albania. But Chinese tourism numbers have been slow to expand due to fears about Albania's poor public security.[84]

Under the policy of "using the local to surround the center", the CCP uses sister city links and local government investment schemes to influence central governments and promote China's agenda. China has included Albania in its city diplomacy efforts,[85] sponsoring its participation in global city diplomacy events.[86] China is planning to "twin" Tianjin with Tirana.

Foreign academics are a common target of CCP united front work. China offers them trips, paid talks, research funding, honours and distinctions. Several Albanian scholars have participated in the CCP's High-Level Symposium of Think Tanks of China and CEECs.[87] In 2015, China's General Administration of Press and Publication agreed to subsidise the translation into Chinese of 50 Albanian books.[88] The project aims to shape positive public opinion. In 2016, the Tirana International Books Exhibition was held in the Albanian Parliament Building. The Association of Albania Publishers, the Tirana Confucius Institute, the Chinese Embassy and China's Foreign Language Teaching and Research Press of Beijing University

---

[81] Munich Security Conference (2019), https://securityconference.org/en/publications/munich-security-report-2019/.

[82] "Çollaku: Albania, Waiting for Chinese Tourists," August 7, 2017, http://al.chineseembassy.org/eng/zgyw/t1482926.htm.

[83] "Albania and China to Boost Cooperation and Simplify Visa Procedures," August 26, 2016, https://invest-in-albania.org/albania-and-china-to-boost-cooperation-and-simplify-visa-procedures/.

[84] Chenger, "The Sorrow of a Nation: Albanian Stealing Chinese Style," Franceqw, November 11, 2014, http://www.franceqw.com/article-37296-1.html; Gao Anhua, "Albania Impression: Dirty Mess," Annie's Spring Princess Blog, July 30, 2013, http://blog.sina.com.cn/s/blog_97f7e2c10101m0rc.html.

[85] "World Canal Historical and Cultural Cities Cooperation Organization Development Strategy Expert Meeting Held in Yangzhou," December 10, 2016, http://www.whcccco.org/DetailImageInfo.php?pid=0&cid=2&num=2&id=104.

[86] Li Shaopeng, "Yangzhou Hosts "City Celebration Day" Series Activities," CRI, December 2, 2015, http://news.cri.cn/gb/42071/2015/10/02/8334s5121728.htm.

[87] *Report on the 2nd High Level Symposium of Think Tanks of the People's Republic of China and Central and Eastern European Countries,* (Bled: 2014), http://mzz.arhiv-spletisc.gov.si/fileadmin/pageuploads/foto/1409/Porocilo_2_O_SIMPOZIJU__ZBRANI_PRISPEVKI__ab__01.pdf.

[88] "China and Albania Sign Agreement for Translation of Classic Books," April 29, 2015, http://al.china-embassy.org/chn/zagx/zajw/t1259339.htm.

participated in the exhibition to promote Sino-Albanian publications.[89] In 2018, academics from the Albanian Academy of Social Sciences joined in an "Albaniology" conference hosted by Beijing International Studies University's Department of Albanian Language.[90] In 2017, Beijing International Studies University announced a major investment in subsidised Albanian-language studies (along with other CEEC languages) to train diplomats and other professionals to further China's 17+1 BRI strategy.[91] Over a 7-year period, 20 undergraduates per year will be trained in Albanian, 20 in Bulgarian, 20 in Slovenian, 20 in Czech (Slovak) and 20 in Hungarian.

4.5 China's Global Strategic Communication Strategy and Albania

Albania has a small media market, so many of the CCP's united front media management efforts are via China-CEEC joint activities. The CCP's key message directed at Albania emphasises economic links and aims to create a positive picture of Sino-Albanian relations that will help erase the negative memories of the past. Radio Peking broadcast in Albanian during the 16 years of Sino-Albanian militant friendship, but this ended after the rupture in relations.[92] The first tendrils of Sino-Albanian media cooperation resumed in 2012, when China Radio International and Albania's Radio Televizioni Shqiptar signed a Programme Cooperation Memorandum to exchange economic-related programmes between the two countries.[93] The stated goal of this collaboration is to encourage more Sino-Albanian economic links and to create positive public opinion. In 2013, China Radio International set up an Albanian-language FM channel in Tirana.[94] In 2017, chief executive officers (CEOs) of 11 Albanian media organisations were invited to a "media friendship" meeting at the PRC embassy in Tirana.[95] As they do in other states, PRC diplomats in Albania

[89]This link has now been erased from the website https://www.fltrp.com/c/2016-11-15/489771.shtml.

[90]"An Albanology Department at Beijing University," *Tirana Times*, November 9, 2018, https://www.tiranatimes.com/?p=139215.

[91]"2017 Beijing Second Foreign Language College Penetrating Talent Training Project," May 3, 2017, https://zs.bisu.edu.cn/art/2017/5/3/art_6741_139624.html.

[92]Steinberg and Paxton (2016), p. 727.

[93]This link has now been erased from the website. http://www.cri.com.cn/2014-1-14/dc31d22c-bad9-ddc2-4de1-57bbe327bb2d.html.

[94]Embassy of the People's Republic of China in the Republic of Albania, "China and Albania," http://al.china-embassy.org/eng/zagx/sbgx/t1245474.htm.

[95]"PRC Embassy Hosts New Year Party in Albania," November 24, 2017, http://al.china-embassy.org/chn/zagx/zajw/t1513586.htm.

publish op eds in the local media promoting China's foreign policy perspective.[96] In 2015, Zhonghua Book Company and Onufri Publishing House co-published "Xi Jinping Classical Quotations and Interpretation" in Albanian language.[97]

4.6 CCP Policies Towards the Chinese Diaspora in Albania

According to official statistics, there are only 200 ethnic Chinese permanent residents in Albania.[98] However, this figure does not take into account Chinese passport holders in Albania on other visas. Chinese companies in Albania use Chinese labourers for construction projects and mining. There are also Chinese traders, students and others on temporary visas. The CEEC region has a significant illegal migrant population from China.[99]

The Tirana PRC embassy keeps close ties with the resident Chinese community via cultural events such as the annual Lunar New Year Reception and associated community events.[100] Senior Albanian political figures also commonly attend these celebrations. CCP united front work organisations also connect to the Albanian Chinese migrant community via free Chinese medicine clinics and Chinese food days.[101,102]

---

[96]This link has now been erased from the website http://www.mfa.gov.cn/mfa_chn/dszlsjt_602260/t1001496.shtml.

[97]This link has now been erased from the website http://www.fmprc.gov.cn/mfa_chn/wjdt_611265/zwbd_611281/t1274718.shtml; Liu Lihang, "Interpretation of Xi Jinping's Classic Quotations Published in Albanian," China.com, December 3, 2015, http://news.china.com.cn/world/2015-12/03/content_37224911.htm.

[98]This link has now been erased from the website http://fec.mofcom.gov.cn/article/gbdqzn/upload/aerbaniya.pdf.

[99]"EU Announces Negotiations with China and Other Countries to Discuss Illegal Immigration," *SINA*, November 30, 2002, http://news.sina.com.cn/w/2002-11-30/15408308s.html.

[100]"Ambassador to Albania Ye Hao comforts overseas Chinese in Albania during Chinese New Year," January 28, 2012, http://al.china-embassy.org/chn/zagx/zajw/t899473.htm; Ministry of Foreign Affairs, the People's Republic of China, "Albanian President Holds First Chinese Spring Festival Reception for Chinese in Albania," January 24, 2014, https://www.fmprc.gov.cn/mfa_eng/wjb_663304/zwjg_665342/zwbd_665378/t1124590.shtml.

[101]Yuan Jing, "Spicy Chinese Medicine in Sichuan Cuisine Sets off Bashu Culture," *Sichuan Daily*, May 31, 2019, http://www.zgscys.com/news/20190531/12493.html.

[102]"Chinese Szechuan Cuisine World Taste" Series of Activities Adds Glory to the 70th Anniversary of the Establishment of Diplomatic Relations Between China and Albania," April 29, 2019, http://www.zytzb.gov.cn/wqfw/308866.jhtml.

4.7 Assessing the Impact of Xi-Era United Front Work in Albania

Xi-era CCP united front work in Albania follows a formulaic and predictable approach: the promotion of BRI, efforts to access strategic natural resources and economic stimulus projects for Chinese companies; the quest to seek transportation link alternatives for Chinese exports; and expansion of the BeiDou global navigation system via Huawei. The CCP has tried to co-opt the Albanian elite to support and promote China's foreign policy goals. China's global strategic communication in Albania aims to suppress critical perspectives on the CCP and to advance the CCP agenda in Albania. The CCP uses united front work in Albania to manage relations with the Chinese diaspora. But what is in this for Albania? And what impact, if any, is CCP united front work having on Albanian domestic politics and foreign policy? Successive Albanian governments have welcomed the CCP's new initiatives and activities since 2012 because China is a potential source of financial aid, soft loans and investments and has a massive market. China's BRI loans are generally much easier to obtain than EU ones, which have strict lending criteria. Albania is the fourth poorest country in Europe and needs economic assistance and new markets.

Nevertheless, if we cut through the rhetoric, Albania's participation in China's signature BRI infrastructure projects is surprisingly small. Albania has a modest amount of trade with China. Albania has taken up few loans from China and none via BRI. China ranks only ninth among Albania's top foreign direct investment (FDI) partners.[103] Despite the CCP's efforts to influence Albanian elites, Albania and China remain far apart on important political issues.[104] While the Albanian government recognises the "One China" principle and keeps its relations with Taiwan to a minimum, the PRC refuses to recognise the Republic of Kosovo and maintains close relations with Serbia. In 2018, China supported Serbia in excluding Kosovo from Interpol.[105] Membership in Interpol would help Kosovo fight organised crime, a major problem for both Kosovo and Albania. The political alignment of Albania has always been important to neighbouring states and great powers that wish to dominate in Europe.[106] Albania has a long history of colonisation and being used as a pawn by

[103]Invest in Albania, "Who Were the Largest Foreign Investors in Albania in Q1?" June 25, 2019, https://invest-in-albania.org/who-were-the-largest-foreign-investors-in-albania-in-q1/.

[104]Arlind Qori, "Albania and China: The Re-emergence of an Old Friendship?" *Left East*, November 1, 2017, http://www.criticatac.ro/lefteast/albania-and-china-the-reemergence-of-an-old-friendship/.

[105]N1, "Serbia Thanks China for Being Against Kosovo in Interpol," November 19, 2018, http://rs.n1info.com/English/NEWS/a437054/Serbia-grateful-for-China-s-opposition-to-Kosovo-s-Interpol-membership.html.

[106]Central Intelligence Agency, *Albania*, (Langley: 1947), https://www.cia.gov/library/readingroom/document/cia-rdp78-01617a001400050001-0.

foreign powers, and Albania has a long experience of foreign political interference.[107]

Xi-era China-Albania relations have revived some elements of the Cold War relationship, including bombastic political rhetoric. But unlike during the Hoxha era, Albania now has a range of political and economic partners. China is a useful counterbalance to other political relationships and an important investment source. But China is no longer Albania's only strategic partner. Albania learned the hard lesson of the failure of the policies of the Hoxha years. One of the biggest lessons was that neither autarky nor developing a relationship with one great power was the solution to a small state's security.

Recent history tends to lead many Albanians to take a somewhat ironic, and even cynical, view of the CCP government.[108] The negative history of the Mao-Hoxha years perhaps makes Albanians more resilient than most societies against being influenced by CCP united front work. Albania signed an agreement on BRI, but it has been careful not to take any actions that might harm its relationship with NATO. Albania is a staunch ally of the United States.

The Albanian government is attracted to China's investments and markets, but it is even more attracted to meeting the criteria to obtain EU membership. Albanian Prime Minister Rama has said that for Albania, joining the EU was about "finally having the possibility to place ourselves in a safe zone from the curse of history".[109] Rama has urged the EU and US not to neglect Albania and "leave a space for other countries to fill".[110] In 2019, Rama stated that Russia, China or Islamist radicals will fill the vacuum if the EU does not commit to Albania.[111]

Assessment of Xi-era Albania-China relations from the perspective of united front work activities reveals a familiar pattern with local variations, but it also demonstrates how a small state can engage with China in a constructive way while limiting potentially negative impacts of those interactions. Like many other small states in a geographically significant location, Albania is trying to avoid the mistake of becoming over-reliant on one great power or becoming a pawn in a great power conflict. It is guaranteeing its political, economic and societal security via relations with a broad number of diplomatic partners and by membership in multilateral organisations like NATO and the EU.

---

[107]Central Intelligence Agency, *OBOPUS BGFIEND VOL. 20 (BGFIEND OPERATIONS)_0012*, (Langley), https://www.cia.gov/library/readingroom/document/519a2b7a993294098d50fd47.

[108]Qori, "Albania and China."

[109]Shaun Walker, "Edi Rama, Albania's Unconventional PM Who Wants to Escape the 'Curse of History'", *The Guardian*, June 10, 2019, https://www.theguardian.com/world/2019/jun/10/edi-rama-albania-pm-escape-curse-of-history.

[110]Thomas Escritt and Andreas Rinke, "Don't Turn Your Back on Us, Albania PM Tells EU," *Reuters*, April 26, 2018, https://af.reuters.com/article/worldNews/idAFKBN1HW1K3.

[111]Walker, "Albania's Unconventional PM."

References

Bieber F, Tzifakis N (2019) The Western Balkans as a geopolitical chessboard? Myths, realities and policy options. BiEPAG, Belgrade, http://biepag.eu/wp-content/uploads/2019/08/The_Western_Balkans_as_a_Geopolitical_Chessboard.pdf
Brady A-M (2017) China as a polar great power. Cambridge University Press, Cambridge
Dreher A, Fuchs A, Parks BC, Strange AM, Tierney MJ (2017) China loans $126 million for Bushat hydro power station in Albania. AidData, Williamsburg, https://china.aiddata.org/projects/42265
International Crisis Group (2001) Bin Laden and the Balkans: the politics of anti-terrorism. University of Essex, Essex, https://www1.essex.ac.uk/armedcon/world/europe/south_east_europe/macedonia/MacedoniaBinLadenandtheBalkans.pdf
Kircher J, Matthews N (2018) Technology transfer in the hydropower industry: an analysis of Chinese dam developers' undertakings in Europe and Latin America. Energy Policy 113:546–558
Marku Y (2017) China and Albania: the cultural revolution and cold war relations. Cold War History 17(4):367–383
Munich Security Conference (2019) Munich Security Report 2019: the great puzzle: who will pick up the pieces? Munich Security Conference Foundation, Munich, https://securityconference.org/en/publications/munich-security-report-2019/
Steinberg SH, Paxton J (eds) (2016) The Statesman's Year-Book 1969-70: the one-volume encyclopaedia of all Nations. Springer, New York, p 726
Tubilewicz C (2007) Taiwan and post-communist Europe: shopping for allies. Routledge, Abingdon, p 145
Yu X, Cristiano R, Mario T, Ziccardi FE, Li G (2018) China's belt and road: the initiative and its financial focus, vol 2. World Scientific Publishing Co. Pte. Ltd, Singapore, p 196

Anne-Marie Brady is the NATO partner project director (PPD) of the Small States and the New Security Environment (SSANSE) Project, funded by NATO-SPS from 2017 to 2020. She is an expert on Chinese politics, polar politics, Pacific politics and New Zealand foreign policy. Professor Brady is a Global Fellow at the Woodrow Wilson Centre in Washington, DC. In 2014, she was appointed to a 2-year term on the World Economic Forum's Global Action Council on the Arctic.

Hiromichi Higashi (pseudonym) was formerly a graduate student at the University of Canterbury, Christchurch, New Zealand, working under the supervision of Professor Anne-Marie Brady.

Chapter 5
Small States, Great Powers, and Armed Drones

James Rogers

5.1 Introduction

According to Thorhallsson's 'shelter theory', the unique vulnerabilities of small states 'can be categorized as being of three types: political, economic and societal. Accordingly, small states are dependent on the economic, political, and societal shelter provided by larger states and/or regional and international organizations.'[1] This chapter draws and builds upon Thorhallsson's body of work, and also that of Bailes and Thorhallsson, to argue that whilst a small state may be somewhat 'dependent' on a larger state, this does not necessarily make it powerless or without leverage. Indeed, as will be argued in this chapter, small states can profit from what Thorhallsson argues as 'political sheltering', a case in point being from the small state hosting of great power armed drones. A state such as Niger, which is the focus of this chapter, shows us that the hosting of American drones can boost economic security and national security, alongside regional political status. For example, multimillion-dollar investments in infrastructure, equipment, and military training, alongside cash investments for the leasing of land, are just a few of the ways in which a small state can make gains. Joint military operations with great powers are another broader benefit that can increase a regime's regional credibility and regional power status, especially if drones, foreign special forces, and national forces work together to tackle terrorism, fight organised crime, and strengthen borders. It is the 'Drone + Special Forces + Proxy Forces' model that the US has chosen as a framework for its involvement in a number of small states.

[1]Thorhallsson (2010), p. 216. Also see Bailes and Thorhallsson (2012), pp. 99–115. https://doi.org/10.1080/07036337.2012.689828.

J. Rogers (✉)
University of Southern Denmark, Odense, Denmark
e-mail: jrg@sam.sdu.dk

A.-M. Brady, B. Thorhallsson (eds.), *Small States and the New Security Environment*, The World of Small States 7,
https://doi.org/10.1007/978-3-030-51529-4_5

There are, however, certain risks that should not be overlooked by both the host and the great power. The risks depend on the small state under analysis, yet each risk outlined in this chapter is intended as a lesson worthy of consideration by any small state and great power looking to establish a working relationship. The erosion of sovereign power and the rule of law will be discussed alongside public disquiet, regime instability, and the influx of other great powers into the region. The main conclusion is that, although there is the potential for considerable gain, the hosting of drones may, if the risks are not mitigated, undermine the benefits for both parties and could even prove counterproductive.[2]

5.2 The Allure of the Drone

Niger, Djibouti, Burkina Faso, and the Seychelles are just a few examples of the small states and micro-nations that have facilitated the launch of American drones. Cameroon, the Central African Republic, Chad, Ethiopia, Gabon, Ghana, Kenya, Mali, Senegal, Somalia, South Sudan, Uganda, Algeria, Botswana, Namibia, São Tomé and Príncipe, Sierra Leone, Tunisia, and Zambia are other nations that have hosted, or continue to host, smaller American sites—often called 'lily pads'—which have the potential to facilitate drone systems in the future.[3] Other North Atlantic Treaty Organization (NATO) powers, such as France and Britain, benefit from the ability of hosting their own armed drone systems in Niger and Cyprus, respectively.[4] In addition to this, nations such as Italy, China, Russia, Turkey, Iran, Israel, the UAE, and Saudi Arabia are expanding their own drone programmes and may further expand their relationships with smaller states to include the hosting of these hi-tech remote control systems.[5] As a result, there is potential for an increasing number of smaller states to join the ever-expanding list of drone-hosting nations over the coming years. To begin, it is worth considering what this altered environment may look like and what the complex implications of these new drone-based relationships may be for both the small states and the great powers involved.

---

[2]Delina Goxho, "Foreign Policy: How the EU Can Improve Its Role in the Sahel," VoxEurop, July 2, 2019. https://voxeurop.eu/en/2019/foreign-policy-5123141.

[3]Mick Turse, "The US Military's Best-Kept Secret," *The Nation*, November 17, 2015, https://www.thenation.com/article/the-us-militarys-best-kept-secret/.

[4]Personal Interview with French Ministry for the Armed Forces (Anon), September, 2019. Also see Jean-Baptiste Vilmer, "The French Turn to Armed Drones," War on the Rocks, September 22, 2017, https://warontherocks.com/2017/09/the-french-turn-to-armed-drones/.

[5]During 2019 and 2020 Turkey and the UAE joined the list of state powers who host bases in other nations. In this case, Libya became the focus as both nations took conflicting sides in the political and military struggle that plagues the nation. See Dan Sabbagh, Jason Burke, and Bethan McKernan, "'Libya is ground zero': drones on frontline in bloody civil war," *The Guardian*, November 27, 2019, https://www.theguardian.com/news/2019/nov/27/libya-is-ground-zero-drones-on-frontline-in-bloody-civil-war.

In this novel environment, small states are likely to take on a role of increased importance when it comes to assisting great powers with threats to their national security. As a result, small states will obtain a certain leverage, control, and power in international politics, deciding, in theory, which great powers can operate drones from within their territorial boundaries as a means to counter terrorism, organised crime, or insurgency. Increased agency may be a welcome benefit for a small state in this new environment. Great powers may find themselves competing for the same access to a small state, meaning the mistakes of past drone hosting, and also the tantalising benefits offered to other states, may be taken into account by a small state when deciding which great power they can cooperate with/benefit from. So the actions of a great power, both now and in the future, take on increased importance, setting norms of behaviour for the drone-hosting process. This, of course, all depends on the small state being discussed. In practice, some small states may find it difficult to reject the advances of one great power, or even multiple great powers, in this new environment, especially if debt, colonial links, or trade links are heavy influencers on the process.

One worry is that upon accepting the advance of one great power, a small state may simply become saturated with competing or even cooperating drone powers. This is important for small states to consider. We only need to look at the swarms of large states competing in Djibouti (especially China, Japan, US, Spain, France, and Italy) or the lack of communications between allied powers operating in Niger (France-US-etc.) to see some of the complexities and risks for a host nation.[6] Another possibility is that the small state may use the opportunity to play great powers off against one another, accepting the assistance of multiple rival state actors. This is a dangerous game, with the small state reaping the benefits whilst the great powers compete and contest in their national borders. Yet with the increased role for small states in mind, it is important to consider these potentially appealing factors. It is, however, also important to consider the drawbacks of these partnerships. A focused analysis of Niger, now a veteran of drone hosting, allows us to explore and learn from some of the experienced profits and some of the risks that have arisen from such an agreement. These lessons provide a useful, albeit tentative, framework to help explore the complexities of this increasingly important issue.

---

[6]Personal Interview with Niger civil society (Anon), September, 2019. Also see, Gordon Lubold, and Jeremy Page, "Laser From Chinese Base Aimed at U.S. Military Pilots In Africa's Skies, Pentagon Charges," *The Wall Street Journal*, May 3, 2018, https://www.wsj.com/articles/laser-from-chinese-base-aimed-at-u-s-military-pilots-in-africas-skies-pentagon-charges-1525351775. Also see U.S. Department of Defense. "Department of Defense Press Briefing on the results of the Investigation into the October 4, 2017, Ambush in Niger," U.S. DOD, May 10, 2018, https://www.defense.gov/News/Transcripts/Transcript-View/Article/1518332/department-of-defense-press-briefing-on-the-results-of-the-investigation-into-t/.

5.3 Give Me Shelter? The Case of Niger

Niger is not only a small state but, according to the UN, also one of the poorest and least developed in the world.[7] The drone partnership between the US and Niger began in 2013, when President Obama announced that he would send 100 American military personnel to establish a new drone base in the country.[8] Built to track and target terrorist groups across the broader Sahel and Sahara region, this base was just one of a number of drone bases situated in strategically important locations around the globe. Niger is important because it is caught at an insecurity crossroads. Threats from Boko Haram are manifest in the south of the country,[9] whilst more importantly for the US, the various franchises of the Islamic State of Iraq and Syria (ISIS), Al-Qaeda (AQ), and other terroristic groups threaten towns and villages from Mali in the west and Libya in the north and have the potential to export terrorism globally.[10] The beleaguered United Nations peacekeeping mission, the United Nations Multidimensional Integrated Stabilization Mission in Mali (MINUSMA),[11] and the French-led Operation Barkhane are designed to help combat such groups, but the threats and issues in the region are not limited to radical terrorism.[12] Organised criminal gangs—who in some case are not disconnected from such terroristic actors—use the country's porous borders to smuggle migrants, arms, drugs, and refugees through the vast region, an issue that has become a priority for European

---

[7]The UN CEDAW Committee stated that "82% of the Nigerian population lived in extreme poverty". For a breakdown of the report, see Amnesty International, "Niger 2017/2018," Amnesty International, 2018. https://www.amnesty.org/en/countries/africa/niger/report-niger/.

[8]Barack Obama, "Letter from the President -- Concerning Niger," The Office of the Press Secretary, February 22, 2013, https://obamawhitehouse.archives.gov/the-press-office/2013/02/22/letter-president-concerning-niger.

[9]Boutellis and Mahmoud (2017), pp. 80–84. https://doi.org/10.1080/15423166.2017.1331748.

[10]"Five Killed by Boko Haram in Niger Attack," News24, March 26, 2018. https://www.news24.com/Africa/News/five-killed-by-boko-haram-in-niger-attack-2018032. Also see Browne, Ryan. "US Warns of Growing African Terror Threat." CNN, April 19, 2018. https://edition.cnn.com/2018/04/19/politics/africa-isis-al-qaeda-threat/index.html.

[11]The UN mission in Mali has been plagued by shortfalls in peacekeeping, meaning that additional external military support has been brought in to bolster the military and surveillance capability of the UN. This, it is argued, has created a more 'robust peacekeeping mission'. For more on the (in)effectiveness and shortfalls of UN Peacekeeping see Rogers and Kennedy (2014), pp. 658–672. https://doi.org/10.1080/13533312.2014.972035.

[12]Here it is important to note that military drones are used by a variety of actors to assist the UN Peacekeeping mission in the Sahel and the French Operation Barkhane. Unarmed German military drones and French military drones (soon to be armed) assist the operations efforts; specifically in Mali and on the border with Niger. For more on the United Nations and the utility of drone to aid in UN Peacekeeping operations see Kennedy and Rogers (2015), pp. 211–227, https://doi.org/10.1080/13642987.2014.991217.

nations due to the ongoing migrant crisis.[13] As a result, Niger has become a point of interest and focus not only for the United States but also for European powers.

This is not wholly an unwelcome attention. The Issoufou government (democratically elected in 2011 after a military coup in 2010, and due to democratically transion in 2020) has struggled to counter insurgency, fight terrorism, and patrol Niger's vast borders. As a result, Western powers have been welcomed in by the Issoufou regime. Issoufou himself is seen as 'everything the West wants in an African leader' due to his pro-Western stance and continued cooperation on issues of international security.[14] It is for this reason that the EU invested 610 million euros in 2016 to help curb migration and smuggling routes in Niger, whilst France has invested additional money, military personnel, and close air support to assist the 'G5 Sahel' to combat terrorism in the region.[15] This group is made up of troops from Mali, Niger, Chad, Burkina Faso, and Mauritania.[16] Denmark is escalating its military presence in the Sahel region by contributing one million euros to the G5 Sahel and by deploying a large aircraft transporter and 60 troops to the UN mission to Mali. Germany, Italy, Britain, and Canada are all involved in the deployment of remote warfare, with drones and/or special operation forces in the region. Yet this is only the start of the external military interest in Niger and the broader Sahel. The addition of new US military and Central Intelligence Agency (CIA) drone bases marks an acceleration of external support.[17]

The world's superpower, the United States, has chosen Niger as a central node for its Africa Command (AFRICOM) operations in the region whilst also allowing the CIA to expand drone operations in the country. The CIA operation is based in Dirkou and is part of an expanded drone programme under President Trump. Access to Dirkou allows the agency to conduct surveillance and strike operation over

[13]During primary interviews in Niger, the term 'Jihadi Banditism' was used on a number of occasions to describe the mix of opportunist criminal gangs working in regions under the control of terroristic actors. Personal Interview with Niger Govt Advisor (Anon) in Niamey, Niger. June, 2019. For more on human smuggling see Luca Raineri and Neil Howard, "Human Smuggling: the Pride of Niger's Economy." OpenDemocracy, August 30, 2017, https://www.opendemocracy.net/beyondslavery/neil-howard-luca-raineri/human-smuggling-pride-of-nigers-economy. For information on ISIS and the broader terrorist drones threat see Rogers, James. "The Dark Side of Our Drone Future." Bulletin of the Atomic Scientists, October 8, 2019, https://thebulletin.org/2019/10/the-dark-side-of-our-drone-future/.

[14]Alex Thurston, "Niger's Issoufou Is Everything the West Wants in an African Leader" *World Politics Review*, September 12, 2017, https://www.worldpoliticsreview.com/articles/23116/niger-s-issoufou-is-everything-the-west-wants-in-an-african-leader.

[15]Ibid.

[16]Ministère de l'Europe et des Affaires étrangères, "G5 Sahel Joint Force and the Sahel Alliance," France Diplomatie: Ministry for Europe and Foreign Affairs. Accessed October 24, 2019. https://www.diplomatie.gouv.fr/en/french-foreign-policy/defence-security/crisis-and-conflicts/g5-sahel-joint-force-and-the-sahel-alliance/.

[17]Kyle Rempfer, "New in 2019: Two New US Air Bases in Africa Nearing Completion," *Air Force Times*, January 4, 2019. https://www.airforcetimes.com/news/your-air-force/2019/01/03/new-in-2019-two-new-us-airbases-in-africa-nearing-completion/.

southwestern Libya, 'a notorious haven for Al Qaeda and other extremist groups that also operate in the Sahel region of Niger, Chad, Mali and Algeria'.[18] The AFRICOM plan is different in its aims. It involves the use of armed drones, originally flown from Niamey Airport (within Niger's capital), alongside the training and deployment of Nigerian forces as proxies/partners on the ground. This is important for Niger. Traditionally, the nation has had an under-equipped and fractured military. Military coups have been a regular occurrence in the poor and unstable nation since obtaining independence from France in 1960. With the hosting of armed drones, plus the training of Nigerian military forces, comes the opportunity to invest in the military, strengthen borders, increase security, and keep the governmental regime strong. At a senior command level, the military appears content. The government, with the help of the military, has quashed all recent attempted coups by disenfranchised minorities.[19]

Thanks to US assistance, Niger now boasts 2000 special operations personnel in its ranks.[20] Col. Maj. Moussa Salaou Barmou (the officer in charge of the Nigerian special forces) stated, 'it's important to still have support from the U.S. to help train my men, to help with our shortfalls'.[21] Stability and security for the state appear to be positive side effects of the cooperation. The US and other NATO powers have, however, also benefited from this partnership. The 'drone + special forces + proxy forces' strategy appears to have paid dividends. The US is able to carry out high-profile drone strikes in Libya and Somalia and also help provide an 'eye in the sky' to protect and assist Nigerian ground forces as they cut off smuggling routes towards the shores of Europe. As *The New York Times* reported in March 2018, American drones flew from Niger to Libya and carried out the targeted killing of Musa Abu Dawud, a high-ranking official in Al Qaeda in the Islamic Maghreb.[22] In addition, according to Chatham House, the once booming smuggling routes through Niger have been interrupted, reducing the illegal movement of people and goods across the country.[23] So the foreign presence in the country is here to stay, and in fact in the coming years, activity will actually increase in Niger.

---

[18]Joe Penney, Eric Schmitt, Rukmini Callimachi, and Christoph Koettl, "C.I.A. Drone Mission, Curtailed by Obama, Is Expanded in Africa Under Trump," *New York Times*, September 9, 2018. https://www.nytimes.com/2018/09/09/world/africa/cia-drones-africa-military.html.

[19]"Niger Holds 13 over Failed December Coup," News24, January 13, 2016, https://www.news24.com/Africa/News/niger-holds-13-over-failed-december-coup-20160113-2.

[20]Eric Schmitt, "A Shadowy War's Newest Front: A Drone Base Rising from Saharan Dust," *New York Times*, April 22, 2018, https://www.nytimes.com/2018/04/22/us/politics/drone-base-niger.html.

[21]Ibid.

[22]Eric Schmitt, "American Drone Strike in Libya Kills Top Qaeda Recruiter," *New York Times*, March 28, 2018. https://www.nytimes.com/2018/03/28/world/africa/us-drone-strike-libya-qaeda.html.

[23]Chatham House has stated that the efforts (both military and monetary) by foreign powers have "reduced numbers of migrants" passing through Niger. Quie Marissa, "EU Pays to Stop Migrants." Chatham House, January 25, 2019, https://www.chathamhouse.org/publications/twt/eu-pays-stop-migrants.

A large patch of desert outside of the city of Agadez, in the north of Niger, has been transformed into a new military hub. At 110 million USD to build and 15 million USD a year to run, the base is the second largest in the region, and according to US Air Force officials, it is the largest troop labour construction project in US history.[24] The base, operational as of late 2019, boasts both MQ-9 Reaper drones and US Army Special Operations Forces (SOF). According to AFRICOM spokesperson Samantha Reho, the strategic location in Agadez improves 'US Africa Command's capability to facilitate intelligence-sharing that better supports Niger and other partner nations, such as Nigeria, Chad, Mali and other neighbors in the region and will improve our capability to respond to regional security issues'.[25] After almost a decade of US assistance, therefore, it appears that Niger has grown to be a more secure nation, albeit in an insecure regional environment. A myriad of attractive investments, alongside increased military capacity and drone support, have allowed it to take on a central role in the G5 Sahel and tackle broader regional security issues. Such advances have, however, come at a price and are by no means guaranteed for a further decade.

The case of Niger not only highlights the benefits of drone hosting, but it also shows some of the potential pitfalls of the agreement. The worries expressed from within Nigerian society are diverse, but each seems to stem from an underlying public mistrust about the intentions of foreign actors and the proximity of the nation's government to said actors. The American construction of the large new drone base in a remote part of the nation has become the focus of this tension.[26] Niger's colonial past may help to explain this distrust, and certainly fuels it, but there are also concerns about transparency, with the public kept in the dark 'due to national security reasons' about what is actually being undertaken in the country.[27] As *The Intercept*'s Joe Penney revealed in February 2018, people in Niger worry that the American drone base and the fight against terrorism might well be a front for the extraction of the nation's gold, oil, uranium, or underground water reserves. As Penney explained, '[i]n my two weeks in Niger, I heard theories that the Americans were fomenting the terrorists themselves, digging for gold, or they're after uranium, or oil, or even possibly the natural water aquifer beneath the Sahara, one of the largest in the world. Other than government officials, no one believed the Americans

---

[24]The Associated Press, "US Builds Drone Base in Niger, Crossroads of Extremism Fight," *Defense News*, April 23, 2018. https://www.defensenews.com/unmanned/2018/04/23/us-builds-drone-base-in-niger-crossroads-of-extremism-fight/.

[25]Ibid.

[26]Personal Interview with Civil Society Organisation (Anon) in Niamey, Niger. June, 2019.

[27]There is a point worth raising here about the French legacy in the country. During fieldwork in Niger in 2019, it became clear from interviews with a number of civil society actors (who will remain nameless for agreed anonymity) that the perception of the French remains very negative in the former colonial nation; far more negative than any other large state operating in the region (including the US). This is something to keep in mind as the French plan to arm their Reaper drones in the country. Personal Interview with Civil Society Organisation (Anon) in Niamey, Niger. June, 2019.

were here for security.'[28] Although such claims may seem fantastical, there is a serious side to these concerns. Public distrust in foreign actors and the national government's inability to address these concerns may lead to public unrest.

The rapid emergence of WhatsApp, Facebook, and 4G connectivity has fuelled the fires of misinformation.[29] It should be remembered that Niger is a nation with a strong history of coups and public uprisings. There are those within rival political factions who have already begun to harness the anti-Western narrative to attack the Issoufou government.[30] This is at a time when the government is attempting to enact major social and economic reforms, with a large and unpopular suppression of civil society being undertaken as a means to bring in new finance laws, control the price of amenities, and drive economic diversification.[31] The reforms, it is argued by the Issoufou government, will generate more income for the state and build private industry, but it is also likely to drive up the cost of living.[32] As such, it is a turbulent time for Niger, and mitigating public worries about great power involvement in the nation may help strengthen the regime. Increased public consultation and/or information dissemination about American and allied actions within the country may help to quell some of these concerns. It is true that some limited interactions have taken place between the Americans and sections of the local population, yet this has largely been carried out through training workshops on basic hygiene.[33] According to local aid groups, academic experts, and journalists, the local population would prefer more direct aid but also some engagement on the specifics of US involvement in the country and how it may affect their lives.[34] Indeed, a diverse range of groups within Niger—from human rights groups to the elements of nation's military—are worried about the nature of the military cooperation with the US and also more

[28]Joe Penney, "A Massive U.S. Drone Base Could Destabilize Niger - and May Even Be Illegal Under Its Constitution," *The Intercept*, February 18, 2018. https://theintercept.com/2018/02/18/niger-air-base-201-africom-drones/.

[29]Personal Interview with Civil Society Organisation (Anon) in Niamey, Niger. June, 2019.

[30]Ibid.

[31]Personal Interview with Philippe Frowd, June 6th, 2018. Also see Frowd (2019), pp. 1–19, https://doi.org/10.1080/01436597.2019.1660633.

[32]President Issoufou calls his reforms the 'Niger Renaissance Programme', stating that his 'administration has worked hard to ensure that Niger is open for business" he said. "We are investing across a number of sectors and looking for strategic long-term partners. The country is northern Nigeria's most important trading partner and we offer a haven of stability in the region'. African Media Agency, "President Issoufou Presents Niger Renaissance Programme at Economy Series in New York," AMA. http://mediaagency.com/president-issoufou-presents-niger-renaissance-programme-economy-series-new-york/.

[33]Personal Interview with Philippe Frowd, June 6th, 2018. Also see Joe Penney, "A Massive U.S. Drone Base Could Destabilize Niger - and May Even Be Illegal Under Its Constitution," The Intercept, February 18, 2018, https://theintercept.com/2018/02/18/niger-air-base-201-africom-drones/.

[34]Personal Interview with Philippe Frowd, June 6th, 2018.

prosaic issues like noise pollution, traffic, and most importantly movement limiting curfews.[35]

With increased American military involvement on the ground in Niger, varying groups within the nation's military have begun to raise concerns. Although the original remit was for training, American special forces now 'assist' Nigerian forces on the ground. With overhead drone and helicopter support, they engage in kill or capture missions near the border with Mali. This has led to a split narrative in the Nigerian military. Despite positive statements coming from the military elites, lower ranking factions are concerned about the influence of American military might. The concern is that great power involvement undercuts the Nigerian military's monopoly on the legitimate use of force and undermines its traditional role as an arbiter of power in Nigerian politics.[36] As Nigerian civic leader Nouhou Mahamadou has stated, 'the presence of foreign bases in general and American in particular is . . . a serious attack on the morale of the Nigerien military'.[37] Yet the military is not the only group with concerns. There is also anxiety within the general populous, with a disenfranchised public specifically worried that American drones are only in the country to fulfil American aims and not to help with the rising threat of Boko Haram in the south of the nation. It should be noted that despite spokespeople for the US military frequently referencing the fight against Boko Haram in the country, there has been little known engagement by the Americans to counter the attacks in the south of Niger.[38] In fact, the most important impact on civilian life thus far has been the foreign assistance to close off smuggling routes, a business that was once a vital lifeline for the local populous.[39] So the worry is that great powers are operating in the country yet with little regard for the concerns and security of the Nigerian population.

Of course, the US is not alone in being the target of public unease; French forces now operate up to 2000 troops in the nation, with over 5000 military personnel deployed in the region as part of the broader Operation Barkhane (as of 2020). There

---

[35]Delina Goxho, "How the EU can improve its role in the Sahel,"*VOXeurop*. Retrieved from: https://voxeurop.eu/en/2019/foreign-policy-5123141.

[36]Personal Interview with Philippe Frowd, June 6th, 2018.

[37]The Associated Press, "US Builds Drone Base in Niger, Crossroads of Extremism Fight," *Defense News*, April 23, 2018. https://www.defensenews.com/unmanned/2018/04/23/us-builds-drone-base-in-niger-crossroads-of-extremism-fight/.

[38]When it comes to American military involvement in the south of Niger against Boko Haram, details become 'a little hazy'. This is, of course, due to special forces operations—but we know some training of both Nigerian and Nigerien forces in the south-east of Niger and some involvement in the Diffa region. This, according to the NYT, was to counter broadly defined IS affiliated forces. Charlie Savage, Eric Schmitt and Thomas Gibbons, "U.S. Kept Silent About Its Role in Another Firefight in Niger," *New York Times*, March 15, 2018, https://www.nytimes.com/2018/03/14/world/africa/niger-green-berets-isis-firefight-december.html.

[39]Personal Interview with Civil Society Organisation (Anon) in Niamey, Niger. June, 2019. Also see Vanda Felbab-Brown, "In the Eye of the Storm: Niger and Its Unstable Neighbors," Brookings, June 13, 2017. https://www.brookings.edu/blog/order-from-chaos/2017/06/13/in-the-eye-of-the-storm-niger-and-its-unstable-neighbors/.

are also 470 Italian troops are in the north of Niger to help stop smuggling, and Germany has frequently expressed its intent to assist in counterterrorism missions, with a German airbase planned in Niamey and German drones currently operating over in Mali.[40] One point to note here is that with increasing numbers of great powers conducting both special forces and drone missions in the region, there is a possibility for things to go wrong and for 'blue on blue' incidents to take place. As Phillippe Frowd, an expert on Nigerian border security, has stated, 'the worry is that Niger is becoming a playground for foreign militaries'.[41] It was only in November 2017 that American special forces stepped up their role in the country, joining Nigerian forces (and watched over by American drones) on a mission to kill or capture a key IS leadership target.[42] In this mission, the group was ambushed, the drone was unable to pick out friend from foe, and nine American and Nigerian personnel were killed.[43] It was only 3 h later that French Mirage jets were called in to perform a show of force, leading experts like Frowd to conclude that the French knew little about the operation in advance.[44] With so many forces working in the same region, it is vital that communication between allied forces is maintained as a means to avoid strikes on allies or innocent civilians. Indeed, this leads us to another, prominent, concern expressed within Niger, specifically the risk of drone strikes on civilians.

The concern here is that American drones may, through accident or error, cause the death of Nigerian citizens. Nigerian human rights groups are well versed in the controversies of previous American drone operations in Afghanistan and Pakistan and understand that when things go wrong, the people or government of the host nation has little chance of obtaining justice. These concerns are not unwarranted. Finalised in January 2013, the US-Nigerien Status of Forces Agreement outlines a number of legal stipulations and waivers that provide support for the Nigerians' concerns. It is important to add that this agreement was signed without the agreement of the Nigerian parliament, thus creating legal ambiguity within the document. A

[40]As Chancellor Merkel stated during a visit in 2016 "There is a strong link between illegal migration and the trafficking of illicit arms in conflict zones, and we will help Niger to fight this phenomenon by providing Niger's army with equipment, notably vehicles, other materials and expertise". "Expanding Assistance for the Niger." Archiv der Bundesregierung: Expanding assistance for the Niger. Accessed October 24, 2019. https://www.bundeskanzlerin.de/Content/EN/Reiseberichte/2016/2016-10-10-merkel-in-niger_en.html.

[41]Personal Interview with Philippe Frowd, June 6th, 2018.

[42]US DoD, "Department of Defense Press Briefing on the Results of the Investigation," U.S. Department of Defense, Accessed October 24, 2019. https://www.defense.gov/News/Transcripts/Transcript-View/Article/1518332/department-of-defense-press-briefing-on-the-results-of-the-investigation-into-t/.

[43]US DoD, "Department of Defense Press Briefing on the Results of the Investigation," U.S. Department of Defense. Accessed October 24, 2019. https://www.defense.gov/News/Transcripts/Transcript-View/Article/1518332/department-of-defense-press-briefing-on-the-results-of-the-investigation-into-t/.

[44]Ibid.

major concern is the provisions it puts in place for dealing with civilian casualties. As the agreement stipulates,

> the Parties waive any and all claims (other than in contractual claims) against each other for damage to, loss, or destruction of the other's property or injury or death to personnel of either Party's armed forces or their civilian personnel arising out of the performance of their official duties in connection with activities under this Agreement.[45]

In short, the concern here is that American military personnel, contractors, or even armed drone operations are not accountable to the civilians they fly over or to the government of the country they fly from. There is a process by which third parties can make a claim against the US, but this would be processed under US law and by the US system. With the controversies around civilian casualties during previous American drone operations and also recent crashes by American drones in other small states, it is clear to see why there are concerns about this legal waiver. We only need to look at the two US drone crashes in the Seychelles between 2011 and 2012 or the crash of a US Reaper drone into Niamey airport in Niger (2016) and the three reported crashes around Agadez (2020) for pertinent examples of the mistakes that can happen.[46] In addition, as Amadou Roufai, a Nigerien administration official, stated, '[w]e are afraid of falling back into the same situation as in Afghanistan, with many mistakes made by American soldiers who did not always know the difference between a wedding ceremony and a training of terrorist groups'.[47] Abbas Yahaya, a prominent imam in Niger, added to this sentiment by arguing, '[a] drone is manned by people on a military base in America, and many times they make mistakes, killing people who aren't extremists'. As he concluded, '[t]his won't solve anything; it will only bring more insecurity'.[48]

[45]Department of State, "Agreement Between the United States of America and Niger," Department of State, January 2013. https://www.state.gov/documents/organization/205314.pdf.

[46]Abdoulaye Massalaki, Phil Stewart, and Matthew Bigg, "U.S. Drone Crashes on Landing at Airport in Niamey: Niger Sources," Reuters, October 20, 2014. https://www.reuters.com/article/us-niger-usa-drones/u-s-drone-crashes-on-landing-at-airport-in-niamey-niger-sources-idUSKCN0I92CF20141020. Also see, Emily Chow, Alberto Cuadra, and Craig Whitlock, "Drone Crashes Database: 237 of the Worst Drone Accidents since 9/11," *The Washington Post*, Accessed October 24, 2019. https://www.washingtonpost.com/graphics/national/drone-crashes/database/. And for details on the Seychelles see, "Drone Crashes in Seychelles, Second in Four Months." Reuters, April 4, 2012. https://www.reuters.com/article/us-seychelles-drone/drone-crashes-in-seychelles-second-in-four-months-idUSBRE83312O20120404.

[47]The Associated Press, "US Builds Drone Base in Niger, Crossroads of Extremism Fight," *Defense News*, April 23, 2018. https://www.defensenews.com/unmanned/2018/04/23/us-builds-drone-base-in-niger-crossroads-of-extremism-fight/.

[48]Joe Penney, "A Massive U.S. Drone Base Could Destabilize Niger - and May Even Be Illegal Under Its Constitution," *The Intercept*, February 18, 2018, https://theintercept.com/2018/02/18/niger-air-base-201-africom-drones/.

5.4 Conclusion

Overall, by harnessing the broader intellectual framework of sheltering theory, and the case of Niger, it is possible to see that the small state and great power can both make major gains when a drone hosting relationship is entered into. Yet, as this case study of Niger shows, issues of transparency, sovereignty, public disquiet, and national stability must be carefully managed if the relationship is to remain stable and the positives maintained. Armed drones are, in particular, a major point of contention within Niger. Indeed, as the US, Germany, Italy, and France (to name but a few nations) increase their military footprint in this small state and the US utilises its new major drone base in the north, it is important to consider and dwell upon some troubling factors that have been raised by the people of Niger. Transparency is lacking in Niger, and the public lacks trust in the relationship between the Nigerian government and foreign actors. Added to this is the continued insecurity brought to the population by Boko Haram attacks in the south of the country, a problem that is still to be fully engaged with by the US military. The Nigerian military add their own concerns, worried that they are being marginalised from their traditionally prominent roles in both defence and politics.

Finally, the Issoufou government is implementing unpopular financial, social, and market reforms in the country, providing political rivals with strength and public support. It is at this point that we should consider whether another larger US drone base, and increased foreign activity in the nation, may destabilise, as opposed to strengthen, this small state. If transparency continues to be stifled and the public disconnected from actions within their sovereign borders, could a simple mistake by a US drone pilot, be it technical fault or accidental death, act as a catalyst for unrest? The words of Joe Penney should give us pause for thought here and lead to some important questions being asked about American and allied policy in Niger. As Penney stated, '[a]rmed drones are a major issue anywhere the US uses them, but in Niger, the American base is in a major city not far from potential drone targets. Judging from the secrecy and lack of trust thus far, it's not hard to envision a future in which an errant drone strike causes the population of Agadez to turn against the base.'[49] If Niger and the Issoufou government, a vital and stable ally in the region, were to fall—in part due to a US or allied drone mishap—the power void that would open could lead to an increase in the terroristic and criminal activity, both in the region and internationally.

References

Bailes AJK, Thorhallsson B (2012) Instrumentalizing the European Union in small state strategies. J Eur Integr 35(2):99–115. https://doi.org/10.1080/07036337.2012.689828

[49]Ibid.

Boutellis A, Mahmoud Y (April 2017) Investing in peace to prevent violent extremism in the Sahel-Sahara Region. J Peacebuilding Dev 12(2):80–84. https://doi.org/10.1080/15423166.2017.1331748

Frowd PM (2019) Producing the 'Transit' migration state: international security intervention in Nige. Third World Q:1–19. https://doi.org/10.1080/01436597.2019.1660633

Kennedy C, Rogers J (2015) Virtuous drones? Int J Hum Rights 19(2):211–227. https://doi.org/10.1080/13642987.2014.991217

Rogers J, Kennedy C (2014) Dying for Peace? Fatality trends for United Nations peacekeeping personnel. Int Peacekeeping 21(5):658–672. https://doi.org/10.1080/13533312.2014.972035

Thorhallsson B (2010) The Icelandic crash and its consequences: a small state without economic and political shelter. In: Steinmetz R, Wivel A (eds) Small states in Europe: challenges and opportunities. Ashgate Publishing, Farnham, p 199

James Rogers is DIAS Assistant Professor in War Studies, within the Center for War Studies, at the University of Southern Denmark and Associate Fellow of LSE IDEAS at the London School of Economics.

Chapter 6
How to Defend Society? Baltic Responses to Hybrid Threats

Margrarita Šešelgytė and Neringa Bladaitė

6.1 Introduction

Since their independence in 1991, Estonia, Latvia, and Lithuania have successfully managed through either external shelter or their own efforts (building a buffer from within)[1] to ensure political, military and economic security. The immense military imbalances between Russia and the Baltic states are mainly sheltered though their membership in NATO and collective defence under Article 5 of the North Atlantic Treaty. All three countries regard NATO and the US as the main pillars of their military security.[2] After the annexation of Crimea, these guarantees have been reinforced by NATO's Enhanced Forward Presence. This means one multinational battle group deployed in each Baltic state and other security measures provided by NATO, such as increased presence in the form of military exercises and restructuring of the regional defence. All three states have also built an internal buffer. Latvia and Lithuania increased defence spending, committing to gradually reach 2% of the gross domestic product (GDP), meanwhile Estonia has maintained its defence spending at the level of 2% of the GDP since 2015. Lithuania has reintroduced conscription and increased a total number of troops of volunteer Territorial Defence Forces. All the Baltic states sped up the modernisation programmes of their armed

[1]Thorhallsson (2015).

[2]Riigikantselei, National Security Concept of Estonia, 2017, https://riigikantselei.ee/sites/default/files/content-editors/Failid/national_security_concept_2017.pdf; KAM (2017); National Security Strategy of Republic of Lithuania, https://kam.lt/en/title.html; MOD (2015); The National Security Concept of Latvia, Informative section. https://www.mod.gov.lv/~/media/AM/Par_aizsardzibas_nozari/Plani,%20koncepcijas/NDK/NDK_ENG_final.ashx.

M. Šešelgytė (✉) · N. Bladaitė
Vilnius University, Vilnius, Lithuania
e-mail: margarita.seselgyte@tspmi.vu.lt

A.-M. Brady, B. Thorhallsson (eds.), *Small States and the New Security Environment*, The World of Small States 7,
https://doi.org/10.1007/978-3-030-51529-4_6

forces.[3] In the economic sector, relations with the EU has secured an important and sufficiently sustainable shelter, which helped the Baltic states to move towards a market economy, reduce economic interdependence with Russia and integrate into Western markets. A successful recovery of Baltic states after the global financial crisis and a subsequent accession of all three to the eurozone indicate that the EU ensures shelter vis-a-vis global economic instabilities.

Protracted deterioration of relations between Russia and NATO after the annexation of Crimea turned Baltic states into NATO's "new front-line states"[4] and exposed them to the new type of challenges. Covert Russian offensive measures that fall under NATO's Article 5 threshold and function directly through vulnerabilities that exist in the societal sector of security[5] prevail as the main security concerns in the Baltic states. The 2018 Lithuanian National Security Threat Assessment Report indicates that these operations are meant to "antagonise society and to reduce its trust in democratic process, state institutions and officials".[6] Current academic debates conceptualise these new challenges under the term hybrid warfare.[7] Hybrid measures are situation specific and are based on strategic context defined by a targeted country's geographical, sociocultural, historical and political aspects.[8] They include information and cyber operations, use of proxies, manipulation of economic and political influence and clandestine measures.[9] Although many authors argue that hybrid activities (with the exception of the use of sophisticated modalities and modern technologies) do not represent conceptually new ways of warfare, the use of the term is useful for both academic and practical purposes as this categorisation broadens the perspectives of how to perceive security challenges, exceeding the traditional security concept, and what measures are necessary to address them. The traditional security concept places a strong emphasis on a state as the main referent object and securitises independence and sovereignty as key priorities of national security policies, where all other sectors are subordinated to this priority.[10] However, hybrid activities do not always attack states directly.

---

[3]Gotkowsaka and Szymański (2017), p. 5, http://www.centrumbalticum.org/files/2157/BSR_Policy_Briefing_1_2017.pdf.

[4]Lucas (2015), https://1f3d3593-8810-425c-bc7f-8988c808b72b.filesusr.com/ugd/644196_302ae06eff3a4f20ab59888b0ed73a0f.pdf.

[5]Buzan and Waver (1998).

[6]State Security Department of Republic of Lithuania (VSD) and Second Investigation Department Under the Ministry of National Defence (AOTD), National Threat Assessment of Lithuania, 2018, https://www.vsd.lt/wp-content/uploads/2018/03/ENG.pdf, p. 58.

[7]A. Raczh, "Russia's Hybrid War in Ukraine: Breaking the Enemy's Ability to Resist," Finnish Institute of International Affairs, FIIA Report 43, 2015, https://storage.googleapis.com/upi-live/2017/01/fiiareport43.pdf.

[8]D. Johnson, "Russia's Approach to Conflict –Implications for NATO's Deterrence and Defence," NATO Defence College. Research Paper 111, 2015, p. 16.

[9]Chivvis (2017), pp. 3–4, https://www.rand.org/content/dam/rand/pubs/testimonies/CT400/CT468/RAND_CT468.pdf.

[10]Vitkus (2017), p. 149.

The chapter argues that due to the dominance of the traditional security concept in Baltic states,[11] both internal and external policies are not ready to cope with these challenges. Moreover, societal vulnerabilities existing in all three have been substantially under-addressed.[12] According to Barry Buzan, societal security is ensured by preserving sustainability of societal identities, which may include language, cultural, religious and national identities.[13] The challenges for the societal security may evolve in the form of social cleavages, conflicts and disloyalty, which by extension might threaten the integrity and identity of a state. These challenges require refocusing attention from state sovereignty to sustainability of certain identities within the state.

This chapter argues that due to the lack of attention to societal security, Baltic states have not managed to develop a strong internal buffer to respond to the external challenges directed against societal vulnerabilities. Therefore, having in mind the significant imbalance of capabilities that exist between Baltic states and Russia, they should be looking for an external societal shelter (as in the cases of political and economic security). Baldur Thorhallsson argues that small states seek societal security shelter from external providers in order to avoid self-isolation within small societies and to get instant access to high-level cultural practices and "networks of innovations".[14] We argue that this definition should be expanded for the purposes of the current context of the security in the Baltic states. Apart from the empowerment function, which could be more relevant in a more peaceful environment, the concept of societal shelter should also include a protection vis-à-vis hybrid activities, including manipulation of existing societal vulnerabilities (social exclusion, decreasing population, societal polarisation). The chapter investigates the main societal security challenges in Baltic states and aims to discover strategies and tools that Baltic states employ in responding to these challenges. In addition, the strategies and tools will be examined in order to determine if the states are trying to build a buffer from within or to seek for an external shelter. Three Baltic states are analysed in separate sub-chapters based on three dimensions: their main societal vulnerabilities, their experience of Russian interference activities and, finally, the strategies and instruments they employ to cope with societal challenges. Our analysis of societal vulnerabilities is based on national security documents, surveys and expert assessment. The chapter aims to assess two hypotheses. First, Russian interference operations in three Baltic states differ, and these differences are based on the particularities of Baltic societal security vulnerabilities. Second, aiming to ensure societal security, the Baltic states try to build a buffer from within rather than rely on an external shelter.

[11]Jakniūnaitė (2016), p. 8; Šešelgytė (2013), p. 51.

[12]Sprūds and Vizgunova (2018), p. 10.

[13]Buzan et al. (1998).

[14]Thorhallsson (2018), p. 27, https://www.um.edu.mt/sst/docs/SST-1-1-Thorhallsson.pdf.

6.2 Latvia

Russian interference operations in Latvia manipulate three main vulnerabilities, Latvian society's ethnic diversity, socio-economic cleavages and low trust in state institutions, and are aimed at affecting societal identities. In 2017, ethnic Latvians constituted 62% of the total population, whereas Russians are 25.4%, Belarusians 3.3%, Ukrainians 2.2%, Polish 2.1% and "others" 5%, respectively.[15] Meanwhile, 11.8% of Latvian inhabitants are "stateless", not holding any citizenship.[16] On the other hand, 37.2% of the Latvian population use Russian as their first language, and the majority of the others understand it.[17]

Arguably, the ability of Latvian society to understand Russian as well as ethnic cleavages has become the main vulnerability as it opens opportunities for Russia to directly access the Latvian population through interference operations. These operations involve the application of programmes and policies related to the concepts of compatriots and the Russian World (Russkyi Mir), which justify Russian actions in "Near Abroad" under the pretext of defending its interests and those of the Russian diaspora.[18] Socio-economic cleavages are a further vulnerability used by Russia.[19] Although, along with other Baltic states, Latvia has managed to benefit from double accession (EU, NATO) over the years and has experienced substantial economic advance, the benefits of growth have been unevenly distributed. Economic development mostly concentrates in the capital, Riga, while Latvia's other regions suffer from underdevelopment. The high levels of socio-economic polarisation in Latvia contributes to feelings of dissatisfaction within the society (77% of Latvians are dissatisfied with the economic situation in the country).[20] Low trust in state institutions is a third vulnerability. In 2009, Latvians demonstrated the lowest score of trust in their governmental institutions at the EU, which not only undermines the general feeling of security and confidence in the state but also affects the parts of the state identity related to the successful statehood and membership of Western democracies. These three vulnerabilities are manipulated using various tools of

[15]European Commission, Eurydice, Latvia, 2018, https://eacea.ec.europa.eu/national-policies/eurydice/content/population-demographic-situation-languages-and-religions-40_en.

[16]Kuczynska-Zonik (2017), https://doi.org/10.11649/en.1438.

[17]Central Statistical Bureau of Latvia, "At home Latvian is spoken by 62% of Latvian population; the majority – in Vidzeme and Lubāna county," 2013, https://www.csb.gov.lv/en/statistics/statistics-by-theme/population/census/search-in-theme/1442-home-latvian-spoken-62-latvian-population.

[18]M. Laruelle, "The "Russian World: Russia's Soft Power and Geopolitical Imagination," Centre on Global Interests (CGI), pp. 8–10, http://globalinterests.org/wp-content/uploads/2015/05/FINAL-CGI_Russian-World_Marlene-Laruelle.pdf.

[19]Berzina (2018), p. 1, https://www.aei.org/wp-content/uploads/2018/02/Mitigating-Nonmilitary-Vulnerabilities-of-Latvia.pdf.

[20]European Commission, Standard Eurobarometer 86: Public Opinion in the European Union, December 2016, 22, http://ec.europa.eu/commfrontoffice/publicopinion/index.cfm/Survey/getSurveyDetail/yearFrom/1974/yearTo/2016/surveyKy/2137.

interference. The 2016 Latvian Security Policy Annual Report marked out three directions of Russian offensive activities targeting Latvian society: (a) information manipulation activities, (b) systemic attacks on the links between the society and the state and (c) Russian compatriot policy directed towards the Russian-speaking minority.[21]

Technological advances in the area of information and communication have enhanced the opportunities of Russia to manipulate foreign societies via various information platforms. In Latvia, Russia operates within the "traditional" media, including TV channels, radio stations and the press. In 2017, around 26% of Latvians regularly watched Russian television.[22] Moreover, Russia extensively uses social networks such as Twitter and Facebook,[23] where it spreads disinformation exploiting users with false identities and computer-generated bots. Russia also relies on the assistance of certain "opinion leaders" and "experts", who are typically Russian academics and journalists but occasionally also local ones. The narratives and messages disseminated by Russia aim to manipulate existing vulnerabilities and are tailored to particular social groups. Russia does not exclusively target the Russian diaspora but by manipulating existing social cleavages aims to affect domestic political dynamics, as well as to promote Russia's geopolitical interests and foreign policy goals.

Russia does have a focus on the Russian minority, however, and part of its interference activities falls under the compatriot policies. By funding various initiatives, groups as well as marginal organisations, which are portrayed as official representatives of the local Russian community, Russia attempts to influence the legal and political processes in Latvia.[24] During the last few years, Russia's compatriot activities have focused on three main areas: "defending the rights" of Russian compatriots, disseminating interpretations of Latvian history promoted by Russia and circulating narratives about failures of the Latvian government at the same time as supporting Russia's foreign policy.[25] Over the last years, a number of protests were organised and petitions signed over the alleged "discrimination" against Russian language in Latvia. However, it might be argued that the Russian-speaking diaspora is quite heterogeneous and its activities are not coordinated. Although Russia insists that there are around 750,000 compatriots in Latvia, Berzina argues that the number is at least three times lower; only around 263,000 Russian speakers consider Russia as a part of their identity.[26] Despite the lack of unity and coordination among the compatriots, Russian interference activities targeting the

[21] Latvia Security Police, Annual Report, 2016, 12–18, 19–22, https://vdd.gov.lv/en/useful/annual-reports/.

[22] Berzina, 3.

[23] Latvia Security Police, Annual Report, 2018, 23, https://vdd.gov.lv/en/useful/annual-reports/.

[24] Kudors (2014), p. 74.

[25] Latvia Security Police, Annual Report, 2018, 18.

[26] Berzina, 3.

Russian-speaking minority have a significant impact on Latvian society and political processes.

Throughout the years, the Latvian government has developed strategies to reduce existing cleavages and to ensure the resilience of society against undesired interferences. In the information security field, efforts were invested to create alternative sources of information in Russian language, to strengthen an independent media environment as well as to promote media literacy. Latvian non-governmental organisations (NGOs) and think tanks organise trainings for journalists in Latvia and beyond, conduct journalistic investigations and produce research on strategic communication and related issues.[27] More restrictive measures are also employed in order to counter disinformation, such as fining or suspending media platforms that display overt biases.[28] Both the radio station Autoradio Rezekne and television channel PBK have been fined for spreading biased information (the PBK has been fined several times since 2014).

It might be argued that the strategies above addressing Russian influence operations are the main ones that Latvia chooses in order to respond to Russian interference activities. On the one hand, this does reflect the high activity of Russia in this field. On the other hand, though these approaches are still not sufficient, they are mainly directed towards the tools employed by Russia and, to a lesser extent, address the root causes of existing vulnerabilities. Reducing societal vulnerabilities requires more comprehensive, expensive and time-consuming strategies, which could be implemented if societal security is prioritised as the key security concern and if there is a political will to allocate efforts and resources to search for solutions. But at the moment, Latvia relies on a traditional state-oriented security concept, and this contributes to a quite limited approach towards Russian interference activities. It might be argued that Latvian strategies to deal with Russia are also internal; it relies on its own efforts to try to build a buffer from within, rather than searching for external shelter.

6.3 Lithuania

Ever since Lithuania re-established its independence in 1991, Russia has been attempting to interfere politically and economically in its domestic affairs. The interference activities draw on close ties between the Russian regime on one side and certain political parties or politicians in Lithuania on the other side. The main aim of these activities is to influence various decision-making processes in order to achieve outcomes favourable for Russia. One of the most illustrative examples revealing the scope of Russian interference into the politics of Lithuania was the

[27] Potjomkina and Vizgunova (2018), p. 126.

[28] A. Wiktorek Saro, "Fighting Disinformation in Baltic States," FIPRI, 2017, https://www.fpri.org/article/2017/07/fighting-disinformation-baltic-states/.

impeachment case of former President of Lithuania Rolandas Paksas. This political scandal evolved in 2003, on the eve of Lithuanian membership in the EU and NATO. A few months after the inauguration of Paksas, the Lithuanian State Security Department released information about suspicious links between the President's office and a Russian businessman, who was the largest financial supporter of the President's electoral campaign and allegedly had links with Russian organised criminal groups and secret services. Igor Borisov, the owner of helicopter manufacturer Aviabaltika, contributed up to $400,000 (350,000 euros) to Paksas' presidential campaign and, in exchange, according to parliamentary investigators, received preferential access to the President's office.

Over the years, political links between Russia and Lithuania contracted, leaving fewer opportunities for Russia to manipulate them. Public opinion towards Russia has become very negative in Lithuania. In 2019, over 68% of Lithuanians considered Russia an unfriendly country.[29] So it would be damaging for a Lithuanian politician or a political party to now have an open pro-Russian stance or close links with Russia. Therefore, most of Russia's interference activities in Lithuania aim to target society directly, and they are conducted either from Russia or through third countries. Russia tries to exploit already existing vulnerabilities, manipulating them in order to antagonise society, and to hamper support for liberal values, democratic institutions and loyalty to the Lithuanian state. Unlike Latvia and Estonia, the Russian minority in Lithuania is relatively insignificant and makes up only 5.8% of the total population; Poles amount to 6.6%, while ethnic Lithuanians are in the majority at 84.2%.[30] This relatively ethnically homogenous society prevents Russia from manipulating ethnic divisions as much as they do elsewhere. In Lithuania, Russia consequently aims to exploit other societal cleavages, primarily aiming at those who understand Russian language such as the Russian and Polish minorities.

Lithuania's 2017 National Security Strategy indicates five major challenges within the societal security sector: social and regional exclusion, social poverty in some sectors, corruption, organised crime and a demographic crisis.[31] A 2017 survey on societal threat perceptions reflects those challenges; Lithuanians consider high prices, emigration and social inequality more pressing than an external military threat.[32] These vulnerabilities are exploited by Russia, employing similar tools as in the case of Latvia. Russia utilises a broad range of resources: pro-Kremlin Internet news portals, TV channels, NGOs funded by Russia as well as social networks. Propaganda messages targeting Lithuanian audience play on Soviet nostalgia, as

[29]Vilmorus, "Apklausa: draugiškiausia valsybė- Latvija, didžiausią grėsmę kelia Rusija. Lzinios.lt, 2019, https://www.lzinios.lt/Lietuva/apklausa-draugiskiausia-valstybe-latvija-didziausia-gresme-kelia-rusija/280952.

[30]Lietuvos statistikos departamentas, Lietuvos gyventojai 2011 metais. 2011 m. gyventojų surašymo duomenys, 2013, https://news.err.ee/852030/the-grey-passport-issue-ministry-of-the-interior-s-response.

[31]KAM, National Security Strategy of Republic of Lithuania, 2017, 6–7, https://kam.lt/en/title.html.

[32]Matonytė et al. (2017), p. 17.

well as social unrest, and they portray Lithuania as in an economic breakdown;[33] they can be also specifically constructed and tailored to particular groups.[34] One of the leading streams of Russian propaganda in Lithuania is systemic attacks on Lithuanian statehood and history. Russian reinterpretations of Lithuanian history attempt to raise doubts in the society about the legitimacy of Lithuania's statehood, undermine ties between society and the state and create conditions for further interference activities.[35] The research conducted by A. Ramonaitė et al. demonstrates that sympathy for the Soviet past correlates with a positive attitude towards the Russian regime and a consumption of Russian media.[36] A second frequent stream targets Lithuania's membership in NATO and the EU and its pro-Western foreign policy direction. In the last few years, Russia orchestrated a number of purposeful information attacks against the NATO presence in Lithuania.[37] In 2017, only a few days after the German Enhanced Forward Presence (EFP) battle group was stationed in Lithuania, a fake-news message claiming that German soldiers had raped an underage Lithuanian girl circulated in various media outlets.[38]

Similarly, in all Baltic states, due to a particular definition of cybersecurity in Russia encompassing the information element itself, information warfare and cyber offences from Russia are often interrelated. The 2017 report of Lithuania's National Cyber Security Center notes that the number of cyberattacks has increased over the last years, especially in the areas related to national or public security.[39] There are various ends for cyber operations, and often they are employed in order to meddle with the official information. For instance, in 2015, during the NATO exercises Saber Strike, hackers attacked the website of Lithuanian joint NATO staff and inserted a message stating that the aim of the exercises was to prepare for the annexation of Kaliningrad district. The official websites of Lithuania's Ministries of National Defence and Foreign Affairs experience recurrent cyberattacks.

Lithuania uses a number of tools to address Russian offensive information operations. Similarly to Latvia, Lithuania has several times suspended broadcasting

---

[33]State Security Department of Republic of Lithuania (VSD) and Second Investigation Department Under the Ministry of National Defence (AOTD), National Threat Assessment of Lithuania, 2019, 44, https://www.vsd.lt/wp-content/uploads/2019/02/2019-Gresmes-internetui-EN.pdf.

[34]Bajarūnas and Keršanskas (2018), p. 144, https://www.tspmi.vu.lt/wp-content/uploads/2018/10/lietuvos-metine-strategine-apzvalga-2017-2018-t-16.pdf.

[35]State Security Department of Republic of Lithuania (VSD) and Second Investigation Department Under the Ministry of National Defence (AOTD), National Threat Assessment of Lithuania, 2019, 46, https://www.vsd.lt/wp-content/uploads/2019/02/2019-Gresmes-internetui-EN.pdf.

[36]A. Ramonaitė, ed., "Kas eitų ginti Lietuvos: pilietinio pasipriešinimo prielaidos ir galimybės, Vilnius, 2018, pp. 155–157; Jastramskis (2017).

[37]National Threat Assessment of Lithuania, 2018, 43.

[38]"Lithuania looking for source of false accusation of rape by German troops, Reuters, 17 February, 2017, https://www.reuters.com/article/us-lithuania-nato/lithuania-looking-for-source-of-false-accusation-of-rape-by-german-troops-idUSKBN15W1JO.

[39]Nacionalinis kibernetinio saugumo centras prie Krašto apsaugos ministerijos, 2017 metų nacionalio kibernetinio saugumo būklės ataskaita, https://www.nksc.lt/doc/NKSC_ataskaita_2017_%5blt%5d.pdf.

or imposed fines on Russian-language channels that display overt biases. One of the most renowned cases was the blocking of Russian NTV Mir Lithuania broadcasting for 3 months in 2013 due to a false interpretation of information about the events of 13 January 1991, which led to Lithuanian independence. Other tools utilised by Lithuania to counter Russian disinformation include the strengthening of independent media, improving media literacy within society and building resilience within society. Interestingly, one of the most successful initiatives to counter information operations emerged from Lithuanian society. A group of over 5000 Lithuanian volunteers, who call themselves the "Lithuanian Elves", fight against pro-Russian trolls online by exposing them, highlighting their disinformation and initiating fact checks.[40] It might be argued that most of the efforts addressing Russian interference operations in Lithuania were directed towards information and cybersecurity and aimed at increasing societal resilience against Russia and building a buffer from within. In 2019, Lithuania was ranked fourth position in the UN global cybersecurity index.[41] In 2017, Lithuania proposed a project to the EU within the framework of Permament Structured Cooperation (PESCO), aimed at creating Cyber Rapid Response Teams (CRRTs) at the EU level, thereby helping member states to better respond to cyber incidents. This initiative can be regarded as an attempt to proactively create an external shelter vis-a-vis any new threats. Lithuania's response to Russian hybrid activities within the societal sector mostly relies on a buffer from within, in particular strengthening resilience in the information and cyber fields, and only indirectly seeks shelter from the EU and NATO.

6.4 Estonia

Estonia's National Security Concept lists demographics, uneven regional development, social inequality, poverty, manifestations of intolerance and polarisation of society as the main societal security challenges.[42] In the context of Russian interference activities, Estonia is somewhat vulnerable due to a large Russian minority. The ethnic composition of Estonia consists of 69% ethnic Estonians, 25% ethnic Russians, 1.7% ethnic Ukrainians and 0.8% Byelorussians.[43] The main goal of

---

[40]Kremlin Watch Report, "Ranking of countermeasures by the EU28 to the Kremlin's subversion operations," European Values, 2018, 65. http://www.kremlinwatch.eu/userfiles/2018-ranking-of-countermeasures-by-the-eu28-to-the-kremlin-s-subversion-operations.pdf.

[41]Verslo žinios, Išankstiniame Jungtinių Tautų (JT) skelbiamame globaliame kibernetinio saugumo indekse Lietuva užima ketvirtą vietą, pirmadienį pranešė Krašto apsaugos ministerija, Verslo Žinios, 2019, https://www.vz.lt/verslo-aplinka/2019/04/01/pasauliniame-kibernetinio-saugumo-indekse-lietuva-uzeme-ketvirta-vieta#ixzz5nQwOaYOv.

[42]Riigikantselei, "National Security Concept of Estonia," 2017, 6, 21, https://riigikantselei.ee/sites/default/files/content-editors/Failid/national_security_concept_2017.pdf.

[43]European Parliament, "Democratic Transition and Linguistic Minorities in Estonia and Latvia," In-depth Analysis, 2018, 8, http://www.europarl.europa.eu/RegData/etudes/IDAN/2018/604952/

Russian interference operations in Estonia is to increase polarisation and hostility between Estonians and the Russian minority.[44] Unsurprisingly, Estonian Russian speakers are the most targeted audience for Russia's intensive and sophisticated propaganda campaigns in Estonia.[45] A study commissioned by the Estonian Ministry of Defence in 2018 demonstrates that ethnic divisions are correlated with differences in political attitudes, in particular on the issues of Estonian foreign policy such as NATO and relations with Russia. Seventy-five per cent of Estonians trust NATO, and only 15% consider cooperation with Russia as a key priority of Estonian foreign policy, whereas the numbers are in reverse in the attitudes of non-ethnic-Estonian respondents: 37% of them trust NATO, and 46% support good relations with Russia.[46] These differences are vigorously targeted by Russian information operations, which aim at increasing anti-Western (especially anti-NATO) sentiments among Estonian Russian speakers and strengthening polarisation between societal groups.

Ethnic diversities in Estonia coincide with socio-economic divisions. Even during the years of general rapid economic growth, Northeast Estonia was falling behind the rest of the country, with a lack of regional development and high unemployment figures. In 2010, the unemployment rate in Northeast Estonia was 25.8%, falling to 20.3% in 2011 compared to the national average of 12.5%.[47] Narva, a town in Northeast Estonia bordering Russia, is predominantly Russian speaking (90%), and a large number of the inhabitants do not have Estonian citizenship. The average income in Narva is the lowest in Estonia.[48] Moreover, the majority of the Narvan population rely on Russian language media for their information, so the Russian minority exists in a "separate informational space" from the rest of the Estonian population. Fears of a "Narva scenario", which was extensively debated by Western analysts after the annexation of Crimea, imagined an instigation of ethnic disturbances and a clawing of Narva into Russia.[49]

Information operations are the main tool that Russia uses in Estonia to shape societal attitudes. Similarly to Latvia and Lithuania, the main narratives employed by Russia revolve around Estonian history and critiquing Estonia's pro-Western

---

IPOL_IDA(2018)6049.52_EN.pdf; World Population Review, Estonia, 2019, http://worldpopulationreview.com/countries/estonia-population/.

[44]Lucas and Pomeranzev (2016), p. 21, https://cepa.ecms.pl/files/?id_plik=2773%2021.

[45]S. Svenson, "Russia and the Baltic States: Why Language Matters," Inkstick, 2018, https://inkstickmedia.com/russia-baltic-states-language-matters/.

[46]Kivirähk (2018), p. 4, http://www.kaitseministeerium.ee/sites/default/files/elfinder/article_files/public_opinion_and_national_defence_2018_october.pdf.

[47]Purju (2013), https://www.eesc.europa.eu/sites/default/files/resources/docs/qe-30-12-149-en-c.pdf.

[48]Statistics Estonia, "Average monthly gross income per employee increased last year, News Release," 2018, https://www.stat.ee/news-release-2018-052.

[49]Josh Rubin, "NATO Fears That This Town Will Be the Epicenter of Conflict With Russia," The Atlantic, January 24, 2019, https://www.theatlantic.com/international/archive/2019/01/narva-scenario-nato-conflict-russia-estonia/581089/.

foreign policy and human rights. Russia exploits "opinion leaders", the Russia-loyal media as well as fake news to spread these narratives. For instance, in May 2016, the mainstream Russian Vesti-Rossiya 24 TV station depicted a gigantic Victory Day march in the Russian-speaking Estonian town of Sillamäe, which never took place.[50] Russia manipulated ethnic divisions and the different interpretations of World War II legacy with regard to the removal of the Bronze Soldier World War II memorial in 2007, which resulted in riots and massive cyberattacks. Online services of Estonian banks, media outlets and government bodies were taken down for several weeks by unprecedented levels of Internet traffic, allegedly coming from Russia.[51]

It might be argued that within the societal security domain, Estonia has developed a comprehensive approach to ensure better societal resilience against hybrid threats. Estonia's National Security Concept proposes developing civil protection and psychological defence, which includes extensive strategic communication that involves the whole society.[52] In 2018, the Government of Estonia approved the Civil Protection Concept, which sets out activities for civil protection.[53] To counter Russian information operations, Estonia has launched an alternative Estonian channel in Russia language (ETV)[54] and bolstered blogs and counter-propaganda websites. Creative tools have been introduced to counter Russian influence in Narva and to speed up integration of the region. For instance, in 2018, Estonian President Kersti Kaljulaid moved her office from Tallinn to Narva for 1 month. The Estonian government is also pouring in development funds and using arts and culture (even punk rock festivals) in order to better integrate Narva's inhabitants into the cultural life of Estonia.[55] All these efforts have borne fruit. According to Dmitri Teperik, chief executive of the Estonian-based think tank International Centre for Defence and Security (ICDS), Estonia has now managed to better integrate around 90% of the Russian-speaking population, so ethnic divisions are less urgent a problem than many assume.[56] It might be argued that Estonia's approach to countering societal security threats is the most comprehensive in the Baltics. On the other hand, it should also be noted that most of the challenges in Estonia are concentrated around ethnic

---

[50]Lucas and Pomeranzev (2016), p. 21, https://cepa.ecms.pl/files/?id_plik=2773%2021.

[51]T. McCulloh, R. Johnson, "Hybrid Warfare," Joint Special Operations University Report, No. 13–4, August 2013, http://www.dtic.mil/dtic/tr/fulltext/u2/a591803.pdf.

[52]Riigikantselei, "National Security Concept of Estonia," 2017, https://riigikantselei.ee/sites/default/files/content-editors/Failid/national_security_concept_2017.pdf.

[53]Republic of Estonia Government, "The Government approved a comprehensive approach towards development civil protection," 2018, https://www.valitsus.ee/en/news/government-approved-comprehensive-approach-towards-developing-civil-protection.

[54]Kuczynska-Zonik (2017), p. 53, https://doi.org/10.11649/sn.1438.

[55]G. Gray, "Fearing Russian Influence, Estonia Trust to the Arts, New York Times, November 1, 2019, https://www.nytimes.com/2019/01/11/arts/estonia-russia-narva.html.

[56]P. Goble, "Experts: Estonia has Successfully Integrated 90% of Its Ethnic Russians", Estonian World, 2018, https://estonianworld.com/security/experts-estonia-successfully-integrated-nearly-90-ethnic-russians/?fbclid=IwAR0RhF_IuZIjTbK6dG4ESPViywPdleQ8YRIHDw2KLdrQTWUV8yOYoToTQXo.

divisions (social, economic and so on), so it might be simpler to concentrate efforts on the societal domain. Most of Estonia's specific measures to deal with Russian interference are focused on trying to build a buffer from within rather than trying to seek external shelter.

6.5 Conclusions

Russian interference activities in Baltic states after the Ukrainian crisis have augmented, but due to fading interdependencies between Russia and the Baltic states in various sectors, Russia has changed the targets. It now tries to focus on existing societal vulnerabilities and, by manipulating them, to directly affect the societies. Differences in the structures of Baltic societies means that Russia chooses different targets for its interference operations. Ethnic divisions are exploited in Latvia and Estonia, whereas in Lithuania due to a relatively ethnically homogenous population, Russia seeks to manipulate socio-economic divisions. In this respect, it is not ethnic identity but rather the ability to understand Russian language (a large part of the older population in all three Baltic states still speak Russian) becomes an important factor for a channel of communication to the Russian media. In all three states, the segments of societies that speak Russian are in many cases also more vulnerable socially and economically. This allows Russia to combine various narratives and achieve better results. The low trust in state institutions that exists in Latvia and Lithuania is also manipulated in relation to ethnic and socio-economic grievances with the same aim, to question the loyalty of society to the state and its Euro-Atlantic direction.

Although societal vulnerabilities in Baltic states differ somewhat, the goals of Russia in all of them are the same: to strengthen societal divisions, to reduce the loyalty of society to their own state and its institutions and to change the policies of the state to be more favourable towards Russia and its foreign policies. The narratives that Russia employs in the three Baltic states are similar, albeit tailored for particular target groups. In all three countries, Russia attempts to manipulate their histories, trying to promote a more positive image of the Soviet past, and to downplay advantages of both EU and NATO memberships. In Latvia and Estonia, the messages also revolve around perceived discrimination on the rights of Russian speakers. Russian information operations are also often conducted in parallel with cyber operations.

The nature and scope of vulnerabilities differ in Baltic states. It might be argued that Latvia and Estonia are more vulnerable vis-à-vis Russian interference operations than Lithuania, which does not have a big Russian minority. However, in Lithuania (similarly to Latvia), socio-economic differences and low trust in state institutions have moved beyond the boundaries of ethnic groups, which makes it more difficult to implement a comprehensive security strategy. It might be argued that due to the most complex vulnerabilities, Latvia is the most vulnerable to Russian interference operations among the Baltic states.

Similar methods to respond to the new security challenges have been undertaken in all three states: all of them have devoted most of their resources and efforts to reduce the links between their societies and Russian propaganda. On one hand, these strategies are less expensive and time consuming than those directed to reduce existing vulnerabilities. On the other hand, due to the reliance on state-oriented security concept, societal security remains under-addressed in all three states. In order to address Russian interference operations, all Baltic states were mostly building a buffer from within rather than seeking for external shelter. First of all, it is easier to maintain links within a given society, and this has become a key vaccine against information operations at the national level. Second, it is the function of domestic politics to address societal vulnerabilities, so the interference of external players might be regarded as a challenge for national sovereignty. Third, neither NATO nor the EU has as yet developed specific strategies that could provide societal shelter for Baltic states against Russia. Last but not the least, it should be noted that due to the complexity of societal security, the wider effects of Baltic states' EU and NATO membership might also be considered as contributing to societal shelter. Rules of international low and strong democratic institutions, which have been some of the conditions for the accession to the EU and NATO, are paramount in sustaining the loyalty of society towards the state.

References

Bajarūnas E, Keršanskas V (2018) Hibridinės grėsmės: turinio, keliamų iššūkių ir priemonių įveikti jas analizė. Lietuvos Metinė Strateginė Apžvalga 16:144, https://www.tspmi.vu.lt/wp-content/uploads/2018/10/lietuvos-metine-strategine-apzvalga-2017-2018-t-16.pdf

Berzina I (2018) Mitigating non-military vulnerabilities of Latvia, vol 1. American Enterprise Institute, Washington, D.C., https://www.aei.org/wp-content/uploads/2018/02/Mitigating-Nonmilitary-Vulnerabilities-of-Latvia.pdf

Buzan B, Waver O (eds) (1998) Security: a new framework for analysis. Lynne Rienner Publishers, Boulder

Chivvis SC (2017) Understanding Russian "Hybrid Warfare" and what can be done about it. RAND Corporation, Santa Monica, pp 3–4, Testimony, https://www.rand.org/content/dam/rand/pubs/testimonies/CT400/CT468/RAND_CT468.pdf

Gotkowsaka J, Szymański P (2017) Russia and security in the Baltic Sea region: some recommendations for policy-makers, Baltic Sea policy briefing series. Centrum Balticum, Turku, p 5, http://www.centrumbalticum.org/files/2157/BSR_Policy_Briefing_1_2017.pdf

Jakniūnaitė D (2016) Changes in security policy and perceptions of the Baltic States. J Baltic Secur 2(1):8

Jastramskis M (2017) Auditorijos reakcija: Rusijos propagandos poveikis Lietuvoje. In: Vaišnys A et al (eds) Rusijos propaganda: analizė, įvertinimas, rekomendacijos. Rytų Europos studijų centras, Vilnius

Kivirähk J (2018) Public opinion and national defence, analysis ordered by Estonian Ministry of Defence. Turu-uuringute, Tallinn, p 4, http://www.kaitseministeerium.ee/sites/default/files/elfinder/article_files/public_opinion_and_national_defence_2018_october.pdf

Kuczynska-Zonik A (2017) Non-citizens in Latvia: is it a real problem? Sprawy Narodowościowe. Seria nowa (49):53. https://doi.org/10.11649/sn.1438

Kudors A (2014) Russian soft power and non-military influence: the view from Latvia. In: Winnerstig M (ed) Tools of destabilization Russian "Soft Power" and non-military influence in the Baltic States. FOI, Stockholm, p 74

Lucas E (2015) The coming storm, Baltic Sea security report. Center for European Policy Analysis, Washington, D.C., https://1f3d3593-8810-425c-bc7f-8988c808b72b.filesusr.com/ugd/644196_302ae06eff3a4f20ab59888b0ed73a0f.pdf

Lucas E, Pomeranzev P (2016) Winning the information war: techniques and counter-strategies to Russian propaganda in Central and Eastern Europe. Center for European Policy Analysis (CEPTA), Washington D. C., p 21, https://cepa.ecms.pl/files/?id_plik=2773%2021

Matonytė I, Morkevičius V, Lašas A, Jankauskaite V (2017) Grėsmių visuomenės gerovei suvokimas: socialnio optimizmo, socialinio ir institucinio pasitikėjimo bei pasitikėjimo savimi įtaka. Politologija 85(1):17

Potjomkina D, Vizgunova E (2018) Societal security in Latvia: new wine in old bottles? In: Sprūds A, Vizgunova E (eds) Societal security in the Baltic Sea Region: expertise rapping and raising policy relevance. Latvian Institute of International Affairs, Riga, p 126

Purju A (2013) Economic and social situation in the Baltic States: Estonia. European Economic and Social Committee, European Union, Brussels, https://www.eesc.europa.eu/sites/default/files/resources/docs/qe-30-12-149-en-c.pdf

Šešelgytė M (2013) A midget warrior: security choices of Lithuania. In: Rublovskis R, Šešelgyte M, Kaljurand R (eds) Defence and security for the small: perspective from the Baltic States. Centre for Small State Studies, Institute of International Affairs, Reykjavik, p 51

Sprūds A, Vizgunova E (eds) (2018) Societal security in the Baltic Sea Region: expertise rapping and raising policy relevance. Latvian Institute of International Affairs, Riga, p 10

Thorhallsson B (2015) Do small states need shelter? The economic and political turmoil in Iceland. In: Baldersheim H, Keating M (eds) Small states in the modern world: vulnerabilities and opportunities. Edward Elgar, Cheltenham

Thorhallsson B (2018) Studying small states: a review. Small States Territories 1(1):27, https://www.um.edu.mt/sst/docs/SST-1-1-Thorhallsson.pdf

Vitkus G (2017) Societal security in Lithuania: what's so different about it? In: Sprūds A, Vizgunova E (eds) Societal security in the Baltic Sea Region: expertise rapping and raising policy relevance. Latvian Institute of International Affairs, Riga, p 149

Margarita Šešelgytė is a director of the Institute of International Relations and Political Science (IIRPS), Vilnius University, and co-director of the SSANSE Project. Previously, Dr. Margarita Šešelgytė worked as deputy director of studies at IIRPS, Baltic Defense College (Tartu, Estonia) and Jonas Žemaitis Military Academy of Lithuania. She teaches international politics and security studies and defence policy. Margarita has published a number of articles and book chapters in the field of security and defence.

Neringa Bladaitė is a PhD candidate at the Institute of International Relations and Political Science (IIRPS), Vilnius University. She currently serves as a young researcher for the project on Small States and the New Security Environment (SSANSE), which is funded by NATO's Science for Peace Programme. Neringa's research interests include societal security, transatlantic security policy and security issues of the Baltic Sea region.

Chapter 7
North Atlantic Small State Security 2025: The West Nordic Security Zone

Robert P. Wheelersburg

7.1 Introduction

Byers has hypothesized that due to the Arctic ice cap melting, three sub-strategic hard security threats would emerge.[1] He argues that these include new territorial/resource claims by Arctic Council members and rogue (i.e. out-of-area) states, terrorism and criminal activity such as drug smuggling, weapon dealing and human trafficking. Today, North Atlantic states have a variety of security policies, objectives and structures focused mainly on strategic operations such as air policing, which makes Arctic nations vulnerable to future security challenges below the strategic level. Multiple existing command structures limit effective security relationships in the region. The US alone has several commands there—the Northern Command, the Pacific Command, the European Command, the Coast Guard and the reactivated Second Fleet.[2] To increase command efficiency over forces confronting future sub-strategic hard security threats, NATO should divide the North Atlantic into operational areas.

The Nordic countries, along with Canada and the United States, have recently produced Arctic security policies and plans that embraced a future perspective by detailing new security organizations and equipment, along with improved command structures to utilize them rapidly and efficiently. For example, in 2016, the Norwegian Defence Minister called for increased command and control over NATO forces by adopting a "stronger regional orientation to our command structure to better

[1] Byers (2009).

[2] B. Finley, "US Navy Revives 2nd Fleet as Russians Patrol North Atlantic," Military.com, 25 Aug 2018, https://www.military.com/daily-news/2018/08/25/us-navy-revives-2nd-fleet-russians-patrol-north-atlantic.html.

R. P. Wheelersburg (✉)
Centre for Arctic Policy Studies, University of Iceland, Reykjavik, Iceland

A.-M. Brady, B. Thorhallsson (eds.), *Small States and the New Security Environment*, The World of Small States 7,
https://doi.org/10.1007/978-3-030-51529-4_7

utilize situational awareness and operational insights".[3] To develop increased command and control, the author recommends that NATO divide the North Atlantic into two security zones, the East Nordic Security Zone and the West Nordic Security Zone (WNSZ). The WNSZ addressed in this chapter would be comprised of the region's small states, including Iceland, northern Norway and Ireland, along with the semi-autonomous Faroe Islands, Greenland and Nunavut.

Why might NATO be unable to handle future security problems at the sub-strategic level in the North Atlantic? The answer lies in the lack of will and resources of larger states in the alliance, which leads to inability to respond rapidly and effectively to threats toward smaller states involving sovereignty, border control and internal security. A shelter framework explains why those larger states like the US may be unable to provide future protection to small states with whom they have security agreements.[4]

The shelter framework posits that due to their sizes, small states have vulnerabilities that create a lack of public administration and resources to address important aspects of governance like security. This chapter focuses on political vulnerability, which includes security crises that arise, which a small state cannot confront without assistance from a large state or international alliance (e.g. NATO). In Iceland's case, the country may have perceived the unilateral withdrawal of US troops from the Keflavik NATO base in 2006 as having left the country without the security necessary to withstand security crises. As described below, there was never any capability of the Icelandic Defence Force to confront Soviet aggression in the country on a large scale. To acquire that ability, Iceland negotiated bilateral agreements with both NATO and non-NATO members. Although closer security relationships formed with other Nordic countries may establish capabilities to confront a crisis, Iceland appears more vulnerable today than when a permanent American presence was in the country.[5]

Yet that appearance may have no basis in reality due to the nature of the US troops stationed at the Keflavik NATO base. Although the NATO troops at Keflavik formed the Icelandic Defence Force (IDF), those troops included only Air Force and Navy ground personnel, along with a security company of Marines. Together, select ground personnel such as Air Force security troops and Marines formed the base defence. Reserve Army troops in the US reinforced that local capability; specifically, US Army Iceland (ARICE) and the 187th Separate Infantry Brigade trained both in the states and on Iceland to provide follow-on support for an attack on the base. Together, these units, along with the aviation assets at Keflavik, formed the Icelandic Defence Force; however, there was never any intent to use the forces for security crises outside of the base and the immediately surrounding area.

---

[3]Søreide (July 12, 2016), Features, NATO in Context: Geopolitics and the Problem of Russian Power, Center for Complex Operations, Washington, D.C.

[4]Thorhallsson (2017), pp. 3–4.

[5]Thorhallsson (2018), pp. 61–82.

It is ironic that the American presence in Iceland during World War II may have actually given the country's population a false sense of security during the last half of the twentieth century, which lasted until today.[6] The 50,000 American soldiers—US Army troops stationed there in WWII—probably prevented the Germans from attacking Iceland to use it as a staging area for an invasion of North America. The Americans left following the war but returned in 1951 as a NATO base. However, the composition of the troops was different during the later time, leaving the country without shelter in sub-strategic security challenges. Unlike the Army troops in WWII, the NATO base had as its mission strategic-level anti-submarine patrols and bomber intercepts of Warsaw Pact forces entering the so-called Greenland, Iceland, United Kingdom (GIUK) Gap. That means the bulk of the troops at Keflavik were Navy and Air Force, with only a small Marine detachment for base security. While many Icelanders opposed the NATO base, they may have believed falsely that it was providing territorial and internal security functions.

US Marines and other ground-based personnel, along with combat aviation assets like Air Force jets and helicopters, provided hardened security against assaults on the NATO base itself. US Army Reserve and National Guard forces also held base defence responsibilities with the potential to expand security protection to the country beyond the base. Units like the Army Reserve 187th Separate Infantry Brigade and later the National Guard 29th Infantry Division provided additional ground troops in the 1990s to secure critical sites (such as power plants) needed to run the country. While exercises allowed the American troops to train and practice the logistical steps necessary to send the troops to Iceland, these reserve forces were not a viable force against an enemy well-trained and equipped for Arctic combat. For example, exercises like Northern Viking took place every few years in summer. Once outside the base housing facilities, the Army units had neither the training nor the equipment to survive and fight in the Arctic environment during the summer, let alone in winter.

More importantly for a sheltering framework, without direct air support provided by jets, attempts at retaining base security or performing tactical combat operations against a hardened and determined enemy in the Arctic could have resulted in a slaughter of the American reserve ground forces. One can surmise what could have happened to troops mobilized for combat in Iceland using the World War II Aleutian Islands Campaign as a model. Although the Allied force that attacked Kiska to retake it included Canadian and US Special Forces trained and equipped for Arctic combat, earlier the American Seventh Infantry Division assaulted Attu Island against 500 Japanese troops, despite being untrained and poorly equipped. While retaking the island in 1943, the Americans suffered more non-battle casualties attributed to weather,

[6] Bailes and Kristmunder (2014), pp. 1–15. Institute of Public Administration and Politics, Reykjavik.

disease and terrain than to combat.[7] One can hypothesize from the Aleutian Islands Campaign that using unprepared ground troops to fight in the Arctic disrupts logistics and drains resources beyond the value of the security they provide.

A more recent test of the shelter framework related to the US and Iceland occurred on 13 October 2018 as part of the NATO exercise Trident Junction 2018 (Iceland). As described by NATO, Trident Junction 2018 was "the largest NATO live exercise since 2002, over 40,000 troops, 250 aircraft and over 40 ships deployed to central and northern Norway in October 2018".[8] The author reconstructed the Icelandic scenario after observing the exercise hosted by the Icelandic Defence Office and Coast Guard. The author did not attend formal briefings before or during the exercise, and the reconstruction was impressionistic from informal interviews with US and Icelandic personnel. Terrorist elements of an unidentified group breeched the perimeter fence at the Keflavik NATO base secure area. Following grenade and machine gun fire, the terrorists confronted the Icelandic Coast Guard and civilian security employees outside the NATO Control and Reporting Center (CRC) Keflavik, killing some and taking others hostage. The terrorists threatened to kill their hostages unless the Coast Guard surrendered the CRC. The Coast Guard requested help from the Icelandic Police, and an hour later, the Viking Squad attempted to retake the CRC, killing a terrorist outside the blast doors. However, the police were unable to dislodge the attackers without inflicting mass casualties on the hostages. The Prime Minister called the NATO command in Naples, Italy, requesting assistance. Within 1 day, the US 24th Marine Expeditionary Unit left Camp Lejeune, arriving 30 h later off the Icelandic coast. After failing to conduct a planned amphibious assault due to surf conditions, the Marines conducted an air assault from the USS Iwo Jima. Using V-22 Ospreys and CH-53 Super Sea Stallions, elements of a Marine rifle company accompanied by the company commander landed near the CRC, attacking it with machine guns and mortars.

Trident Juncture 2018 (Iceland) continued the next day after the exercise with realistic training, although it did not involve simulated combat. Slightly less than a thousand Marines over 2 days made a forced march through the Þjórsárdalur Valley in the southern Iceland highlands, where they set up bivouac. According to the 24th Marine Expeditionary Unit press release, the training allowed the Marines to use their cold weather uniforms and equipment in Iceland's autumn climate to prepare for their simulated air and amphibious assaults in Norway during Trident Juncture 2018. Apparently, the Marines successfully accomplished the amphibious landing and simulated combat in Norway. The second part of Trident Juncture in Norway showed the true capabilities of a military force to support NATO's ground mission. Yet the exercise illustrated several limitations with using strategic-level American

---

[7]American Battle Monuments Commission, Remembering the Aleutian Campaign of World War II, 2018, https://www.abmc.gov/news-events/news/remembering-aleutian-campaign-world-war-ii, accessed May 11, 2018.

[8]NATO, "Trident Juncture 2018, Media Resources. https://www.nato.int/cps/en/natohq/news_158620.htm, accessed October 31, 2018.

troops in an anti-terrorist crisis, including a lack of rapid response, inability to navigate the Arctic terrain and poor logistical support. The exercise illustrated several limitations with using American troops in an anti-terrorist crisis, including a lack of rapid response, inability to navigate the Arctic terrain and poor logistical support.

The first limitation involved the lack of a rapid response. Although the Marines were supposed to conduct the assault on 12 October 2018, the delay in the American Iwo Jima Amphibious Readiness Group's arrival provided the fictional terrorists with over 24 h to disrupt Coast Guard operations and to attack other targets in Iceland. The second limitation was the seeming inability of the Marines to conduct an amphibious assault on Iceland's southern shore despite relatively good weather conditions. The decision to forgo the amphibious assault, apparently made by command authorities thousands of miles away lacking on-site situational awareness, not only caused them to use aviation assets, but it also led to the third problem with the assault. A successful amphibious assault would have provided the Marines with their own transportation, enabling the troops to move themselves to the CRC. As it was, arriving by aircraft without their own ground transportation, the Marines had to rely on tourist buses arranged by the Icelandic government. Thus, a recent NATO exercise involving an internal security crisis in Iceland that depended upon their shelter country to resolve failed due to several actual command and control events. The conclusion to draw from the sheltering framework as applied to Iceland's current security position is that the country and small states in the region need to develop their own capability to respond to sub-strategic threats using indigenous resources and those of other small states in the North Atlantic as part of a West Nordic Security Zone.

7.2 The Problem with Future North Atlantic Security

During the past three decades, North Atlantic security evolved to a completely different level, moving from a strategic nuclear confrontation to a local enforcement of borders and internal security. At the height of the Cold War, Tom Clancy's World War III scenario in *Red Storm Rising* (1986) laid out a frightening future for the countries that make up the GIUK Gap. The fictional account depicted a Soviet cruise missile attack destroying the Keflavik base, followed by amphibious troops invading Reykjavik to take control of the Reykjanes Peninsula. While Clancy's book was disturbing enough, the release 3 years later of the computer simulation *Harpoon* made the threat credible to large numbers of gamers. Larry Bond, the simulation designer and *Red Storm Rising* co-author with Tom Clancy, had been a naval officer involved with the 1970s actual war game Sea Control Tactical Analysis Game (SEATAG). SEATAG, like the 1980s land-based exercises Return of Forces to Germany (REFORGER), staged the planned NATO military response to a Soviet invasion of Western Europe during the Cold War. By the end of the 1980s, NATO was "loaded for bear" literally and figuratively to meet the threat. The US

Department of Defence's (1990) annual inter-agency publication *Soviet Military Power* predicted that the USSR would be a formidable military machine well into the next century. At that time, few "experts" could have anticipated the collapse of the Soviet Union in 1991, which led to the so-called Peace Dividend that saw defence funding collapse and militaries gutted.

After the fall of the Soviet Union in 1991, the US gradually withdrew strategic forces (e.g. anti-submarine patrols and bomber intercepts). Eventually, the North Atlantic became a security vacuum as various organizations from the Keflavik base departed to join the fight in the Global War on Terrorism. By the time the base closed in 2006, it did not provide any permanently stationed strategic assets to the North Atlantic alliance. The base's weekly newspaper, *The White Falcon*, tells the story during the base's last few years of operation. When the Navy stripped its P-3 Orion sub hunters from the air station, followed shortly by the Air Force bomber interceptors, NATO lost its security posture in the region. Base personnel spent the last few years as an impotent and unhappy military force complaining about having no dental clinic or Wendy's restaurant. Crime (e.g. 1 murder) and drug use increased on the base and command put some Keflavik bars off limits. The base's Air Force rescue helicopters, now with no mission because the jets whose crews they protected were gone, spent their flight hours plucking Icelandic mariners off foundering trawlers.

Another problem with lacking security abilities below the strategic level is that some scholars[9] and government officials continue to proclaim the Arctic peaceful, with conflict between member states handled by the Arctic Council. Statements like the one from the current Norwegian Defence Minister, "[c]ompared to most quarters of the world, the Arctic is a region of stability, respect for international law, and well-functioning multilateral institutions", are commonplace.[10] In that view, there is no need to improve small states' security in today's North Atlantic since there is no threat to the region.

As articulated in their national policies, large nation states like Russia and the US will pursue their own interests in the Arctic, creating their own security structures there. They demonstrate their independence through actions such as Russian territorial claims over the Lomonosov Ridge or the US's insistence that the Northwest Passage is open international water. That one-sidedness could increase following the opening of the Trans-Arctic Route, leading to conflicts involving member nations, rogue states, non-governmental organizations (NGOs), private corporations or criminal organizations. For example, the presence of unregulated maritime traffic following the ice cap melting, along with emerging national sovereignty claims, could lead to skirmishes such as those in the 1970s during the Cod Wars between Iceland and Great Britain. Importantly, the Arctic Council is not an effective body for

[9]Bailes (2015), pp. 23–41.

[10]Søreide (2016), p. 49, Features, NATO in Context: Geopolitics and the Problem of Russian Power, Center for Complex Operations, Washington, D.C.

solving conflicts because its founding declaration prevents the body from discussing military issues.[11]

Without appropriate shelter for sub-strategic crises and with no ability to handle large-scale terrorism or other threats, some within Iceland are calling for the country to "strengthen its domestic institutions responsible for security and defence, such as the Icelandic Coast Guard".[12] In the author's opinion, at present the country's inability to protect itself from sub-strategic threats creates a weak spot in the North Atlantic. That weakness increases the possibility of threats unanticipated in Iceland's 2009 Risk Assessment Report, which drove most of the country's current security policies and structures.[13]

Iceland does not need to wait until 2025 to see sub-strategic security threats or the country's inability to meet them. The devastating 2016 murder of Birna Brjánsdóttir showed how competent Iceland's police and Coast Guard are; however, it also revealed their inability to counter a more elaborate (larger or multiple events) security threat. In brief, a crewmember from a Greenlandic trawler, Polar Nanoq, murdered Birna and subsequently departed with his ship into the North Atlantic. To prevent his escape, the Icelandic Coast Guard airlifted the police Viking Squad to intercept the trawler, which they boarded while underway to search it and arrest two suspects (Bilefsky and Bjarnason 2017).[14] While successful, the operation completely taxed the Icelandic security structure such that a simultaneous event happening elsewhere would have been difficult to address.

7.3 Improving Future Small State Security in the North Atlantic

To reduce reliance on sheltering nations and improve the ability of small states to handle their own sub-strategic security needs quickly and effectively, NATO should develop a new command structure focused on regional threats. A future NATO

---

[11]Arctic Council, "Declaration on the Establishment of the Arctic Council," Joint Communique of the Governments of the Arctic Countries on the Establishment of the Arctic Council. Ottawa, Canada, 1996. https://oaarchive.arctic-council.org/bitstream/handle/11374/85/EDOCS-1752-v2-ACMMCA00_Ottawa_1996_Founding_Declaration.PDF?sequence=5&isAllowed=y. Accessed September 19, 1996.

[12]B. Thorhallsson, "A Small State Seeking Shelter: Iceland's Search For Shelter. Small States and the New Security Environment. Policy brief no. 16, June 4, 2017. Paper presented at the conference "Small States and the Changing Global Order: New Zealand Faces the Future" at University of Canterbury, Christchurch, New Zealand, 3-4 June 2017

[13]Bailes and Kristmunder (2014), pp. 1–15. Institute of Public Administration and Politics, Reykjavik.

[14]D. Bilefsky, E. Bjarnason, "Woman Was Thrown into Ocean, Autopsy Says, In Murder that Shook Iceland," *New York Times*, February 7, 2017. https://www.nytimes.com/2017/02/07/world/europe/iceland-murder-victim-birna-brjansdottir-autopsy.html.

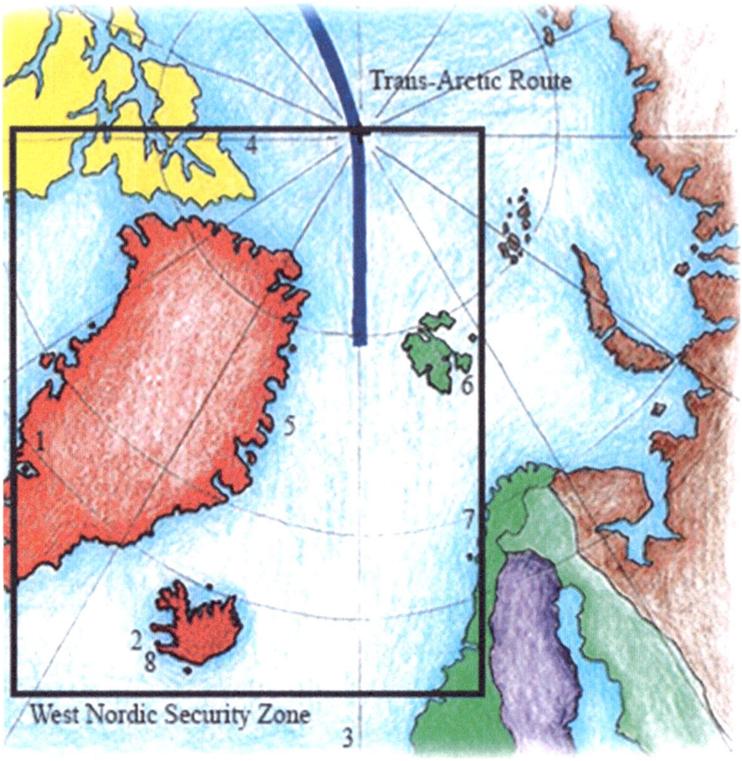

Fig. 7.1 West Nordic Security Zone and Trans-Arctic Route (blue line). Map by Elin Flóki Storeide

regional command structure would place responsibility for sub-strategic security into the hands of Nordic policymakers who control most of the surface and maritime territory in the region. A regional headquarters structure utilizing local forces as part of multinational coalitions could facilitate rapid response to threats while conforming to individual states' national Arctic policies.

The specific command structure should start with NATO Headquarters in Brussels. Member states in the North Atlantic could adapt the Nordic Defence Cooperation relationship to create command capabilities, located in one of the Scandinavian capitals from which it could control both the West and East Nordic Security Zones. The West Nordic Security Zone should have two operational commands forming a regional security force (Fig. 7.1; numbers in text correspond to map numbers). Those two commands would be the HQ Joint Arctic Command (Ground) in Nuuk, Greenland (#1), and the HQ Joint Arctic Command (Maritime) at the Keflavik NATO base (#2).

The proposed WNSZ force structure includes the following units. The 1st Battalion (Galway) of the Irish Reserve Army (#3) could provide two dismounted rifle companies and a fire support company (approximately 500 combat troops). The First

Canadian Ranger Patrol Group in Nunavut and North West Territories (#4) could provide winter open-range security throughout the region (approximately 500 combat troops). The Sirius Dog Sled Patrol assigned to the Danish military training base in Greenland (#5) has the capability for overland reconnaissance (14 combat troops). The Maritime Rescue Coordination Center in Torshavn (#6) could facilitate transport or search-and-rescue operations using maritime resources, along with police units, to assist in security under local circumstances. The Norwegian Coastal Rangers in Trondenes (#7) have their own assault boats and could respond to a WNSZ mission given enough advance warning (86 combat troops). The proposed Icelandic security force headquartered in Keflavik (#8) could provide three infantry companies (light, airborne/airmobile, mechanized) using organic C-130 and helicopter transport (400 combat troops). In addition to aviation support, Coast Guard maritime transport and local ground transport supplied by the Icelandic Association for Search and Rescue units would provide experienced and logistically sound Arctic operations (e.g. vehicles) to support security forces. The total number of small state and autonomous region security troops to support operations in the WNSZ could be 1500 (equivalent to a regiment).

The proposed Icelandic security force could consist of reservists who train regularly but who have no mission outside of the WNSZ. The intent is to provide a rapid response to sub-strategic security crises beyond the scope of police forces, including the Viking Squad and/or the Coast Guard (i.e. because the proposed security force would be capable of conducting ground combat). The security force would not be a viable military unit capable of sustained combat operations against a determined enemy presenting overwhelming odds. These missions could include maintaining or restoring territorial integrity and performing a delaying action to allow NATO or Partnership for Peace forces (e.g. Sweden, Finland) to conduct follow-on operations. In this proposal, sheltering remains a key aspect of North Atlantic strategic security; however, for sub-strategic threats, the initial security response is by forces from small states and/or autonomous areas.

The recommendation complies with the Parliamentary Resolution establishing a National Security Policy for Iceland.[15] Specifically, the proposed security force could "ensure[s] Iceland's independence and sovereignty, territorial integrity, the safety of its citizens, and the protection of its governmental system and social infrastructure". A security force rather than a national guard or other military unit recognizes that Iceland "has neither the resources nor the desire to maintain an army". With a future orientation, the Parliamentary "policy extends to ... military risks [and] give[s] particular consideration to Iceland's ... security interests in the Arctic" while maintaining its membership in NATO, monitoring the ability of the 1951 bilateral defence agreement to meet "military threats" and to "strengthen still further cooperation among the Nordic countries on security and defence". The resolution orders appropriate ministries to "ensure that Iceland has the defence

[15]Parliament of Iceland, "Parliamentary Resolution on a National Security Policy for Iceland," 145th legislative session 2015 – 2016, Parliamentary document 1166 – Case no. 327, No. 26/145.

infrastructure, equipment, capacity, and expertise needed both to respond to the challenges facing the country in connection with security and defence and to honour its international commitments". It also directs that "Government policies take into account other threats that require full attention, such as terrorism [and] organized crime".

7.4 Background Information on Icelandic Culture and Attitudes Towards Defence

The author makes the policy recommendation above based upon over 30 years' experience in Iceland as both a military officer and an anthropologist. Except for members of organizations like *Varðberg* (Organization for Western Cooperation and International Affairs) or the Centres for Small State Studies and Arctic Policy Studies at the University of Iceland, few Icelanders have considered the reality of their nation's hard security (although many condemn the NATO mission and other efforts). Absence of public discussion led the former US Ambassador to Iceland, Robert C. Barber, to make the following address to *Varðberg* on 19 November 2015, entitled "Iceland, the United States, and North Atlantic and European Security":

> The state of the world today presents many challenges to the rule of law, to peace and stability, and to the happiness, which we all deserve and strive to achieve. That is the harsh reality, it is staring us right in our faces, and it means tough decisions lie ahead . . . for the U. S., for NATO, for the Nordics, and for Iceland. . . . I would like to urge all Icelanders . . . to participate in a national discussion about security. Have the conversation. Have the conversation amongst yourselves about Iceland's role and responsibilities in its own security and in North Atlantic and European security more broadly. How will Iceland as a whole bear the costs, economic and otherwise, of its collective defence commitments, in a changed and ever-changing security environment, especially if the costs fall disproportionately on particular geographic areas or sectors of Icelandic society?

Although he presented it diplomatically, Barber asked the Icelandic people to make their voices heard above the din of intellectuals or a few vocal members of Parliament to create a secure nation in a world based on the reality of desperate countries desiring access to Arctic resources or criminals and terrorists seeking plunder and chaos in the north.

A 2016 study of Icelanders' knowledge about the country's security relationships and needs indicates that the people may not understand their situation today and may not understand future security requirements in the North Atlantic. Researchers conducted a few studies of Icelandic attitudes towards national security issues previously, but these tended to focus on the public's perception of the Keflavik NATO base.[16] The most recent large-scale survey in 2016 involved questions on security that test the proposal presented here. Some of the results about global

[16]Hardarson (1985), pp. 297–316.

security issues and Iceland's involvement achieved anticipated viewpoints. Nearly half of the respondents incorrectly thought Iceland is neutral or non-aligned and that the country would not "attack" anyone invading other NATO members. Respondents also indicated that financial crises and natural crises dominated the perceived threats to Iceland, but the recent economic crises and the possibility of natural disasters wreaking havoc on the country possibly influenced that reaction.[17] Fifth and sixth ranked threats to Icelanders were terrorists and organized crime; two of the four threats were posited by Byers.[18] Given that perception, Icelanders might accept a security force that responds above the level of the police but does not constitute a military organization.

Three recent events in Iceland illustrated how a society with no military, no war monuments and no changing of the palace guard lacks the cultural support for a security force. The first event was the Norwegian government giving the Icelandic police machine guns in 2014, which resulted in demonstrations, new civic groups (e.g. Return the Guns) and petitions against the action.[19] The second event was the 2016 announcement about the US Navy renovating the NATO Base in Keflavik seemingly without consultation with the Icelandic government.[20] Both of those actions showed how controversial small-group decision-making about the country's security remains today. The third event was a poll following the 2017 Independence Day celebrations, which showed that less than half of Reykjavik's residents supported armed police providing security for the event.[21] Thus, without the participation of all its citizens, the Icelandic people may meet closed political decisions about hard security measures with resentment and distrust. The resulting decisions and policies may fail as a result as the parties who supported them lose at the ballot box.

[17]S.B. Ómarsdóttir, "Sýn Íslendinga á utanríkis- og öryggismál," [Icelanders Views on Foreign Affairs and Security], *Icelandic Review of Politics & Administration* (Stjórnmál & Stjórnsýsla) 1, no. 2.

[18]Byers, *Who Owns the Arctic?*

[19]P. Fontaine, "Icelanders Object to More Machine Guns For Cops," *The Reykjavik Grapevine*, October 22, 2014, https://grapevine.is/news/2014/10/22/icelanders-object-to-more-machine-guns-for-cops/.

[20]P. Fontaine, "US Encouraged to Re-open Naval Air State in Iceland," *The Reykjavik Grapevine*, August 3, 2016, https://grapevine.is/news/2016/08/03/us-encouraged-to-re-open-naval-air-station-in-iceland/.

[21]E. Þósson, "Police with Guns at All Future Public Gatherings in Iceland," *The Reykjavik Grapevine*, June 13, 2017, https://grapevine.is/news/2017/06/13/police-with-guns-at-all-future-public-gatherings-in-iceland/.

7.5 Conclusion

Global climate change could present new security challenges in the Arctic and the North Atlantic requiring the creation of new policies and structures by 2025, when new transport corridors present easier movement into and out of the region. The author's recommendation is to create a regional NATO command called the West Nordic Security Zone, which provides small states with the ability to participate in decisions and control of forces to protect their own countries from sub-strategic threats. To meet NATO obligations, along with making required spending contributions, small states should increase their security capabilities in the North Atlantic. Iceland should develop a security force to improve the country's ability to respond quickly and appropriately to crises. To do so, leaders should involve the public in discussions about what the future challenges could be, what policies and entities the country should create to meet those challenges and under what circumstances the government would be able to utilize them. The proposal comes at a time when NATO and aspirant members are increasing their defence spending and militaries. Iceland should follow suit and increase its contribution and capabilities both to NATO and to its own security.

There is another reason for Iceland to assume its own security posture and not depend upon the US for shelter. Three years ago, the US looked to be in a good position to respond to coming environmental and societal changes in the North Atlantic and to provide shelter for small states located there. For the first time, an American president visited the Arctic while in office when Obama toured northern Alaska.[22] A new ambassador received an appointment as the senior Arctic representative, and retired Coast Guard Admiral Papp assumed the chair of the Arctic Council. The US had a new National Strategy for the Arctic Region,[23] although many criticized it for lack of specificity, addressed by the subsequent US Coast Guard Arctic Strategy[24] and the Defence Department Arctic Strategy.[25] The congressional budget had funding for new icebreakers and began expanding security facilities like the Keflavik hangers to accommodate the P-8 Poseidon. The North Atlantic NATO air-policing mission was never stronger.

Three years later, the US has no statement from the administration about its intentions in the Arctic. The US currently has no ambassador-level Arctic Council representative. It is unclear whether America will honour its commitments in the Arctic based upon history, agreements, treaties or even laws. The President stripped away funding for the Polar Security Cutter project (i.e. icebreaker) to fund building

---

[22]C. Welch, "Why Obama is the First President to Visit the Arctic," *National Geographic*, September 1, 2015.

[23]B. Obama, "National Strategy for the Arctic Region," The White House, Washington D.C., May 2013.

[24]Papp (2013).

[25]Office of the United States Department of Defence, "Report to Congress on Strategy to Protect United States National Security Interests in the Arctic Region," OUSD (Policy), December 2016.

the wall on the country's southern border, though a commitment was made to build Coast Guard icebreakers in January 2019. Federal agencies such as the Departments of the Interior and Agriculture removed references to climate change from their publications, including websites, and directed funding priorities and scientific committees to eliminate funding from research on Arctic warming. US foreign policy drifts from position to position, with decisions usually the result of whimsical fiat by an unsophisticated and autocratic actor, which leaves America's allies puzzled and its enemies gleeful. It is unclear whether the US under its current leadership could protect itself, let alone provide shelter for smaller states.

In late 2018 and 2019, strategic-level American involvement in NATO operations around Iceland increased somewhat. In fall 2018, Iceland hosted a counterterrorism exercise and Arctic survival training as part of Trident Junction 2018. In February 2019, US Secretary of State Mike Pompeo visited Iceland and met with the Prime Minister and Foreign Minister to discuss security and economic issues.[26] In July 2019, the Icelandic Coast Guard, which operates the Keflavik NATO base, planned to increase the number of troops it could accommodate by 300.[27] On 4 September 2019, US Vice President Mike Pence met the Icelandic Prime Minister, the Foreign Minister and the Mayor of Reykjavik ostensibly to speak about economic and defence issues. The focus of the visit, however, became human rights treatment of homosexuals and asylum seekers in the US. During September 2019, the newly reactivated US Navy's Second Fleet established a temporary Maritime Operations Centre in Keflavik to provide a more regionally oriented command and control capability between the US Naval Forces in Europe and the Second Fleet in Norfolk, Virginia.[28] Finally, the US 2020 Defence budget includes $57 million for improvements of the air operations at Keflavik.[29]

While not the same level of Arctic activities conducted by the Russians in the region, the uptempo of US and NATO activities there are in direct response to Russian efforts to gain the advantage in the North Atlantic as well as China's growing Arctic security interests. The important aspect to understand for the recommendation presented here is that these high-level visits and the increased operational control in and around Iceland involve strategic NATO and US military activities, not

[26]L. Kyzer, "Disappointment and Protest Meet U.S. Secretary of State," *Icelandreview*, February 16, 2019, https://www.icelandreview.com/news/disappointment-and-protest-meet-us-secretary-of-state/.

[27]J. Ćirić, "Expanded Accommodation 'Does Not Mean Permanent Army Base'," *Icelandreview*, July 31, 2019, https://www.icelandreview.com/news/expanded-accommodation-does-not-mean-permanent-army-base/.

[28]G. S. Einarsdóttir, "Pence Focused on Business and Defence During Iceland Visit," *Icelandreview*, September 5, 2019, https://www.icelandreview.com/news/pence-focused-on-business-and-defence-during-iceland-visit/; G.S. Einarsdóttir, "US Navy Establishes Temporary Operations Centre in Keflavik," Icelandreview, September 27, 2019, https://www.icelandreview.com/news/us-navy-establishes-temporary-operations-centre-in-keflavik/.

[29]A. Fontaine, "America Putting $57 Million Towards Icelandic Base," *The Reykjavik Grapevine*, June 25, 2019, https://grapevine.is/news/2019/06/25/american-military-putting-57-million-towards-icelandic-base/.

territorial control and protection capabilities for the country itself to prevent and defeat sub-strategic threats.

Consequently, this chapter presents a proposal for a regional NATO command using the forces of small states and autonomous regions to provide sub-strategic security in the North Atlantic. Some might question whether Nordic and other forces in the region would respond to protect Icelandic security. The answer is that all are members of NATO, and as such, they must respect and respond to an Article 5 threat to a fellow member nation—or leave NATO. As called for here, the creation of a West Nordic Security Zone increases the pre-conflict cooperation and capabilities in the North Atlantic to respond to such sub-strategic threats. The WNSZ implicitly requires Iceland to develop the ability to defend its sovereignty, maintain its border integrity and enhance its internal safekeeping to improve regional security. That means Iceland should create a security force above the police that can provide the ground forces with which to complement the maritime capabilities of the Coast Guard. Other NATO forces in the WNSZ could provide support (e.g. transport) or follow-on operations to the Icelandic security force, not serve as a substitute for it.

References

Bailes A (2015) Small states and security: does size still matter? In: Baldersheim H, Keating M (eds) Small states in the Modern World: vulnerabilities and opportunities. Edward Elgar Publishing, Cheltenham, pp 23–41

Bailes A, Kristmunder Ó (2014) Developments in Icelandic security policy. Icelandic Rev Polit Adm (Stjórnmál & Stjórnsýsla) 10(2):1–15

Byers M (2009) Who owns the Arctic? Understanding sovereignty disputes in the North. Douglas and McIntrye, Vancouver

Hardarson ÓT (1985) Icelandic security and foreign policy: the public attitude. Coop Confl XX (4):297–316

Papp R (2013) United States Coast Guard Arctic strategy. U.S. Government Printing Office, Washington, D.C.

Søreide IE (2016) NATO and the North Atlantic: revitalizing collective defence and the maritime domain. Prism 6(2):49

Thorhallsson B (2017) A small state seeking shelter: Iceland's search for shelter, Small states and the changing global order: New Zealand faces the future. University of Canterbury, Christchurch

Thorhallsson B (2018) A small state in world politics: Iceland's search for shelter. Icelandic Rev Polit Adm (Stjórnmál & Stjórnsýsla) 14(1):61–82, Special Issue on power and democracy in Iceland

Robert P. Wheelersburg holds a bachelor's degree in Anthropology from Ohio State University. He received a master's degree in Anthropology and a doctorate in Arctic Studies (Anthropology) from Brown University. Dr. Wheelersburg was awarded three Fulbright fellowships to Nordic universities, including two Fulbrights to Umeå University and one to the University of Iceland. He has conducted research on past and present Saami reindeer herding for nearly 10 years in Sweden and 5 years on the Kola Peninsula. Dr. Wheelersburg spent 25 years in the US military, including nearly a decade as a member of the Icelandic Defense Force.

Chapter 8
From Nordic Peacekeeper to NATO Peacemaker: Denmark's Journey from Semi-neutral to Super Ally

Rasmus Mariager and Anders Wivel

8.1 Introduction

In contrast to Cold War operations, Danish military activism since the end of the Cold War has varied considerably in size, goals and institutional embeddedness. Some troop deployments are small and aimed only at observation. Others, like the Danish military deployments in former Yugoslavia and Afghanistan, entailed a series of commitments amounting to more than 10,000 troops in both countries and involved peacemaking and protection of civilians, as well as peacekeeping. While the UN held monopoly as the institutional framework for Danish troop deployments from 1948 to 1990, the post-Cold War era has seen Danish troop deployments embedded in multiple institutional frameworks. Consequently, Denmark has been characterized as an "impeccable ally" of the United States and other North Atlantic Treaty Organization (NATO) member states[1] and a "super-Atlanticist"[2] that is "happy to fight".[3] Not surprisingly, observers tend to view Danish foreign policy activism in general as synonymous with military activism.[4]

We would like to thank Clara Lyngholm Mortensen and Daniela Dominguez for research assistance.

[1]Ringsmose and Rynning (2008), pp. 55–84.

[2]Mouritzen (2007), pp. 155–167; Wivel and Crandall (2019), pp. 392–419.

[3]Jakobsen and Rynning (2019), pp. 877–895.

[4]Pedersen and Ringsmose (2017), pp. 339–357.

R. Mariager · A. Wivel (✉)
University of Copenhagen, Copenhagen, Denmark
e-mail: rmariager@hum.ku.dk; aw@ifs.ku.dk

A.-M. Brady, B. Thorhallsson (eds.), *Small States and the New Security Environment*, The World of Small States 7,
https://doi.org/10.1007/978-3-030-51529-4_8

Denmark's military activism contrasts with fundamental assumptions on small state security in the research literature.[5] We would expect small states to "play it safe" and keep a low profile in international relations in order to avoid exposing themselves to danger.[6] However, in Denmark, a broad coalition of centre-right and centre-left political parties agree on an "activist" Danish foreign policy. Danish foreign-policy makers continue to seek influence and brand Denmark on traditional "Nordic" issues such as climate policy and gender equality.[7] However, since the early 1990s, military activism has been an important aspect of Danish foreign policy activism in general.

We would expect small states to prefer diplomatic and institutional instruments to promote their national interests.[8] However, since the end of the Cold War, Denmark has engaged in unprecedented military activism, sometimes even embedded in ad hoc coalitions rather than established international institutions. We would expect small states to promote a strong and peaceful international society.[9] However, Denmark has been willing to take sides between the great powers even when this involved the risk of undermining international society. This was the case when great power disagreement contributed to a split in the UN Security Council in the Kosovo War in 1998–1999. It was also the case in 2003, when disagreement between Denmark's most important cooperation partners—the United States and the United Kingdom on one side and France and Germany on the other—constituted a European and transatlantic crisis in the run-up to the Iraq War. Finally, it is often assumed that small states will balance the most powerful great powers.[10] However, Danish military activism after the Cold War is characterized by close cooperation with the United States and great responsiveness to the preferences of the superpower regarding participation in military operations.[11]

This chapter traces Denmark's transformation from a Cold War semi-neutral Nordic peacekeeper to a post-Cold War "impeccable ally" of the United States willing to deploy its troops in the most dangerous places and even when facing opposition from parts of international society. We unpack Denmark's development as a military actor and discuss the relevance of two contemporary theses on small state foreign policy—shelter seeking and status seeking—for understanding Denmark as a military actor. We proceed in three steps. First, we briefly situate Denmark's military activism in the security studies literature. Second, we trace the origins of Denmark's position on military activism. Finally, we discuss the findings

---

[5]For recent overviews of this literature, see Baldacchino and Wivel (2020); Wivel et al. (2014), pp. 3–25.

[6]Jesse and Dreyer (2016).

[7]Wivel (2018), pp. 419–434.

[8]Wivel et al. (2014), pp. 3–25.

[9]Thorhallsson and Steinsson (2017).

[10]Waltz (1979), p. 127.

[11]Mariager and Wivel (2019) and Wivel and Crandall (2019).

of the analysis and the implications of our analysis for Denmark and small states in general.

8.2 Small States in International Security

The security studies literature typically views small states as bargaining chips. Small states only enter into the equation when they upset or alter the balance of power and thereby affect the dynamics of the system and the action space of the great powers.[12] Despite recent advancements in understanding the security policy and military strategy of small states,[13] the security studies literature remains primarily concerned with the great powers setting the parameters for the security order. Small states are viewed as "structurally irrelevant", "impotent in international power politics" and "easily ignored" states.[14]

Two theoretical perspectives challenge this general neglect and marginalization of small states in the literature. First, a number of scholars have observed how many small states accept some measure of dependency as a necessary cost to enjoy the benefits of bilateral or multilateral relationships with stronger powers providing shelter. Typically, a small state gains military protection in return for accepting great power influence over its foreign policy. In essence, the small state accepts a restricted foreign policy action space in return for the protection of its national security.[15] Recently, this observation has been developed into so-called shelter theory, making three points nuancing our understanding of small state foreign and security policy.[16] First, military security should not be viewed in isolation: shelter may be military, economic, political or societal, and restrictions of small state action space vary across sectors. Second, because of their relative and absolute weakness, small states are willing to trade off more autonomy compared to larger states in order to seek economic, political and societal security. Finally, defensive and offensive strategies are closely connected. Thus, while seeking shelter from the risks and security threats of international anarchy is by definition a defensive strategy, it is often a condition for pursuing more offensive goals in promoting the small state's interests and values. Moreover, shelter seeking may in itself be offensive. A notable contribution to the battlefield and support for military operations or controversial policies may help secure for the small states the political and military backing of great powers.

Shelter theory unpacks how small states accept restrictions on their foreign policy action space in return for national security. Proponents of the status seeking theory

---

[12] Wivel et al. (2014), pp. 3–25.

[13] Bailes et al. (2014), pp. 26–45; Edström et al. (2019).

[14] Maass (2017).

[15] Krause and Singer (2001), pp. 15–23; Morrow (1991), pp. 904–933.

[16] Bailes et al. (2016), pp. 9–26; Thorhallsson (2019).

points out how status in international affairs "confers tangible benefits in the form of decision-making autonomy and deference on the part of others concerning issues of importance, including but not limited to security and prosperity".[17] Status is as a "collective belief about a given state's ranking on valued attributes" such as wealth, moral standing, military capabilities, population, democracy and diplomatic influence.[18] Status is particularly important for small states because their relative lack of material power means that "the power game is generally not an option".[19] In this context, status seeking is a compensatory strategy. Power capabilities would allow a small state to protect and promote its national interests, but in the absence of power, international status and visibility may be the best bet for the small state when seeking to increase security and influence. Status seeking is a means to increasing a state's foreign policy action space by strengthening the state's standing as a valuable ally, cooperation partner or member of international society in general: "small states achieve status through making themselves *useful* to greater powers. Great power status is about being a state to be reckoned with; small-power status is about being noticed or seen".[20]

On the face of it, both shelter seeking and status seeking seem to be relevant for understanding Denmark's military engagement. Shelter arguments are largely consistent with the political discourse of a large centre-right/centre-left majority in the Danish Parliament.[21] Status-seeking arguments are largely consistent with some of the recent academic literature on Danish security policy.[22]

8.3 From Nordic Peacekeeper to NATO Peacemaker

As for most European states, using military means to achieve political aims is an integral part of Danish history. Military power and the ability and willingness to go to war were essential for the establishment of a Baltic Sea empire under the Danish Crown in the fourteenth century. Denmark continued as the leading naval power in the Baltic Sea until the early seventeenth century, and in the seventeenth and eighteenth centuries, the army was vital in Denmark's efforts to maintain its status as a leading Nordic power and subsequently as an independent state, when Sweden gradually overtook Denmark's dominant position in Scandinavia. The military

[17] Larson et al. (2014), pp. 18–19.

[18] Larson et al. (2014), p. 7.

[19] de Carvalho and Neumann (2015), p. 1.

[20] Ibid, 1–2.

[21] For an analysis of the arguments of Danish policy-makers in relation to participation in the wars in Kosovo, Afghanistan and Kosovo, see Wivel (2019), pp. 363–539. For a recent official statement of the continued importance of the United States for Danish National Security, see the official Danish foreign and security policy strategy: Danish Government (2018).

[22] E.g. Jakobsen et al. (2018), pp. 256–277.

demise of Denmark was sealed when Denmark lost most of its fleet after British attacks on Copenhagen in 1801 and 1807 and subsequently in 1864 when it lost the three duchies Schleswig, Holstein and Lauenburg in a war with Prussia and Austria.

8.3.1 1864–1945: Denmark as an Anti-militaristic Small State

After the 1864 defeat, Denmark lost its status as a European middle power, and both domestic and foreign elites now saw the country as a small state unable to change the European balance of power and inconsequential for future European developments. Consequently, 1864 has since been considered a watershed moment in Danish history, a "Stunde Null",[23] signalling the birth of Denmark as a small state and leading to a fundamental rethinking of Danish foreign policy and Denmark's international role.

Initially, Danish policymakers disagreed on whether Danish military weakness was a temporary position to be reluctantly accepted until the country had a chance to rebuild its armed forces or whether it was to be accepted as a "new normal" for foreign-policy making. However, in the latter half of the nineteenth century, consensus gradually emerged that Denmark was for better or worse a small state and that recognizing Danish weakness was a necessary and inescapable starting point for Danish foreign policy. Consequently, Denmark embarked on an almost ideal-type small state foreign policy. Danish policymakers tended to view the use of armed forces as dangerous to national security—possibly endangering the survival of the state, as had been the case in 1864—and morally dubious.[24]

Building on the lesson of 1864 as well as social liberal ideology and inspiration from the international peace movement, Denmark was to pursue a new foreign policy. In the short term, the Danish small state aimed at pragmatic, non-provocative adaptation to the interests of the great powers (from 1864 to 1945 primarily Prussia/Germany). An important aspect of this was political and military non-alignment in order not to alienate or provoke any great powers. Hedging its security bets, Denmark stayed neutral in World War I, pursuing non-provocation towards Germany while seeking security shelter from the United States. Thus, Denmark bought munition from the United States and sold the Danish Caribbean colony, Danish West Indies, to the United States in order to avoid it falling into the hands of the Germans in case of German victory in the war.[25] In the long term, Denmark aimed at creating a more peaceful world with stronger international institutions and peaceful conflict resolution. The means to these ends were diplomatic, and on achieving the latter aim in particular, Denmark worked with other small states, most often Sweden and Norway. In sum, Denmark pursued a status as

[23]Glenthøj (2018), pp. 566–598.

[24]Rasmussen (2005), pp. 67–89.

[25]Wivel and Crandall (2019), p. 399.

non-threatening and inconsequential—a typical small state aiming for peace, adapting to the interests of its strongest neighbouring power (Germany) and hedging its security bets by occasionally seeking shelter from other states such as the United States.

8.3.2 1945–1989: Military Activism in the Service of International Society (and Danish Status Seeking)

It took another war to change the role of the military in Danish foreign policy. The 1920s and 1930s had seen subsequent cuts in the Danish defence budget, leaving Denmark defenceless at the outbreak of World War II. After five years of German occupation, the Danish armed forces were virtually non-existent. Consequently, a coalition of political parties began a gradual rebuild of the Danish armed forces. Building on a Danish brigade initialized in 1944 in Sweden; the Danish armed forces were reorganized and expanded in the following years. This resulted in the creation of a unified Ministry of Defence, the Royal Danish Air Force (in addition to the existing Royal Danish Army and Royal Danish Navy), a Joint Chief of Staff and a defence college educating military officers from all three services. Still in the immediate aftermath of the war, the aim and rationale of the Danish armed forces were uncertain: Were they instruments for deterrence, surveillance, stabilization or something else? What would be the grand strategies of the remaining great powers, and would relations among them remain peaceful? As consequence of this uncertainty, Denmark continued its pre-war non-aligned hedging strategy by procuring military equipment from the East and West in the immediate aftermath of the war.[26]

Politically, Denmark was on the margins of international society because of the Danish authorities' cooperation with Germany during the Second World War. Danish policymakers chose two instruments to secure Denmark's re-admittance to international society, institutional activism and military activism, and Britain played a decisive role in providing the necessary conditions for both strategies. In institutional politics, Britain secured Denmark's re-admittance into international society by promoting Denmark as a founding member of the United Nations (UN). In military politics, Denmark contributed 45,000 Danish troops to the British military occupation of Germany from 1947 to 1958.[27] This was Denmark's first military engagement in the 1945–1989 period and the only one not under the auspices of the UN. In total, Denmark deployed military personnel to 12 UN missions during the Cold War. During the entire Cold War period, Denmark participated in all but three UN missions, and Danish troops alone amounted to seven per cent of all UN peacekeeping troops between 1948 and 1989.[28]

---

[26]Petersen (2011), pp. 276–280.

[27]Mortensen and Wivel (2019).

[28]Jakobsen (2011), pp. 287–293; Jakobsen and Kjærsgaard (2017), p. 386.

UN peacekeeping was an effective status-seeking policy for Denmark. In fact, this was a semi-official Danish foreign policy during the Cold War. As formulated by Danish Foreign Minister Per Hækkerup in 1965, the UN was one of the four cornerstones in Danish foreign policy and the primary channel for Danish value promotion in international society.[29,30] This platform successfully branded the Nordic countries as a social-liberal avant-garde international affairs. Today, it continues to place Denmark at or near the top of international rankings on contributions to peace and human development.[31]

Politically useful, the UN provided no shelter against the security threats to Denmark emanating from the Cold War. After initially negotiating with Norway and Sweden on a potential Scandinavian Defence Union, Denmark decided in favour of NATO and became a founding member of the alliance. However, in the alliance, Denmark earned a reputation of being quasi-neutral. Defence budgets remained low throughout the Cold War, fluctuating between 2 and 3 per cent of gross domestic product (GDP) and with a downward trend never rising above 2.5 per cent from 1969 onwards.[32] Even more significant, Denmark (like Norway) had important reservations in regard to official NATO policy. Denmark refused to allow foreign bases and troops on its territory in peacetime (since 1953)[33] and did not accept nuclear weapons on Danish territory, including Danish waters (since 1957). The Danish approach to NATO was pragmatic and functionalist, viewing NATO with the backing of the US primarily as a supplier of security shelter against the Soviet Union rather than an "Atlantic community". NATO membership was a cornerstone in Danish foreign policy, but mainly because of its importance for preserving Denmark's territorial integrity, security and survival.[34]

Scandinavia played a double role in Denmark's development as a military actor during the Cold War. On the one hand, it served as a platform for status seeking in UN peacekeeping missions. The Nordic welfare states provided an ideational starting point for the values underpinning Danish UN policy. Nordic cooperation on UN peacekeeping led to the development of a Nordic model for peacekeeping training and its implementation, which had significant impact on the UN.[35] On the other hand, the very same values served as a way of legitimizing low defence expenditures. Nordic politicians saw Scandinavia as an exceptional area of low tension. Nordic policymakers argued that the national securities of the Nordic states

---

[29]Hækkerup (1965).

[30]The other cornerstones were NATO (security and defense), EFTA/EC (trade and economic growth) and the Nordic Council of Ministers (identity politics).

[31]Marcussen (2018), pp. 240–253.

[32]SIPRI, SIPRI Military Expenditure Database: Data for all countries 1949–2017 (excel spreadsheet). https://www.7.org/databases/milex, accessed 16 January 2019.

[33]With the notable exception of Greenland, which was used as a bargaining chip in Denmark's relationship with the United States.

[34]Due-Nielsen and Petersen (1995), pp. 11–54.

[35]Jakobsen (2006), pp. 381–395.

were interdependent. Therefore, continued peacefulness depended on a delicate "Nordic balance", which would be upset if either of the superpowers insisted on normalizing the region, i.e. if the United States and NATO insisted that Denmark and Norway always followed official NATO policy. This would allegedly provoke a reaction from the Soviet Union, limiting the action space of Sweden and Finland, increasing tension in the region.[36] According to this argument, Denmark should be allowed to pursue non-provocative policies towards the Soviet Union while enjoying the military shelter following from NATO membership.[37]

As in the pre-war period, Denmark adapted to the great powers perceived as pivotal for Danish security interests. The Soviet Union was viewed as the major threat and the United States as the most important shelter. NATO membership secured access to this shelter. Scandinavia allowed for hedging this security bet with a Nordic security identity and non-provocative policies towards the nearby Soviet superpower. The UN provided a platform for status seeking by showcasing Denmark as a willing and able contributor to international society.

8.3.3 1990–2019: Taking Advantage of Unipolarity

Even though the end of Cold War left Denmark (and other Nordic countries) with a sense of "Nordic nostalgia",[38] Danish decision-makers tended to view the new security environment as "a unique window of opportunity" for a foreign and security policy based on so-called active internationalism.[39] Danish policymakers viewed the new security environment as benevolent to small states. There was virtually no military threat to small NATO member states, and a new broad security agenda allowed for small state influence on a number of issues. Moreover, the demand for small state contributions to international military operations quickly increased as a number of conflicts, which had been overlain by superpower conflict, came to dominate the new security order.

Denmark was quick to meet this demand. In 1990, Danish corvette Olfert Fischer participated in the US-led coalition against Iraq in the Persian Gulf. From 1992 to 1996, Danish forces participated for the first time in a NATO operation in the form of Sharp Guard in the Adriatic, where three Danish corvettes contributed to maintaining the maritime embargo on former Yugoslavia. From 1990 to 1999, Denmark contributed to 17 UN operations compared to 12 UN operations during the entire 1945–1999 period. In 1998, the Danish Parliament for the first time authorized Danish participation in a military operation without authorization from the UN, i.e. NATO's Operation Allied Force in the Western Balkans. The majority of

[36]Noreen (1983), pp. 43–56.
[37]Mouritzen (2001), p. 298.
[38]Wæver (1992), pp. 77–102.
[39]Holm (2002), pp. 21, 22–23.

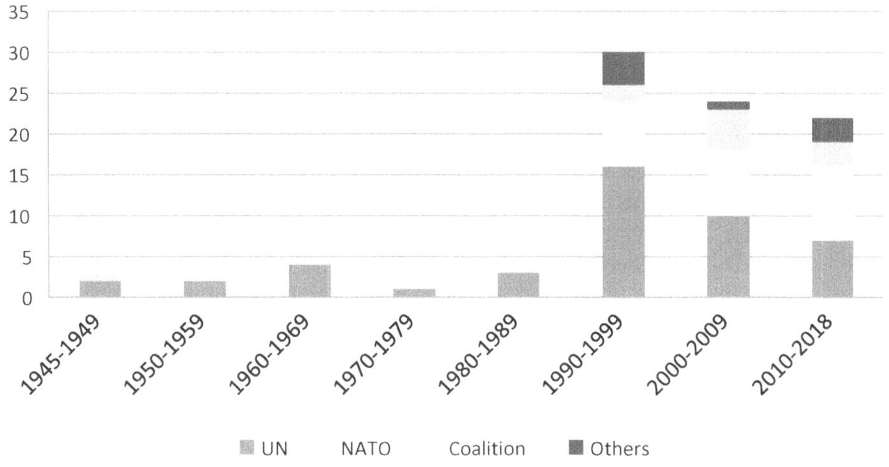

Fig. 8.1 Denmark's military contributions to international operations. Numbers indicate Parliamentary decisions authorizing Denmark's military engagement (Mortensen and Wivel 2019)

Parliament argued that this constituted a necessary exemption from Danish UN policy because of the Serbian repression and violence against the Kosovo Albanians.[40] However, behind closed doors, leading members of the government argued that Denmark had a vital interest in staying within the NATO mainstream and not complicate matters in a moment viewed as decisive for the future of the alliance.[41] From this time, and in particular after the terrorist attacks on New York and Washington on 11 September 2001, Denmark emphasized US-led coalitions and NATO-led military missions rather than UN operations. To be sure, the UN has not lost its relevance as an institutional framework for Denmark's military engagement, but it no longer holds a monopoly status when it comes to Danish troop deployments outside the Danish territory. From 1990 to 2018, the UN constituted the institutional framework in 33 out of a total of 76 military operations, while NATO constituted the institutional framework in 25 operations (Fig. 8.1).

Typically, NATO operations are either operations that intend to maintain the sovereignty of NATO countries, as is the case of the operations in the Baltic and Icelandic airspace and the Danish contribution to Enhanced Forward Presence (EFP) in Estonia since 2017, or operations authorized by the UN but carried out by NATO. In addition, Denmark has contributed to operations based on NATO's Article 5, i.-e. Operation Eagle Assist (2001–2002) in US Airspace and Operation Active Endeavor (2001–2004) in the Mediterranean (in addition, the latter was also authorized by the UN) and one operation intended to avoid a humanitarian disaster, Operation Allied Force in Kosovo in the spring of 1999.

[40]Wivel (2019), pp. 382–383.

[41]Mariager and Wivel (2019), pp. 172–177.

International *ad hoc* coalitions formed to carry out specific military operations constitute the other important framework for Denmark's military engagement after the Cold War. In the 1990s, Denmark participated in two ad hoc coalitions, the US-led coalition in the Persian Gulf 1990–1991 and Operation Alba in 1997, an international protection force under the leadership of Italy, under the authority of the UN Security Council and OSCE and at the request of the Albanian government to intervene in the Albanian civil war. Denmark participated in five coalitions during the period 2000–2009: Operation Enduring Freedom in Afghanistan in 2002, International Security Assistance Force (ISAF) in 2002–2003 (before NATO took command), Operation Iraqi Freedom in Iraq (2003–2007), Combined Task Force 150 and 151 (CTF) (formerly part of Operation Enduring Freedom) and Combined Maritime Forces (CMT) in the Gulf of Aden and the Horn of Africa (2008–), as well as the United Nations Command Military Armistice Commission (UNCMAC) (2009–). From 2010 to 2018, Denmark contributed militarily to three coalitions: Operation Odyssey Dawn in Libya (2011), which was replaced by NATO's Operation Unified Protector (also in 2011) in Libya; the French-led Operation Serval in Mali (2013); and Operation Inherent Resolve (OIR) in Iraq and Syria since 2014.[42]

By far the most controversial among these military operations was the decision to participate in the 2003 invasion of Iraq. The controversy in Denmark was not over participating in a coalition, and it was not the first time Denmark chose to go to war without a clear UN authorization. However, to critics, the invasion was too much a reflection of US military interests, and the government had awarded too little attention to the UN and the opportunities for working with Nordic and European partners on the diplomatic and humanitarian aspects of the conflict.[43] Thus, while participation in a coalition against Iraq was not in itself ruled out by the opposition in the Danish Parliament, they were concerned that it was not inclusive enough and did not represent international society. It was the first time Denmark participated in a military operation when the country's most important international partners disagreed (the United States and the United Kingdom were in favour of an intervention, while France and Germany were against). Consequently, it was the first time that Denmark participated in a military operation without a broad consensus between centre right and centre left in the Danish Parliament.

This massive military engagement has been enabled by a transformation of Denmark's defence posture and armed forces since the early 1990s and onwards. During the Cold War, the primary aim of the defence forces had been the defence of the territorial integrity of the Kingdom of Denmark. However, with the collapse of the Soviet Union, Danish decision-makers found that a conventional territorial threat to Danish security was unlikely for decades to come. In contrast, a new set of threats emanated from the end of the Cold War, increasing the demand for expeditionary forces.

[42]Mortensen and Wivel (2019), p. 551.

[43]Wivel (2019), pp. 454–459.

Consequently, from the early 1990s, Denmark initiated a reorganization of the Danish armed forces towards a national defence primarily aimed at international military operations. The establishment in 1993 of the Danish International Brigade was a significant political signal, although it had less operational significance. However, not until 2004 did the defence budgets initiate a fundamental restructuring of the Danish defence posture and the Danish armed forces. In a bold move, Denmark de facto abolished territorial defence in favour of a minor, flexible and deployable force suitable for out-of-area operations. The costs for restructuring were supported by savings on the Cold War mobilization force and through acceptance of a relatively low post-Cold War peace dividend; that is, Denmark reduced its defence spending by less than the average NATO member state.[44] The subsequent two defence budgets followed the same course, while the 2018 defence budget and a subsequent political agreement in 2019 increased the budget to a projected 1.5 per cent in 2023 and refocused the Danish defence posture towards the Baltic Sea area.[45]

The increase and change in Danish military contributions after the Cold War mirror a change in demand and the end of the Cold War stalemate when the UN acted as a clearing house for the superpowers and any military operation took place in the shadow of the risk of a third world war.[46] However, the decision to meet international demand for military operations is made by the Danish government and Parliament. It is the decision of these policymakers that Denmark shadows the policies of the United States (and the United Kingdom). Military activism is not a response to the threat of repercussions from the world's only superpower should Danish decision-makers decide for a different course. In contrast, Danish decisions to contribute to international military operations are done in anticipation of US interests.[47] In some cases, Afghanistan and Iraq in particular, Danish policy positions followed those of the United States from an early stage of the decision-making process. Thus, even though Danish military activism seems to contradict conventional wisdom about small states, as described in the beginning of this chapter, it is fundamentally a reflection of Denmark's status as a small state. Denmark has adapted and has been eagerly forthcoming in assisting the US in military operations.

Denmark's military activism since the end of the Cold War combines shelter seeking with status seeking to the extent that the two now exist in symbiosis. Shelter seeking is conditioned upon status seeking, and status seeking is an important instrument for shelter seeking. To Denmark, small state security seeking in the post-Cold War security environment is about signalling that Denmark is a useful and able partner making an active contribution and meeting the challenges to international security deemed vital by its great power partners, most importantly

---

[44]Rasmussen (2017), pp. 51–73.

[45]Danish Ministry of Defence 2018, Aftale på forsvarsområdet 2018–2023, 28 January 2018. http://www.fmn.dk/temaer/forsvarsforlig/Documents/Forsvarsforlig-2018-2023.pdf, accessed 14 March 2019.

[46]Jakobsen (2015), pp. 5–13.

[47]Mariager and Wivel (2019), p. 22.

the United States.[48] Securing a status as an "impeccable ally" of the United States is viewed as the best bet for keeping the American security shelter. This approach has until recently left little room for hedging. However, recent Russian resurgence combined with a series of US challenges to the principles and institutions of the liberal world order has prompted Danish decision-makers to engage actively with initiatives by France, Germany and the United Kingdom, as well as the Nordic Defence Cooperation.

8.4 Conclusion: Lessons for Small States in Theory and Practice

Denmark's instrumental use of military activism since the end of the Cold War is characterized by willingness as well as ability to meet international demand for participation in international military operations, in particular when this demand comes from the United States. This policy holds lessons for both the practice and theory of small states.[49]

One practical lesson is that military activism may increase access to and information from the US administration to the small state. Thus, Danish foreign-policy makers, diplomats and defence staff find that Denmark's international status as an ally has increased access to key US decision-makers and information on US policy positions.[50] They link this to Denmark's willingness to contribute to military operations, although it is difficult to discern to which extent access translates into influence. A second practical lesson is that taking on a role as a super-Atlanticist and an impeccable ally increases vulnerability. Giving up territorial defence and focusing on Danish expeditionary forces made Denmark vulnerable to Russian resurgence in the wake of Russia's annexation of Crimea in 2014. This development also illustrated Denmark's vulnerability to changes in US foreign policy. The United States now wants Denmark to take on an active role in the Baltic Sea area while continuing to contribute to military operations in the Middle East.

A third practical lesson follows from this experience. Small states by definition suffer from limited capacity. Military activism risks overstretching human and material capacity and wearing down the armed forces with subsequent problems of recruiting staff and maintaining adequate material capabilities. Finally, military activism demands political prioritization and solid administrative procedures for preparing, implementing and evaluating military operations. The Danish experience suggests that small militarily activist states run the risk of catering to international demand without systematically evaluating the costs and benefits and the alignment

---

[48]Cf. Breitenbauch (2015), p. 28.

[49]The practical lessons discussed here draw on Mariager and Wivel (2019) and in Wivel et al. (2018).

[50]Jakobsen et al. (2018).

between national interests and values and the military operations in question. The Danish government rarely conducts systematic cost-benefit analyses on the likely effect of a military operation prior to committing Danish troops, and there has been no procedure for systematic learning from previous military engagements.[51] Without these measures, the political decision-makers lack the necessary tools to navigate current challenges and opportunities and to evaluate past operations.

The Danish experience holds lessons for small state theory as well. The most important lesson is that small state shelter seeking and status seeking become closely intertwined in a dynamic and globalized security environment. The Cold War stalemate allowed small states like Denmark to separate shelter seeking and status seeking, but today status is increasingly a prerequisite for shelter. This reflects a collapse in the traditional division of labour between small states and great powers. Small states are now expected to be security producers as well as security consumers. However, they still need security shelter because of their absolute and relative lack of power. Consequently, contributing to international security becomes a way of achieving status as a good ally worthy of security shelter. A more general lesson follows from this observation. Small states do not face a choice between offensive and defensive strategies. Rather, they need to strategize how to optimize the use of offensive tools to secure the backing and shelter from stronger powers and, in turn, how this backing allows them to further optimize their quest for status, information and influence.

References

Bailes A, Rickli J-M, Thorhallsson B (2014) Small states, survival and strategy. In: Archer, Bailes, Wivel (eds) Small states and international security. Routledge, London, pp 26–45

Bailes A, Thayer B, Thorhallsson B (2016) Alliance theory and alliance 'shelter': the complexities of small state alliance behavior. Third World Thematics: TWQ 1(1):9–26

Baldacchino G, Wivel A (2020) Introducing the politics of small states. In: Handbook on the politics of small states. Edward Elgar, Cheltenham

Breitenbauch H (2015) Uendelig krig?: Danmark, samtænkning og stabilisering af globale konflikter. Djøf Forlag, Copenhagen

Danish Government (2018) Udenrigs- og sikkerhedspolitisk strategi 2019–2020. Ministry of Foreign Affairs, Copenhagen

de Carvalho B, Neumann I (2015) Introduction: small states and status. In: de Carvalho B, Neumann I (eds) Small states and status seeking: Norway's quest for international standing. Routledge, London, pp 1-21

Due-Nielsen C, Petersen N (1995) Adaptation and activism. DJØF Forlag, København, pp 11–54

Edström H, Gyllensporre D, Westberg J (2019) Military strategy of small states: responding to external shocks of the 21st century. Routledge, London

Glenthøj R (2018) 1864 før, nu og i fremtiden. Fortællinger i nyere og ældre dansk 1864-historiografi. Historisk Tidsskrift 117(2):566–598

Hækkerup P (1965) Dansk Udenrigspolitik. Fremad, København

[51] Wivel (2019), pp. 330–333.

Holm H-H (2002) Danish foreign policy activism: the rise and decline. In: Heurlin B, Mouritzen H (eds) Danish foreign policy yearbook 2002. Danish Institute of International Studies, Copenhagen, pp 21–23

Jakobsen PV (2006) The Nordic peacekeeping model: rise, fall, resurgence? Int Peacekeeping 13 (3):381–395

Jakobsen P (2011) Fredsbevarende operationer. In: Den Kolde Krig Og Danmark. Gad, Copenhagen, pp 287–293

Jakobsen P (2015) Danmarks militære aktivisme fortsætter med eller uden USA. Politik 18(4):5–13

Jakobsen P, Kjærsgaard K (2017) Den danske FN-aktivismes storhed og fald 1945–2016. Politica 49(4):386

Jakobsen PV, Rynning S (2019) Denmark: happy to fight, will travel. Int Aff 95(4):877–895

Jakobsen P, Ringsmose J, Saxi H (2018) Prestige-seeking small states: Danish and Norwegian military contributions to US-led operations. Eur J Int Secur 3(2):256–277

Jesse N, Dreyer J (2016) Small states in the international system: at peace and war. Lexington Books, Lanham

Krause V, Singer D (2001) Minor powers, alliances and armed conflict: some preliminary patterns. In: Reiter E, Gärtner H (eds) Small states and alliances. Physica-Verlag, Vienna, pp 15–23

Larson D, Paul T, Wohlforth W (2014) Status and world order. In: Paul, T.V., Larson D, Wohlforth W (eds) Status in world politics. Cambridge University Press, Cambridge, pp 18–19

Maass M (2017) Small states in world politics: the history of small state survival, 1648–2016. Manchester University Press, Manchester

Marcussen M (2018) Scandinavian models of diplomacy. In: Nedergaard P, Wivel A (eds) The Routledge handbook of Scandinavian politics. Routledge International Handbooks, Routledge, London; N.Y., pp 240–253

Mariager R, Wivel A (2019) Hvorfor gik Danmark i krig? Uvildig udredning af baggrunden for Danmarks militære engagement i Kosovo, Afghanistan og Irak. Rosendahls, København

Morrow J (1991) Alliances and asymmetry: an alternative to the capability aggregation model of alliances. American Journal of Political Science 35(4):904–933

Mortensen C, Wivel A (2019) Mønstre og udviklingslinjer i Danmarks militære engagement 1945–2018. In: Mariager R, Wivel A (eds) Hvorfor gik Danmark i krig? Uvildig udredning af baggrunden for Danmarks militære engagement i Kosovo, Afghanistan og Irak. Rosendahls, København, pp 541-638

Mouritzen H (2001) Security communities in the Baltic Sea region: real and imagined. Secur Dialogue 32(3):297-310

Mouritzen H (2007) Denmark's super Atlanticism. Journal of Transatlantic Studies 5(2):155–167

Noreen E (1983) The Nordic balance: a security policy concept in theory and practice. Cooperation and Conflict 18(1):43–56

Pedersen RB, Ringsmose J (2017) Aktivisme i dansk udenrigspolitik: Norden, FN, NATO og EU. Politica 49(4):339–357

Petersen N (2011) Forsvarspolitik. In: Lauridsen JT, Mariager R, Olesen TB, Villaume P (eds) Den Kolde Krig og Danmark. Gads Forlag, Copenhagen, pp 276–280

Rasmussen MV (2005) 'What's the use of it?': Danish strategic culture and the utility of armed force. Cooperation and Conflict 40(1):67–89

Rasmussen M (2017) Nationalists, national liberals and cosmopolitans: Danish foreign policy debates after Brexit and Trump. In: Fischer K, Mouritzen H (eds) Danish foreign policy yearbook, pp 51–73

Ringsmose J, Rynning S (2008) The impeccable ally? Denmark, NATO, and the uncertain future of top tier membership. In: Hvidt N, Mouritzen H (eds) Danish foreign policy yearbook. Danish Institute for International Studies, Copenhagen, pp 55–84

Thorhallsson B (ed) (2019) Small states and shelter theory: Iceland's external affairs. Routledge, London

Thorhallsson B, Steinsson S (2017) Small state foreign policy. In: Oxford research encyclopaedia of politics. Oxford University Press, Oxford

Wæver O (1992) Nordic Nostalgia: Northern Europe after the Cold War. International Affairs 68 (1):77–102

Waltz K (1979) Theory of international politics. McGraw-Hill, New York, p 127

Wivel A (2018) Forerunner, follower, exceptionalist or bridge builder? Mapping Nordicness in Danish foreign policy. Global Affairs 4(4–5):419–434

Wivel A (2019) Hvorfor bidrog Danmark militært i Kosovo, Afghanistan og Irak? En analyse af de offentligt fremførte argumenter for Danmarks militære engagemen. In: Mariager R, Wivel A (eds) Hvorfor gik Danmarks i krig? Irak og tværgående analyser. Rosendals, Copenhagen, pp 363–539

Wivel A, Crandall M (2019) Punching above their weight, but why? Explaining Denmark and Estonia in the transatlantic relationship. Journal of Transatlantic Studies 17(3):392–419

Wivel A, Bailes A, Archer C (2014) Setting the scene: small states and international security. In: Archer C, Bailes A, Wivel A (eds) Small states and international security: Europe and beyond. Routledge, London, pp 3–25

Wivel A, Mariager R, Mortensen C (2018) Denmark at war: patterns and developments in Denmark's Military Engagement, Small States and the New Security (SSANSE), Policy Brief No. 8. http://ams.hi.is/wp-content/uploads/2018/06/Denmark-at-War-Patterns-and-Developments-in-Denmark%C2%B4s-Military-Engagement-1.pdf

Rasmus Mariager is an Associate Professor of History at the University of Copenhagen, where he also serves as director of Danish Culture Courses. His research interests include Danish foreign policy in the twentieth and twenty-first centuries and transatlantic relations in the same time period. His publications include "Danish Cold War Historiography," *Journal of Cold War Studies* (2019).

Anders Wivel is a professor with special responsibilities in the Department of Political Science, University of Copenhagen, Denmark. His research interests include power politics, small state foreign policy and European and Scandinavian politics. His recent publications include articles in *European Security*, *International Studies Review* and *Global Affairs*, as well as two books.

Chapter 9
Security in the Nordic Baltic Region and Russia: Towards Enhanced Regional Defence Cooperation?

Živilė Marija Vaicekauskaitė

9.1 Introduction

In recent years, the strategic environment in Europe's northeast has undergone crucial changes, giving a new impetus to the countries of the region to reassess their defence strategies and cooperation both at bilateral and multilateral levels. The events in Ukraine brought back traditional security concerns and presented new (hybrid) ones, pushing them to the forefront of the political agenda and increasing focus on small states' ability to cope with changing geopolitical landscape. Faced with the deterioration of their immediate security environment, the small Nordic Baltic states found themselves particularly threatened and have begun reviewing their security policies to better address their rising security concerns.

The Nordic Baltic format presents an interesting case for analysis because two countries in the region are North Atlantic Treaty Organization (NATO) partner countries, yet all of them are small states bounded by the same strategic environment—the Baltic Sea region, where they face many of the same security challenges. The security cooperation among these countries has always been a constantly evolving process. However, it has never achieved a regionalised and overarching security and defence cooperation framework that would involve all the countries of the region.[1]

With a recent change in the European security landscape, the Nordic Baltic countries are incentivized to increase their defence and security cooperation. The argumentation for this conclusion is that the assertive nature of Russia and the uncertainty of the US's role in NATO create a strong demand for broader and deeper

[1]Major and von Voss (2016).

Ž. M. Vaicekauskaitė (✉)
Vilnius University, Vilnius, Lithuania

A.-M. Brady, B. Thorhallsson (eds.), *Small States and the New Security Environment*, The World of Small States 7,
https://doi.org/10.1007/978-3-030-51529-4_9

regional defence cooperation.[2] Hence, the predominant expectation is that there are now stronger incentives for the Nordic Baltic states to intensify their regional defence coordination.

Against this backdrop, this article examines the recent changes in Nordic Baltic defence policies. It aims to assess how the countries in the region meet their security challenges and whether the shelter strategy can serve as a catalyst for more enhanced regional defence cooperation. The article focuses on the political component of the shelter theory. Political shelter refers to small states' inability to sustain their military or diplomatic power. This is specifically related to small states' limited military strength and incapacity to defend themselves alone.

This article aims to analyze major shifts of Nordic Baltic security choices after 2014. It progresses through several phases. First, it addresses the implications of the Ukraine crisis for Nordic Baltic security. Second, using official documents, this article examines each of the Nordic Baltic states' security and defence concepts employed after 2014, showing major shifts in their defence policies. Third, it discusses the role of the shelter strategy in current Nordic Baltic defence policies. Last but not the least, it concludes with some practical recommendations on how the shelter strategy could catalyze regional defence cooperation.

9.2 The Ukraine Crisis as a Turning Point in the Security Landscape of the Nordic Baltic Region

The Ukraine crisis had serious implications on the Nordic Baltic region. Russia's assertive actions via land, air, and maritime domains demonstrated a real threat to the neighbouring states, which, being small, felt exposed to a significantly stronger military power. Russia went from being a potential regional partner to a potential threat, posing serious security challenges to the states in the area. The annexation of Crimea, which was first change by force of Europe's borders in decades, generated fear among the small littoral states in the Baltic Sea region that Russia could also attempt to violate their sovereignty or territorial integrity. Given their size and capabilities, the Nordic Baltic states are very limited in maintaining or ensuring their security by themselves. Also, memberships in different organizations and diverging security policies are complicating the situation since not all countries have the same security guarantees.[3] This affected the shared threat perception in the region and also prompted Nordic Baltic countries, together with NATO and the European Union, to reassess defence strategies and policies, as well as adopt new measures to boost their security in the region.[4]

---

[2]Breitenbauch et al. (2017).

[3]Ibid.

[4]Larrabee et al. (2015).

9.2.1 Denmark

Following up on the review of its foreign and security policy in 2016, the Danish government presented a new foreign and security policy strategy. The document noted that changes in the European security environment and its unpredictability have an impact on Danish foreign policy; therefore, maintaining and strengthening international cooperation is important than ever. The new strategy has a particular emphasis on membership in the EU and NATO, as well as bilateral partnerships with its closest allies, including the United States and Baltic Sea region countries.[5]

The latest review of the Danish defence agreement for 2018–2023 articulated the need for a change in defence policy.[6] To cope with rising security challenges, Denmark is increasing defence spending, investing into Armed Forces operational capabilities. The new guidelines aim to strengthen Danish contributions to the collective deterrence of NATO and significantly boost national security efforts. Strong NATO and steadfast transatlantic ties, along with effective multilateral and regional cooperation, are seen as key elements of Danish national security interests.[7]

Developments in the Baltic Sea region play an important role in Denmark's security. Denmark seeks a greater security policy role in the region.[8] Throughout the years, it has developed close relations with regional partners and aims to continue developing strong security ties both with Nordic partners and Baltic allies. In 2015, Denmark and Sweden signed a bilateral military cooperation agreement on air and naval operations. A wider defence agreement was also signed between all five Nordic countries to deal with threats emanating from Russia.[9]

9.2.2 Sweden

The new Swedish national security strategy published in 2017 recognized the wide range of challenges facing Sweden and the entire Baltic Sea region. The new document emphasized that Swedish security interests are closely related to those of Nordic and Baltic countries, in that any military conflict in the region will also have an effect on Swedish security. The document outlined a strong Swedish interest

---

[5]Government of Denmark, "Foreign and Security Policy Strategy 2017-2018," 2017, http://um.dk/en/news/newsdisplaypage/?newsid=030b755e-643a-44db-989a-528847f6671b. Accessed 17 January 2019.

[6]Danish Ministry of Defense, "New Agreement for Danish Defense," 2018, http://www.fmn.dk/eng/news/Pages/New-agreement-for-Danish-Defence-2018-2023.aspx. Accessed 21 April 2018.

[7]Ibid.

[8]Government of Denmark, "Foreign and Security Policy Strategy 2017-2018," 2018, http://um.dk/en/news/newsdisplaypage/?newsid=030b755e-643a-44db-989a-528847f6671b. Accessed 17 January 2019.

[9]Nissen (2017), pp. 139–151.

in keeping the stability in the region, which can be achieved through a strong transatlantic link with the United States, as well as increased defence and security cooperation with Finland and NATO. Strong emphasis is also placed on Sweden's membership in the European Union, which plays an important role in Swedish security policy, especially in terms of crisis management capacity, and provides "soft" security shelter. As noted by Foreign Minister Margot Wallström in her Statement of Foreign Policy to the Riksdag in 2017, "the EU is most important foreign policy arena and Sweden will seek to strengthen the Common Security and Defence Policy".[10]

In 2015, five Swedish political parties agreed on a bill in Parliament on the key defence policy guidelines for the years 2016–2020. The document indicated two main priorities for the upcoming years: to increase the operational warfighting capability of the armed forces and to ensure the collective force of the total defence. Since Sweden remains non-aligned, the bill underlined the importance of solidarity with other regional partners, including security cooperation with the Nordic and Baltic countries. Enhanced bilateral cooperation with the United States and Finland is seen as crucial for Swedish national security.[11]

For a long time, Swedish defence policy was seen as non-participation in military conflict and neutrality in war time. However, lately this approach has been slowly changing. Sweden began considering closer ties with NATO, which resulted in a host nation support agreement, ratified in 2016. The agreement allows NATO to more easily operate on Swedish soil in case of a conflict.[12] Although the country's membership in NATO remains unlikely, Sweden has increased its cooperation with NATO, pursuing a new middle course in its defence policy, somewhere between non-alignment and NATO partnership.[13]

Given the latest developments in Swedish defence policy, it can be noticed that Sweden is seeking partnerships, not alliances. The "Hultqvist doctrine", named after the current Minister of Defence, is guided by two principles: strong national defence and close bilateral partnerships, especially with the United States and Finland. Recently, Sweden has signed several bilateral and trilateral defence agreements with the USA, the UK, and Denmark, among others. The latest Trilateral Statement of Intent, signed by the United States, Sweden, and Finland, further reinforces their existing defence relationship in areas such as increasing interoperability, capability and readiness through training, and expanding practical cooperation in research and

---

[10]Government Offices of Sweden, "Statement of Government Policy in the Parliamentary Debate on Foreign Affairs 2017," https://www.government.se/statements/2017/03/statement-of-government-policy-in-the-parliamentary-debate-on-foreign-affairs-2017/. Accessed 3 January 2019.

[11]Government Offices of Sweden, "Sweden's Defence Policy 2016 to 2020," https://www.government.se/49c007/globalassets/government/dokument/forsvarsdepartementet/sweden_defence_policy_2016_to_2020. Accessed 20 November 2018.

[12]R. Steindish, "Fearing Russian Bear, Sweden Inches Toward NATO," *Foreign Policy*, May 25, 2016, http://foreignpolicy.com/2016/05/25/fearing-russian-bear-sweden-inches-toward-nato-finland-moscow-military/. Accessed 20 November 2018.

[13]Friis and Bredesen (2017).

development.[14] Experts argue that bilateralism currently dominating Swedish defence policy can yield practical benefits for Sweden by strengthening its security and also by keeping many other available cooperation options open.[15]

9.2.3 Norway

Historically, Norway has paid more attention to security cooperation in the High North, where its interests are clearly defined by geography and existing neighbourhood with Russia.[16] However, the latest white paper of the Norwegian government recognized that the European security environment has changed considerably, having significant implications for the country's national security. One of the main Norwegian security concerns is Russia acting aggressively both in the Baltic Sea and the Arctic. Russia's military build-up in the Arctic region threatens to limit Norway's freedom of action and stop any reinforcements if any crisis would erupt in the area. Most of Norway's military cooperation with Russia is suspended, with only a few direct lines of communication remaining open to safeguard security in the Arctic.[17]

In order to respond to the evolving security landscape in its close neighbourhood, Norway seeks to strengthen national defence capabilities, maintain close transatlantic cooperation, contribute to NATO's collective defence efforts, and build closer ties with Nordic countries and European allies. Particular attention is given to developing long-lasting security ties with the United States, which due to historical reasons and its military presence in the country remains the key security ally. Defence dialogues with the so-called selected allies, such as the US, Germany, the UK, the Netherlands, and France, demonstrate Norway's interest in having strong allies and bilateral partnerships.[18]

Norway's multilateral approach to security policy is demonstrated by its support for NATO's ability to adapt to a changing security environment, as well as collective defence capacity. NATO constitutes an important part of maintaining stability in the North by providing a significant level of security. The new white paper reiterates Norway's commitment to NATO's collective defence and cooperative security. This is illustrated by the implementation of the NATO Warsaw Summit decision to deploy four multinational battalions to the Baltic states and Poland, where Norway

[14]Government Offices of Sweden, "Minister of Defence Peter Hultqvist signed US-Swedish Statement of Intent," https://www.government.se/articles/2016/06/minister-of-defence-peter-hultqvist-signed/. Accessed 22 April 2018.

[15]Friis and Bredesen (2017).

[16]Hakon (2018), p. 102.

[17]Ibid.

[18]Ibid.

also participates in the German-led battle group in Lithuania.[19] The security of the Baltic states is understood as part of a collective defence principle, which is of great significance for Norway, itself a small state bordering Russia which alone could not ensure its own security if needed.[20]

With regard to the broader Nordic Baltic region, Norway seeks to intensify the security dialogue with its Nordic counterparts. The other Nordic countries, especially Sweden and Finland, are perceived as a very important part of Norway's national security. Even before the Ukraine crisis, the Nordic states were seen as more capable and stronger military and security partners than the Baltic states, which are smaller and less militarily capable than Sweden, Finland, or Denmark.[21] As noted in the white paper, close Nordic and Baltic security cooperation strengthens all of Europe's security and stability; therefore, close dialogue with Nordic and Baltic countries should be further maintained and strengthened.[22]

9.2.4 Finland

Finland and Sweden are two countries in the region that officially follow the policy of non-alignment and remain outside of NATO. Despite that, both countries are important partners to the Alliance and actively support its activities.

Finland's desire to have more enhanced security and defence partnerships was rather low, partly because the chance of a military conflict in the region was perceived as limited. In addition, the close proximity to Russia influenced the country's decision to follow the non-alignment policy, which could be seen as a strategy to not to provoke Russia.

However, with recent changes in Finland's military operating environment, the demand on defence has increased. The new Finnish defence policy guidelines, adopted in 2017, emphasized the need to boost the country's military readiness, defence capacity, and societal resilience. The primary objective of Finland's security policy remains the same: avoid being involved in a military conflict and make decisions independently. However, the country understands the need to play an active role in the region in case of an emergency and seeks to strengthen its ability to provide or receive security assistance.[23]

Both Sweden and the United States form an important part of Finland's defence concept. In 2016, Finland and the United States signed a Statement of Intent aimed to deepen the practical bilateral defence cooperation through engagements on a regular

---

[19]NATO, "Boosting NATO's presence in the east and southeast," https://www.nato.int/cps/en/natohq/topics_136388.htm?selectedLocale=en. Accessed 22 April 2018.

[20]Ibid.

[21]Hakon (2018), p. 103.

[22]Norwegian Ministry of Foreign Affairs (2017).

[23]Government of Finland (2017).

basis. The agreement charts a path to even closer defence cooperation with the United States in areas such as exchange of information, research and development, and enhancement of readiness, interoperability, and armament.[24]

Finland strongly promotes the development of defence cooperation with the European Union, which is Finland's primary security choice and soft security provider. Cooperation with NATO has also been expanding. Both have signed a Memorandum of Understanding on Host Nation Support allowing NATO to use Finnish territory in case of an emergency.[25] Both countries are also actively taking part in the Enhanced Opportunities Partnership programme, participating in NATO military exercises such as Trident Juncture to test capabilities to operate in a joint action. Sweden and Finland are also part of the enhanced NATO Response Force, aimed at strengthening collective defence capability.[26] Should Finland and Sweden decide to join the Alliance, it would significantly boost security in the region, making the Baltic Sea region an internal NATO sea. Together, Sweden and Finland form a big territory in the region, playing an important role in case of a crisis in the Baltic Sea.[27]

When it comes to public support for NATO, Finns still remain reluctant. A recent poll revealed that only 46 per cent of Finns support close defence cooperation with the NATO Alliance and the United States, while a quarter are sceptical of it. Moreover, only 17 per cent of Finns are in favour of Finland joining NATO.[28] To compare, public support for Sweden's membership in NATO has been shifting upward lately, reaching 43 per cent.[29] In terms of regional cooperation, the newest Finnish defence report re-emphasized the need to further intensify Nordic defence cooperation in the areas of training and exercises, along with cooperation between the Nordic countries and the Baltic states.[30]

---

[24]Ministry of Defense of Finland, "Ministry of Defense of Finland," 2016, http://www.defmin.fi/files/3543/Statement_of_Intent.pdf. Accessed 23 April 2018.

[25]Government Communications Department, "The President of the Republic of Finland," 2014, http://www.tpk.fi/public/default.aspx?contentid=311365&nodeid=44807&contentlan=2&culture=en-US. Accessed 26 April 2018.

[26]Mission of Norway to the EU, "Trident Juncture 2018: Defending the Nordic neighbourhood," https://www.norway.no/en/missions/eu/about-the-mission/news-events-statements/news2/trident-juncture-2018-defending-the-nordic-neighbourhood/. Accessed 23 January 2019.

[27]Dahl (2018), p. 130.

[28]"46% of Finns approve of close defence co-operation with Nato, finds poll," *Helsinki Times*, March 6, 2018, http://www.helsinkitimes.fi/finland/finland-news/domestic/15376-46-of-finns-approve-of-close-defence-co-operation-with-nato-finds-poll.html. Accessed 13 January 2019.

[29]Charlie Duxbury, "Under threat, Sweden rediscovers its Viking spirit," *Politico*, January 30, 2018, https://www.politico.eu/article/under-threat-sweden-rediscovers-its-viking-spirit-nato-russia/. Accessed 5 October 2019.

[30]Government of Finland (2017).

9.2.5 Iceland

Iceland does not have a standing army but belongs to NATO, which remains a key pillar of its national defence and security. Its new national security policy, approved by the Parliament in 2016, gave particular attention to participation in the Alliance and its activities. Although Iceland has no military resources, it actively contributes to NATO with its civilian assets. For instance, in 2018, the country contributed to the NATO Enhanced Forward Presence battle group in Lithuania.[31]

Another very important pillar of Iceland's national security is its bilateral defence cooperation with the United States. Historically, the US has played a crucial role in Iceland's security and has provided Iceland with security shelter. In 1951, both countries signed a defence agreement, as a part of which the US placed troops in Iceland, along with the establishment of an air and naval base in Keflavik. Due to its strategic location and importance in protecting the Greenland, Iceland, and the United Kingdom (GIUK) gap, Iceland formed an important part of US defence policy during the Cold War. This policy changed in 2006, when the US announced that it was withdrawing its troops from Iceland. Following this decision, Iceland had to reorient its security policy since it could not rely solely on US as an external territorial defence provider.[32] However, amid growing tensions with Russia, in 2016 Iceland and the US signed a new joint defence agreement, reaffirming US commitment to Iceland's defence and reconstituting American presence on the island.[33]

The withdrawal of US troops strengthened the European dimension of Iceland security policy. However, without full EU membership, Iceland cannot rely on EU security guarantees provided by mutual solidarity declaration.[34] To ensure its security, Iceland started enhancing bilateral cooperation with other Nordic countries. Iceland participates in the security policy dialogue of the NORDEFCO format and aims to develop cooperation with Nordic countries further.[35]

---

[31]Government Offices of Iceland, "Parliamentary Resolution on a National Security Policy of Iceland," 2016, https://www.government.is/library/01-Ministries/Prime-Ministers-Office/Parl-Res-Nat-Sec-Council-25-145-2016-tr-br-prot-SKIL-310817-.pdf. Accessed 20 November 2018.

[32]Ingimundarson (2007), pp. 7–23.

[33]US Department of Defense (2016).

[34]Ingimundarson (2007).

[35]Government Offices of Iceland, 2016. Parliamentary Resolution on a National Security Policy of Iceland. Available at: https://www.government.is/library/01-Ministries/Prime-Ministrers-Office/Parl-Res-Nat-Sec-Council-25-145-2016-tr-br-prot-SKIL-310817-.pdf. Accessed 20 November 2018.

9.2.6 Lithuania

To respond to growing instability in Europe's east, Lithuania took a whole-government approach, which included an increase in defence spending and investments, enhanced multilateral and bilateral defence cooperation, and a stronger emphasis on its commitment to international security.[36]

Lithuanian national security consists of three main pillars: membership in NATO, membership in the EU, and strategic partnership with the US. NATO remains the key provider of collective defence, while the EU is seen as a "soft" security shelter provider, having the tools needed to counter non-conventional threats.[37]

Lithuania places a huge importance on its strategic partnership with the US, whose active participation in NATO and military presence in the Baltic region remain the top priorities for Lithuania's security and defence agenda. Lithuania's latest military strategy underscores the importance of the US commitment to guarantee the regional security as "the key factor of the security of Lithuania".[38] In 2017, both countries signed a bilateral agreement on US troop deployments, granting the US a special status in Lithuania's security policy.[39]

The new national security strategy pays special attention to strengthening regional security cooperation, including the integration of the Baltic and Nordic countries. Lithuania seeks to deepen its defence cooperation with the other two Baltic states and the Nordic countries, as well as Poland, Germany and the UK.[40] In 2016, Lithuania and Latvia signed an agreement to synchronize military procurements, which should further enhance military cooperation and operational interoperability.[41]

9.2.7 Latvia

The annexation of Crimea shifted Latvia's security and defence policy. The current Russian foreign policy and the way it has been implemented, including the use of

[36]Seimas of the Republic of Lithuania (2017).

[37]Ibid.

[38]The Military Strategy of the Republic of Lithuania, APPROVED by the order No. V-252 of the Minister of National Defence of the Republic of Lithuania, 17 March 2016.

[39]"Lithuania signs agreement with US on troop deployment," *Military Times*, January 17, 2017, Available at: https://www.militarytimes.com/news/pentagon-congress/2017/01/17/lithuania-signs-agreement-with-u-s-on-troop-deployment/. Accessed 20 November 2018.

[40]Seimas of the Republic of Lithuania (2017).

[41]Defense News, "Lithuania, Latvia Sign Deal To Synchronize Defense Procurements," *Defense News*, September 9, 2016, https://www.defensenews.com/global/europe/2016/09/19/lithuania-latvia-sign-deal-to-synchronize-defense-procurements/. Accessed 20 November 2018.

military force and hybrid tactics, remain a major concern to Latvia's security.[42] In response, Latvia has taken major steps to increase its defence capacity and social resilience.

Latvia's new defence concept, adopted in 2016, outlined three courses of action. First and foremost, the reviewed document called for a stronger defence build-up and greater involvement of the society in the national defence.[43] Latvia significantly increased its defence spending and investments in developing additional defence capabilities. Second, both the new defence strategy and the national security concept stressed the importance of NATO and its long-term military presence in the country. Participation in the Alliance remains the main multilateral cooperation format, providing collective defence and security.[44]

The third priority of Latvia's national security policy is the further development of bilateral defence cooperation with the United States, which remains the main strategic partner. Latvia is actively seeking to have an active and long-term US presence in the country.[45] Other important bilateral partners include Canada, Germany, the United Kingdom, and Poland.

Latvia's defence concept outlines the need for a more synchronized, coordinated, and integrated Baltic military cooperation. Lithuania and Estonia remain among Latvia's closest military allies. The country also seeks to enhance regional cooperation with the Nordic states to strengthen security in the broader Baltic Sea area.[46]

9.2.8 Estonia

To effectively respond to arising security threats, Estonia adopted a defence development plan for 2017–2026, which paves the way for further enhancement of national defence forces and defence capabilities.[47] The newly approved document focuses on strengthening territorial defence, increasing civil engagement in national security, and further investing into the nation's defence capabilities. Estonia, as with the other Baltic states, has linked its security to full integration into NATO and the European Union. NATO remains the core of European security, which Estonia views as indivisible from its own security.[48]

---

[42]The Ministry of Defence of the Republic of Latvia, "The National Defence Concept," Approved by the Cabinet of Ministers 24 May 2016.

[43]Ibid.

[44]Ibid.

[45]Ibid.

[46]Ibid.

[47]Estonian Ministry of Defence, "National defence development plan 2017–2026," 2017, http://www.kaitseministeerium.ee/riigikaitse2026/arengukava/eng/. Accessed 20 November 2018.

[48]Ibid.

One of the main tools to enhance national security is strong bilateral and multilateral defence partnerships with NATO allies and regional partners. The strong transatlantic link is the key element of Estonia's defence policy.[49] Regionally, Estonia also seeks to deepen defence cooperation with the Nordic Baltic partners. The current Estonian Minister of Defence, Juri Luik, underscored that the tension within the region's security encourages all Baltic and Nordic countries to engage in closer defence cooperation. Among other bilateral defence partners, Estonia also develops closer cooperation with the United Kingdom, which is the framework nation for NATO multinational battle group deployed in the country.

9.3 The Transatlantic Nature of the Region's Desired Security Shelter

Three major guidelines can be found in all Nordic Baltic countries' defence policy agendas after 2014. First and foremost, a strategic partnership with the US is at the core of all countries' defence policies. All countries rely on the US, seeking to secure its political and security shelter and keep a steadfast transatlantic link. Despite uncertainties of US political and military commitment to NATO, and the US President's rhetoric about "America first", an enduring US presence and military leadership remain a primary goal for Nordic Baltic states to ensure regional security. The US remains an indispensable partner of all regional countries and their desired security shelter provider, and keeping it actively engaged in the region is a top defence policy priority. No other country is viewed as having a similar amount of capabilities and deterrent effect as the US.

Second, along with the US, NATO plays an important part in maintaining stability and providing a significant level of security to the Nordic Baltic region. Both the US and NATO are given primacy in Nordic Baltic defence matters. Sweden and Finland, which remain outside the Alliance and cannot be covered under Article 5, also demonstrated a growing interest in enhancing cooperation with the Alliance by intensifying defence cooperation with NATO, which resulted in host nation support agreements signed between all parties. Although NATO is seen as a security provider, US leadership is required for a strong transatlantic Alliance. As in the Cold War, an extensive US involvement has a reassuring and deterring effect.[50] With capabilities and diplomatic power, the US remains a key pillar of NATO collective defence.

---

[49]The Parliament of the Republic of Estonia, "National Security Concept of Estonia," 2010, http://www.kaitseministeerium.ee/sites/default/files/elfinder/article_files/national_security_concept_of_estonia.pdf. Accessed 20 November 2018.

[50]Michael Howard, "Reassurance and Deterrence: Western Defense in the 1980s," *Foreign Affairs* (Winter 1982/82), https://www.foreignaffairs.com/articles/1982-12-01/reassurance-and-deterrence-western-defense-1980s. Accessed 22 January 2019.

The third common aspect that helps to characterize the Nordic Baltic defence concepts after 2014 is a strong focus on boosting national defence capacity. This has resulted in increased defence spending, a build-up of military capabilities, and modernization of armed forces. Some of the biggest increases in military spending since 2013 have been made by the Baltic countries.[51] The Nordics also seem to recognize the need to further strengthen their militaries.

Regional Nordic Baltic defence cooperation is seen as important. However, by itself it is not sufficient to compensate for the lack of security of small states in the area. Each of the Nordic Baltic security strategies underlines the significance of regional defence cooperation, but only as an additional measure to support already existing security efforts. Additionally, some differences in terms of how Nordic Baltic states perceive regional defence cooperation occur. Nordic countries place more emphasis on cooperation within the Nordic format, while Baltic states underline the importance of broader defence cooperation encompassing all countries in the region.[52] As an example, in 2015, all five Nordic countries signed a wider defence agreement on expanding exercises and sharing of intelligence information to deal with threat emanating from Russia.[53]

9.4 Reinvigorating the Regional Dimension

Recent trends in Nordic Baltic defence policies reveal the growing importance of coordinating regional defence efforts. The United States has underlined the importance of regional efforts and has suggested that Europe should invest more into its own security.[54] The last US Nordic Summit in 2018 reaffirmed US interest in the broader Nordic Baltic region.[55] Since Sweden and Finland most likely will not join the Alliance in the nearest future, regional countries, along with US leadership and support, could benefit from deepening regional cooperation and building credible counterweight against Russia.

The Nordic Baltic countries' defence policies clearly demonstrate the desire to secure US involvement and political shelter encompassing various forms of it—the

---

[51]NATO Public Diplomacy Division, "Defence Expenditure of NATO Countries (2011-2018)," https://www.nato.int/nato_static_fl2014/assets/pdf/pdf_2018_07/20180709_180710-pr2018-91-en.pdf. Accessed February 1, 2019.

[52]Nissen (2017).

[53]"Nordic nations agree on defense cooperation against Russia," Reuters, April 10, 2015, https://www.reuters.com/article/us-nordics-russia-defence-idUSKBN0N02E820150409. Accessed October 14, 2019.

[54]"U.S. Supports Drive for Nordic Defense Cooperation," *Defense News*, May 18, 2015, https://www.defensenews.com/pentagon/2016/05/18/us-supports-drive-for-nordic-defense-cooperation/. Accessed 13 January 2019.

[55]"U.S.-Nordic Leaders' Summit Joint Statement," 2016, https://obamawhitehouse.archives.gov/the-press-office/2016/05/13/us-nordic-leaders-summit-joint-statement. Accessed 1 February 2019.

presence of US troops, US political leadership in NATO with regard to regional security, and additional US assistance and investments in enhancing regional defence capabilities. With both sides being interested in further cooperation efforts, there are mutual benefits that also lead to broader cooperation at a regional level.

The United States values mutually beneficial partnerships and alliances.[56] The Nordic Baltic region provides the US with great strategic value and access to military infrastructure, which is a key to deterrence posture. For instance, Norway is a host nation for US Marines and their military equipment. In Greenland, the US has built an early warning radar station. With Finland and Sweden, the US has bilateral agreements on exchanging information.[57] The Nordic states are also important defence industry partners of the US. The three Baltic countries provided host nation support for US rotational forces after the Ukraine crisis and could offer facilities to increase the US troops readiness navigating in unique operational environment.[58]

When it comes to regional capabilities, such as maritime or air domain, the efficiency of using and employing existing resources is critical. US leadership and role in the region could incentivize regional actors to combine regional efforts with increasing regional defence capabilities. There are at least a couple of significant areas where greater coordination of defence efforts is necessary, one of which is a need for an integrated air defence architecture in Northern Europe. Russia's *anti access area denial* capabilities in the Baltic Sea pose a serious threat to the whole Alliance and its collective defence capabilities. These challenges require collective capabilities that the countries of the region, along with US assistance, could jointly build. The latest report by the Atlantic Council, featuring Gen. P. Breedlove, noted the US's ability to play a leading role in air defence capabilities and help energize regional cooperation in Northern Europe.[59]

Another domain where broader cooperation is needed and where the US could play a role is the maritime domain. The Baltic maritime defence is a recognized NATO priority area regarding increasing deterrence and defence in Europe's north-east. Generating necessary capabilities to secure maritime domain requires resources. However, if efforts were aligned, it would significantly boost NATO's maritime capabilities in the area. The US could generate further cooperation by providing additional assistance or increasing its presence in the region.[60]

---

[56]Summary of the National Defense Strategy of the United States of America, 2018, https://dod.defense.gov/Portals/1/Documents/pubs/2018-National-Defense-Strategy-Summary.pdf. Accessed 1 February 2019.

[57]"The Nordic Countries and U.S. Relations," Congressional Research Service, September 13, 2018, https://fas.org/sgp/crs/row/IF10740.pdf. Accessed 13 January 2018.

[58]Otzulis and Ozolina (2017), pp. 77–97.

[59]Breedlove (2018).

[60]M. Nordenman, "Maritime Defense for the Baltic States," 2018, https://www.atlanticcouncil.org/images/Baltic_States_Maritime_Defence_WEB.pdf. Accessed 17 February 2019.

9.5 Conclusion

The shelter strategy plays an important role in Nordic Baltic defence policies. Given their limited defence capabilities and memberships in different security organizations, the small Nordic Baltic states see the US's role as essential in preserving their security. The newest developments in Nordic Baltic security policies reveal that all countries in the region seek a strong transatlantic link and see the US as their primary security shelter provider. Both NATO and the US are given primacy in Nordic Baltic defence policies. NATO already serves as a security shelter for six out of eight countries in the region. But since two countries in the region remain outside the alliance with unclear prospects of joining it, NATO cannot provide equal security guarantees for all actors in the region. Therefore, the US with its deterrence capacity is being seen as a desired security shelter provider. Incentive to have the US more engaged in regional security affairs may chart a path to enhancing regional cooperation. With both the US and Nordic Baltic countries willing to enhance their partnerships, there is a potential for deeper regional defence cooperation.

References

Breedlove P (2018) Toward effective air defense in Northern Europe. Atlantic Council. https://www.atlanticcouncil.org/images/publications/Toward_Effective_Air_Defense_in_Northern_Europe.pdf. Accessed 17 Feb 2019

Breitenbauch HØ, Kristensen KS, Schaub G Jr, Jakobsson AK, Winther M (2017) Options for enhancing Nordic–Baltic Defense and Security Cooperation. Center for Military Studies, University of Copenhagen. https://cms.polsci.ku.dk/publikationer/options-for-enhancing-nordicbaltic-defence/. Accessed 20 Nov 2018

Dahl A-S (2018) Sweden and Finland, partnership in lieu of NATO membership. In: Dahl A-S (ed) Strategic challenges in the Baltic Sea region: Russia, deterrence, and reassurance. Georgetown University Press, Washington, DC, p 130

Friis K, Bredesen MG (2017) Swedish–Norwegian Defence Cooperation. Norwegian Institute of International Affairs. https://www.nupi.no/en/News/Swedish-Norwegian-Defence-Cooperation-New-opportunities. Accessed 20 Nov 2018

Government of Finland (2017) Government's Defence Report. Prime Minister's Office. https://www.defmin.fi/files/3688/J07_2017_Governments_Defence_Report_Eng_PLM_160217.pdf. Accessed 20 Nov 2018

Hakon SL (2018) Norwegian perspectives on Baltic Sea Security. In: Dahl A-S (ed) Strategic challenges in the Baltic Sea region: Russia, deterrence, and reassurance. Georgetown University Press, Washington, DC, p 102

Ingimundarson V (2007) Iceland's security identity dilemma, the end of a U.S. military presence. Fletcher Forum World Aff 31(1):7–23

Larrabee FS, Wilson PA, Gordon J (2015) The Ukrainian Crisis and European Security: implication for the United States and U.S. Army. RAND Corporation. https://www.rand.org/pubs/research_reports/RR903.html. Accessed 20 Nov 2018

Major C, von Voss A (2016) Nordic-Baltic Security, Germany and NATO. German Institute for International and Security Affairs. https://www.swp-berlin.org/en/publication/nordic-baltic-security-germany-and-nato/. Accessed 20 Nov 2018

Nissen C (2017) Denmark. In: Kellner AM, Optenhögel U, Bartels H-P (eds) Strategic autonomy and the defence of Europe, on the road to a European Army. Dietz Verlag J.H.W. Nachf, pp 139–151

Norwegian Ministry of Foreign Affairs (2017) Setting the course for Norwegian Foreign and Security Policy. Norwegian Ministry of Foreign Affairs. https://www.regjeringen.no/en/dokumenter/meld.-st.-36-20162017/id2549828/. Accessed 20 Nov 2018

Otzulis V, Ozolina Ž (2017) Shaping Baltic States Defence Strategy: Host Nation Support. Lith Annu Strategic Rev 2016–2017, 15:77–97

Seimas of the Republic of Lithuania (2017) National Security Strategy. Seimas of the Republic of Lithuania

US Department of Defense (2016) U.S., Iceland Sign Security Cooperation Agreement. US Department of Defense. https://dod.defense.gov/News/Article/Article/820904/us-iceland-sign-security-cooperation-agreement/. Accessed 13 Jan 2019

Živilė Marija Vaicekauskaitė holds a master's degree in European Studies from the Institute of International Relations and Political Science and currently serves as a young researcher for the project on Small States and the New Security Environment (SSANSE), which is funded by NATO's Science for Peace Programme. Prior to that, Živilė served as a Baltic American Freedom Foundation Fellow working with the Transatlantic Security Initiative in the Brent Scowcroft Center for International Security at the Atlantic Council in Washington, DC. Živilė also served as a chair of the board of the Lithuanian Atlantic Treaty Association and as a coordinator for the Eastern European and Russian Studies programme at the Institute of International Relations and Political Science at Vilnius University. Živilė's principal research interests include transatlantic security policy, Baltic Sea regional cooperation, and Nordic-Baltic security.

Chapter 10
Neutrality and Shelter Seeking: The Case of Malta

Hillary Briffa

10.1 Introduction

The Mediterranean island of Malta is the archetypical small state. It has a small fixed size with a population of 432,053 (in 2018) across 316 km^2 of land. This makes it one of the smallest, yet also most densely populated, countries in the world. There are fewer than 2000 active personnel in the military service, and as the smallest of the EU member states, Malta conforms to many of the structural, economic, and political limitations endemic to small states.

Amongst these typical characteristics, one finds a small domestic market and limited competition possibilities, limited human capital, poor natural resources, constraints upon the labour market, and the insularity and remoteness costs of being an island. However, like several other particularly successful small states, such as Qatar, Singapore, and Bahrain, Malta has managed to achieve high income by leveraging her geostrategic location, educated and specialised workforce, robust legal and parliamentary systems, and integrated financial sectors.

In leveraging these assets, Malta avails of various policy options in order to foster resilience and thereby overcome her inherent vulnerabilities. Resilience becomes policy based and able to be nurtured, rather than states always being subject to insurmountable nature. Foremost amongst these are policies that enable Malta to seek external assistance in order to overcome her innate weaknesses. Therefore, this chapter sets out to examine the pursuit of 'Europeanity' by Malta, which led to her eventual accession to the European Union. In so doing, it examines the means by which she is able to balance external shelter seeking in a way that is compatible with

H. Briffa (✉)
King's College, London, UK
e-mail: Hillary.briffa@kcl.ac.uk

A.-M. Brady, B. Thorhallsson (eds.), *Small States and the New Security Environment*, The World of Small States 7,
https://doi.org/10.1007/978-3-030-51529-4_10

her own security posture of 'neutrality' in order to safeguard her autonomy and still avail of assistance from the international system in the long term.

10.2 Maltese Strategic Culture

In order to understand how Malta pursues a 'shelter seeking' foreign policy, it is first necessary to understand the strategic culture that shapes Maltese decision-making. Assessing the structural and ideological parameters of Maltese policymaking, former Minister for Foreign Affairs Michael Frendo recognised in 2006 that Malta is:

> a country that wholly forms part of Europe and wholly forms part of the Mediterranean. We are an island state. We attained sovereign statehood within living memory, after centuries of colonial rule. We are on a cultural frontier between Europe and North Africa, speaking a language that fuses Semitic and Romance. We are necessarily foreign trade oriented. Our foreign policy must reflect our realities and our Maltese and European values.[1]

This gives us a useful starting point to consider the geopolitical, political, historical, economic, and anthropological foundations upon which Maltese statecraft operates. These factors all come to bear upon one another: for instance, being a small island necessitates an emphasis on foreign trade. In understanding the Maltese strategic calculus, however, it is primarily necessary to further develop an awareness of Malta's colonial inheritance.

Hiding strategies has long been a hallmark of small states determined to preserve autonomy in the international system, yet it is difficult for Malta to hide entirely due to her exposed and valuable geostrategic location, which affords the barren island an importance that far exceeds her size or material capabilities.[2] Malta is situated at the heart of the Mediterranean—amongst the world's busiest waterways and the sea most important to the empires of antiquity and the world's three major religions. Hence, historically every major military and economic power in the Mediterranean sought to establish control over what was a valuable strategic landing spot. The Phoenicians, Carthaginians, Romans, Byzantines, Arabs, Normans, Swabians, Angevins, and Aragonese all left an indelible mark. From a security perspective, historian Dominic Fenech writes that 'until 1530, Malta was effectively indefensible. It could be and was taken by whichever regional power had the strength and wish to do so.'[3]

---

[1]Michael Frendo, "Greater Focus, Stronger Direction," *Times of Malta*, February 10, 2006, https://www.timesofmalta.com/articles/view/20060211/opinion/greater-focus-stronger-direction.63609.

[2]Anders Wivel, "On Small States in the European Union," *Scottish Parliament's European and External Relations Committee*, February 6, 2014, http://www.parliament.scot/S4_EuropeanandExternalRelationsCommittee/Meeting Papers/Anders_Wivel_written_evidence.pdf.

[3]Fenech (1997), pp. 153–163.

Malta's pre-industrial history was marked by the hegemony of the Order of the Knights of Saint John, who arrived in Malta in 1530 to reign for 268 years. The Grand Harbour was expanded, fortifications were constructed around the major cities, and watchtowers were built along the entire coastline. Malta transformed from an indefensible, barren rock to an island fortress. The French conquered Malta in 1798, before being ousted by the British in 1800. After a long and turbulent campaign for sovereign independence, Malta was finally granted independence from the British on 21 September 1964. Then on 13 December 1974, Malta experienced what former Prime Minister Dominic Mintoff called Malta's 'appointment with destiny' as she became a Republic and thereby moved from *de jure* sovereignty to *de facto* sovereignty.

Before independence in 1964, Malta's security depended on the capacity of her colonial protector to defend her as she had no sovereign capabilities for defence. However, the transformation of the nation into a Republic took place without renewing British defence agreements, leading to the rejection of British forces from the islands and the eviction of North Atlantic Treaty Organization (NATO) personnel. This, then, required a shift in economic policy as the Maltese economy was dependent upon Malta's position as a military base. Hence, the island's industry underwent a dramatic shift in order to wean off British dependency. New means of assistance would need to be found to enable Malta to survive and thrive as one of the smallest sovereign actors in the international system.

10.3 Orienting Westward

Following independence in 1964, Malta joined the Council of Europe. This was her first entry into the international community as a small, yet autonomous, state. In his inaugural address at the Assembly on 4 May 1965, Prime Minister George Borg Olivier stated that:

> ...with the recent attainment of independence, Malta regained her sovereignty of old and one of the most ancient nations of Europe returned to take its place among the free countries of this continent...Here we feel truly at home, joined with other members of the family who share our basic concepts and philosophy...[4]

The Western orientation of the Nationalist government was indisputable. This approach is what Alyson Bailes calls a 'declared' strategy: a public strategy designed to create a policy consensus and promote coordination of cross-sectoral actions

[4]George Borg Olivier, "Speech Made to the Parliamentary Assembly," *Council of Europe*, May 4, 1965, http://www.assembly.coe.int/nw/xml/Speeches/Speech-XML2HTML-EN.asp?SpeechID=24.

serving the broader goals of the strategy.[5] Borg Olivier was seeking, through speech acts, to convince neighbours that this arid rock—in a geographically precarious position so close to North Africa, speaking a Semitic language, and with little to offer economically—deserved a seat at the lucrative Western table.

In his address, Borg Olivier told the Assembly that:

> whilst as a European country sharing a common culture, history and way of life, we naturally gravitate towards Europe, our geographical position makes us aware of the importance of North Africa which shares, with six Members of this Council, a common sea, and which has much to contribute to the welfare of the area. We would therefore think that this aspect of European foreign policy could be given some more thought.

Even as Borg Olivier sought to solidify Malta's European identity on the international stage, there was recognition that Malta would never be able to eschew the North African connection. Instead, it could be leveraged for status-seeking purposes as one of the nation's greatest assets, enabling the Maltese to both seek shelter within the European community and take a proactive role in this area of European policymaking.

In addition to his overtures to the Council of Europe, during this period Borg Olivier sought to attain an agreement with the European Economic Community (EEC), with the ambition of eventual membership. As Malta was starting her independent journey, the EEC was viewed as a guarantor of industrial security and long-term prosperity. Hence, an Association Agreement was signed between Malta and the EEC in Valletta on 5 December 1970. Following Greece (1961) and Turkey (1963), this was only the third of such agreement that the EEC entered into with a prospective member state.

The agreement, which came into effect on 1 April 1971, intended 'to bring about in two stages the progressive elimination of obstacles with respect to substantially all the trade between the Community and Malta, leading to the formation of a customs union'.[6] Although the document makes no reference to the prospect of full membership, the Nationalist Party made it clear that this was their long-term intention and that they viewed Malta's natural place as being within the European fold.

---

[5]Alyson J.K. Bailes, "Does a Small State Need a Strategy?" *CSS Publication Series*, November 27, 2009, https://ams.hi.is/wp-content/uploads/old/does_a_small_state_need_a_strategy_bailes_a.pdf.

[6]"Agreement between the European Economic Community and Malta." Joint declaration by the Contracting Parties concerning Co-operation and contacts between the European Parliament and the Maltese Parliament, April 1, 1971, https://wits.worldbank.org/GPTAD/PDF/archive/EC-Malta(English).pdf.

10.4 Increasing Institutionalism

Independent Maltese governance has oscillated under the leadership of the two leading parties: the Nationalist Party and the Labour Party. Under a Labour government, during the 1970s and 1980s, therefore, the European integration efforts stalled as Malta pursued strategic hedging between Eastern and Western partners in order to secure aid from any favourable party. Borg Olivier's successor, Labour Prime Minister Dominic Mintoff, was determined to see Malta develop economically and with a strong infrastructure in order to stand on her own two feet without being tied too closely to any one bloc. In the 1970s, however, the theory of liberal internationalism and institutionalism emerged as the most prominent alternative to the realism that was prevalent at the height of the Cold War.[7] The rule-based order of institutions such as the EEC demonstrated how states may be willing to cede a margin of their autonomy in order to create 'integrated communities'.[8] These would foster economic growth and enable them to 'achieve outcomes unavailable to them individually'.[9]

Diane Stone speaks of the emergence of a 'global agora', defined as 'a growing public space of fluid, dynamic and intermeshed relations of politics, markets, culture and society . . . shaped by the interaction of its actors – that is multiple publics and plural institutions'.[10] If international institutions create a meeting place for such diverse cultures to come together, Malta could use her niche knowledge of the Mediterranean to enhance the institutional depository of information. Beyond tribal partisan politics, geographic positioning was indisputable as Malta's primary strategic asset. Independence, therefore, was slowly enabling Malta to transition from a 'prisoner of geography' at the whim of every overlord with global ambition to wielding geography as the nation's primary advantage within the international community.

In line with this, Malta sought to rapidly expand her membership of international organisations and to promulgate her 'niche' of Mediterranean expertise. Notable in this regard was the establishment, in 1889, of the Inter-Parliamentary Union (IPU), a global inter-parliamentary institution. This was the first permanent forum for political multilateral negotiations. Under the auspices of the IPU, a process known as the Conference on Security and Cooperation in the Mediterranean was developed, with the first meeting held in Malaga in 1990.

In the 1970s, taking a leading role in this organisation seemed like a natural extension of the Mediterranean agenda being advocated by Malta simultaneously at the Conference on Security and Cooperation in Europe (CSCE). In 1995, the second inter-parliamentary Conference on Security and Cooperation in the Mediterranean was held in Malta. The final document from the conference states that 'While having a sense of belonging to the Mediterranean, the peoples of the region have not yet laid

---

[7]Bull and Watson (1984).

[8]Caporaso and Jupille (1999), pp. 429–444.

[9]Hoffman (1999), pp. 159–177.

[10]Stone (2008), pp. 19–38.

the bases of a communal destiny bringing together the wealth of their diversity and differences'.[11] Looking to contribute to this 'communal destiny' demonstrates Malta's increasing recognition of the need to seek shelter and avail of increased multilateral efforts in order to mitigate uncertainty within the region, reduce power politics, and enhance the prospects for regional cooperation.

Whilst pursuing these international avenues, however, it became increasingly evident to the Nationalist Party that they needed to accede to the EEC in order to be fully considered a member of the developed Western international community. The Nationalist Party had even made it clear in their 1981 manifesto that 'we are Europeans, that our place is in the fold of a United Europe, as conceived by the three Christian Democratic Statesmen who are rightly referred to as "the fathers of Europe" ... We will seek full membership of the European Economic Community.'[12] The person to lead this charge would be the staunchly pro-European leader of the Nationalist Party, lawyer Edward Fenech Adami.

10.5 Fenech Adami: Premier with a Vision

Fenech Adami contested the 1987 election on a platform promising 'Our place in Europe on the right conditions. We shall join the European Economic Community which will assist us in carrying out the necessary changes over an extended period.'[13] With a margin of only 4784 votes, the Nationalist Party obtained an absolute majority of the vote on 11 May 1987, and Fenech Adami was subsequently sworn in as the Prime Minister of Malta on 12 May 1987.

As the Cold War paradigm faded into the past, the Nationalist government sought to remedy two major issues: the struggles of the economy in a bid to prevent a slide back into foreign dependency (thereby losing autonomy) and what they perceived to have been the inconsistent and ambiguous policy of the Labour Party (in government between 1971 and 1987) towards Europe (thereby sacrificing influence). These two targets are demonstrably interlinked.

The economic situation that the Nationalists had inherited from the former government was troubled. The Labour Party had endeavoured to foster local self-sufficiency by instituting a command economy based on import substitution. Yet 'bulk buying' had undermined the prospects for the economy to generate sustained growth. Locally manufactured products were of inferior quality and largely

[11] Inter-Parliamentary Union, "Final Document of the Second Inter-Parliamentary Conference on Security and Co-Operation in the Mediterranean." Valletta, Malta, 1995, http://archive.ipu.org/splz-e/valetta.htm.

[12] "Ripe for Change" Nationalist Party Electoral Program Approved by the General Council, Malta Nationalist Party, November 14, 1981, https://www.um.edu.mt/__data/assets/pdf_file/0014/180500/NationalistPartyManifesto1981.pdf.

[13] "PN's Programme for the 1987 Election," Malta Nationalist Party, 1987, https://www.um.edu.mt/__data/assets/pdf_file/0015/180501/NationalistPartyManifesto1987.pdf.

uncompetitive, sustained only as a result of high protectionist barriers that insulated them from competition. As the domestic economy floundered as a result of protectionism, global markets were moving in the opposite direction: removing trade barriers through the World Trade Organization and seeking enhanced regional exchange.

Small state economies must be open; this is not a choice. Following the 1987 election, therefore, the Nationalist government did away with many of their precursor's protectionist policies, and the economy began to improve. However, Patrick Tabone assessed that 'the country faced a competitiveness deficit that it could not resolve without massive, sustained investment in infrastructure and human capital; it needed access to a wider market for its goods and services; and it needed a clear sense of confidence and direction'.[14] The European Union represented, therefore, an inexpensive source of raw materials, an expansive market for Maltese goods and services, and an anchor for Maltese independent identity that had thus far been swinging between every prospective protector that offered shelter.

10.6 Malta and Libya: A Special Relationship

The economic uncertainty was compounded by the increasingly troubling relationship with Malta's closest southern neighbour: Libya. As Gaddafi provided crucial assistance to Malta in the wake of the departure of British troops, Mintoff's Labour government had signed the 1984 Treaty of Friendship and Cooperation. However, this had raised the opposition of the Nationalists on the ground that it was considered too imbalanced in Libya's favour. Fenech Adami's approach was to try to unhook from this relationship whilst avoiding an abrupt rupture. With the Nationalists in government from 1987, Fenech Adami signed a new friendship and cooperation agreement on 19 February 1990, in which the Nationalists scrapped the controversial clause mandating the two countries to exchange military information and which had required Libya to supply military equipment and training to the Mediterranean island. Despite this adjustment, 23 other agreements signed between Libya and Malta from 1968 to 1989 continued to be enforced.[15]

However, this close relationship was clearly unsustainable given the clear desire to situate Malta more firmly within the Western orbit. As Libya looked increasingly isolated in the closing stages of the Cold War, it was necessary to establish further distance from Gaddafi.[16] After Libya was implicated in the 1988 bombing of Pam

[14]Patrick Tabone, and Veronica Nardelli, "Malta's EU Story: How Ten Years of EU Membership Have Changed the Country," *Today Public Policy Institute*, June 2014, 15, http://www.europarl.europa.eu/malta/resource/static/files/malta-eu%2D%2D2-.pdf.

[15]United Press International, "Malta and Libya Sign New Cooperation Agreement." *UPI Archives*, February 19, 1990, https://www.upi.com/Archives/1990/02/19/Malta-and-Libya-sign-new-cooperation-agreement/8472635403600/.

[16]Rudolf and Berg (2010).

Am Flight 103 over Lockerbie, United Nations (UN) sanctions were imposed in 1992. Malta, striving to be an active member of the United Nations, abided and imposed sanctions on Libya as well. Consequently, bilateral economic relations deteriorated and the air traffic arrangements between the two countries were promptly suspended.

Having played the role of a creditor in the past, Libya's usefulness to Malta was much diminished in this period of Nationalist dominance. Following Gaddafi's agreement to pay compensation to the families of the Lockerbie victims, the UN lifted sanctions against Libya. However, US unilateral sanctions were sustained until 2004 due to Libya's pursuit of chemical and nuclear weapons. These sanctions, in turn, took their toll on Libyan investment in Malta. By 2004, Libya owed Maltese companies a total of Lm2 million, including Lm196,000 to the Health Department.[17] In an attempt to restore and sustain the friendly bilateral relations with Malta, Libya agreed to pay back its debt after the suspension of sanctions.

The relationship had reversed from one where Malta—as an economically troubled small state—had been seeking shelter from the Libyans to one where Malta—as a small power with a revitalised economy—was in turn increasingly the provider of shelter for a struggling Libya. This demonstrates the importance of Tom Long's argument that what is important in international relations should be 'the dynamics of the relationships in which these states are engaged' rather than their size.[18] However, Malta still needed to compensate for the changing parameters of this relationship.

10.7 European Shelter Seeking

With the Nationalist government increasingly cognisant that their relationship with Libya may not be able to provide long-term guarantees, the European Union appeared, more than ever, a sustainable source of economic and cultural shelter. Moreover, according to the concept of social shelter, small states also require access to international interactions to benefit from the exchange of ideas, information, and people, which foster change and growth within society.[19] Yet the Maltese government was also engaged in a tussle at the domestic level. Whilst both the major political parties agreed that Malta's relationship with the rest of the world rested on its Mediterranean location and its European identity, there was still a lack of agreement as to how this should be pursued with respect to the European Union. The country stood at a crossroads.

---

[17]Herman Grech, "Stronger Relations with Libya Expected," *Times of Malta*, November 22, 2004, https://timesofmalta.com/articles/view/stronger-relations-with-libya-expected.106340.

[18]Long (2017), pp. 144–160.

[19]Amber Pariona, "What Is a Small Power State?" *World Atlas*, February 6, 2018, https://www.worldatlas.com/articles/what-is-a-small-power-state.html.

Due to their complex history of colonial subjugation, the primary fear for Maltese policymakers was that their country may once again be turned into a base for outsiders or a puppet state; this would cause them to relinquish the final say over national security. Therefore, it was believed that a neutrality policy could safeguard against vulnerability. In 1987, amendments to the Maltese constitution (proposed by Malta's Labour Party—then in opposition—and consolidated by the Nationalist government) explicitly outlined the country's national interest, with Article 3 stating that:

> Malta is a neutral state actively pursuing peace, security and social progress among all nations by adhering to a policy of non-alignment and refusing to participate in any military alliance.

In order not to compromise this strategic orientation that they had fought so hard for, the Labour Party abjured the notion of EU membership in favour of a partnership, which would enable Malta to retain absolute sovereignty. Their 1996 electoral manifesto explicitly outlined their concerns, stating that 'Labour believes that Malta should refrain from seeking full membership of the European Union, which would entail the adoption by Malta of all the Union's policies. Many of these have been designed for big European countries and do not suit the specific economic and social characteristics of small islands like Malta and Gozo. Besides, membership of the EU would also undermine Malta's neutrality.'[20]

Rather than seeing EU membership as a sacrifice of the sovereignty they had fought so hard to attain, the Nationalists, conversely, recognised that seeking shelter from the EU would allow their small state to obtain benefits that were previously only available to their larger counterparts (such as economies of scale and increased competition). Therefore, the Nationalist Party wanted to be an integrated part of the Union, not just a partner. The devolution of some sovereignty would be a worthwhile price for the 'sheltering and amplification features' characteristic of collective security, as well as access to the markets, finances, and infrastructural assistance necessary to galvanise the development of Malta and ensconce it firmly as a modern actor in the European community.[21]

During this period, the Labour Party wrangled with an internal leadership crisis. Conversely, the Nationalists continued to build momentum and found success in three consecutive elections (1998, 2003, and 2008). The run-up to joining was still fraught, however, with challenges in the effort to meet the Copenhagen criteria and gain electoral support for accession. The mandated overhaul of the economy and infrastructure was so extensive and cumbersome that former Chief of Staff to the Ministry of Foreign Affairs (MFA) Patrick Tabone holds that 'only unswerving

[20] "Malta Labour Party Manifesto, 1996," Malta Labour Party, 1996, https://www.um.edu.mt/__data/assets/pdf_file/0005/180491/MLPElectionManifesto1996.pdf.

[21] Lee (2016), p. 52.

political determination on the part of Government could keep the process on track'.[22] In so doing, Fenech Adami maintained that 'the challenge was itself the guarantee of success. It would give us the motivation and the blueprint to reform, to compete.'[23]

10.8 A Clash of Visions

Analysing Malta's prospects for Europeanisation in 2000, Michelle Cini identified two processes that the country had to undertake. First was the rational process of adaptation to the norms and regulations of the EU. Assisted by the European Commission, Malta would undertake domestic reforms to come into alignment with the EU standards. The second, more difficult process contends with Europeanisation as a constructivist process of redefining the national identity. Where the first process leads to 'acting European', the second leads to 'thinking European'.[24]

These two processes were dogged by the resistance of the Labour Party, the only mainstream party in any of the candidate parties to oppose the membership bid. It must be stressed that the Labour Party's apprehension towards the European Union was not an ideological opposition to the organisation itself but stemmed from concerns that the membership conditions would not be compatible with Malta's sovereign national interest; notably, they argued that Malta's neutrality would not be compatible with the European Union's ambition to develop a Common Foreign and Security Policy (CFSP).

The Labour Party felt that Malta's security, in the event of conflict in the Mediterranean, would be better guaranteed through an absolute adherence to neutrality, uncompromised by European Union membership that may cloud perceptions of Malta's allegiance. Yet Malta was already unable to guarantee her security alone: the signature of bilateral agreements with external partners (Italy and Libya, primarily) being indicative of the need for external assurances of assistance. This meant that Malta's neutrality was still inextricably tied to regional military arrangements.

What would happen, for instance, if Italy reneged on its commitment to Malta? What if the bilateral agreement was superseded by the Italian national interest? Roderick Pace further argued, in 1997, that Malta's strategic reliance on Italy, as well as a degree of economic dependency at that time due to receiving Italian financial aid, may result in a transformation of the relationship into one of Italian

[22]Patrick Tabone and Veronica Nardelli, "Malta's EU Story: How Ten Years of EU Membership Have Changed the Country," *Today Public Policy Institute*, June 2014, 19, http://www.europarl.europa.eu/malta/resource/static/files/malta-eu%2D%2D2-.pdf.

[23]Martiin Scicluna, "Malta's European Story," *Times of Malta*, September 30, 2014, https://timesofmalta.com/articles/view/Malta-s-European-story.537974.

[24]Cini (2014), pp. 261–276.

hegemony over Malta.[25] Membership of the European Union—as a security community and not a military alliance—would better serve Maltese security and thereby quell these uncertainties.

The European Commission had indicated that Malta may need to alter the neutrality clause in the constitution in order to participate in the CFSP. Constitutional amendments require two-thirds majority support in Parliament, and under the Labour government the party had made it clear that they viewed Malta's neutrality as *sui generis* and not open to debate. Yet there were already other neutral states in the European Union, such as Austria and Denmark, and hence it was not inconceivable that Malta, too, could be a part of the Union whilst still practicing her own particular brand of neutrality. Denmark, for instance, could refrain from participating in joint actions with defence implications. A similar arrangement would therefore enable Malta to safeguard her constitutional neutrality (ensuring no military bases upon her territory and refraining from participation in any military alliances) whilst still engaging actively in the CFSP.

By remaining aloof (including lack of participation in NATO'S Partnership for Peace, European Union membership, or the peacekeeping missions of the OSCE), Malta would significantly reduce her influence in areas where her history, culture, and human resources could enable her to play a leading role. Conversely, by maintaining her refusal to host military bases, but still actively participating in the CFSP and peacekeeping efforts, Malta could leverage her knowledge and resources towards shaping her own regional environment. This would be a far more active means of safeguarding security than remaining an isolated, sitting duck.

Likewise, the European Union also stood to gain by admitting Malta on the ground that her membership would enhance the Union's Mediterranean security dimension and would 'sensitise' the core countries to the issues on the southern periphery.[26] New dangers creeping up from the south, ranging from migration and human trafficking to organised crime and militant Islamic fundamentalism, meant, according to Dominic Fenech, that Malta's 'tradition of casting itself as a natural bridge between Europe and north Africa renders it a useful asset'.[27] Hence, the Maltese government continued to prioritise membership over any alternate partnership model.

The so-called clash of visions and the hesitancy of the Labour electorate was not insurmountable. From an economic perspective, private enterprises such as the Federation of Industry pushed hard for accession to the Union as a means of surmounting Malta's intrinsic economic vulnerability as a small state. They argued

---

[25] Roderick Pace, "The European Union's Next Mediterranean Enlargement," *Jean Monnet Working Papers in Comparative and International Politics*, January 1997, http://aei.pitt.edu/387/1/jmwp06.htm.

[26] Ibid.

[27] Fenech (1997).

that 'it does not make sense for Malta to stand alone in splendid isolation when its competitors . . . are uniting under the aegis of different regional blocs'.[28]

Moreover, the Labour tactic of demonising the prospect of membership kept backfiring. Richard Cachia Caruana, Malta's chief negotiator and later permanent representative to the EU, claimed that the opposition actually helped the government to bolster the credibility of the EU because their insistence 'that certain things would not be possible in the EU: a good financial package, the 25-mile Fishing conservation zone, Maltese as an official language, hunting, neutrality, restructuring subsidies for the shipyards' and so forth proved unfounded.[29] As the Union compromised to ensure that all of Malta's needs were met, this presented the image of the EU as an institution sensitive to the domestic concerns of a small state and compatible with the pursuit of Maltese strategic interests.

Consequently, the Maltese went to the polls on 8 March 2003 for the pivotal referendum on prospective EU accession. As a result, 90.9% of the population cast their vote (the highest participation rate of all the candidate countries), and it gave the Nationalists a win, with 53.6% of the vote versus Labour's 46.4% (the narrowest margin of all the candidate countries).[30] As the result was non-binding, the Prime Minister called an election for 12 April 2003. The Nationalist Party subsequently won 35 of the 65 seats in Parliament, sealing Malta's fate as an acceding member of the European Union and with access to the sheltering and voice amplification features that membership would provide.

10.9 Sheltered and Thriving

By joining the EU, Malta sealed her position as indivisibly part of 'Europe' and gained access to the political, economic, and cultural shelter afforded by the regional union. Expanding participation in the international community and playing an active role would thereby offset Malta's characteristic insularity and provide valuable voice opportunity to shape supranational policymaking.

Over 17 years of membership, it has been shown that military neutrality does not hold Malta back from being an active player in the region. Constitutionally and structurally unable to contribute to international military combat operations, Malta collaborates in other spheres. These include logistics, the sharing of intelligence, participation in counterterrorism and anti-human trafficking operations, and routine collaboration between the policy and security services and Europol. Although small in quantity (equipped with 11 offshore and inshore patrol vessels), the Maritime Squadron of the Armed Forces of Malta meets the Maltese responsibilities for Search

[28] Roderick Pace, "The European Union's Next Mediterranean Enlargement."

[29] Patrick Tabone and Veronica Nardelli, "Malta's EU Story: How Ten Years of EU Membership Have Changed the Country," 21.

[30] Nohlen and Stöver (2010).

and Rescue operations, participates in enforcement operations with police and customs agencies, and contributes to international commitments, such as Frontex and Atlanta.[31]

In return, Malta has benefited from the sheltering benefits of institutional membership. In assessing the impact of a decade of membership, Tabone concluded that:

> Malta has found in the EU a community of like-minded states that has provided a coherent set of values, an incentive and a blueprint for development, and systems of benchmarking and "peer review" that have helped the country to develop and prosper during difficult times. This clearer sense of who we are and where we want to go has increased our sense of self-assurance, and, together with the larger stage offered by EU membership, has changed and enriched the country's international profile and the way it operates on the world stage.[32]

The security of guaranteed foreign investment and EU funds has made the Maltese economy more resilient. By joining the European Union, Malta has availed of economic shelter and gained increased access to trade agreements, particularly with Northern African and Middle Eastern markets. Fostering strong ties with Malta's immediate neighbours as the bridging link between Europe and the southern shores of the Mediterranean has meant that Malta is considered, according to former Foreign Minister Frendo, 'a safe and stable gateway for investors interested in investing in these countries'.[33]

Capitalising on this, in 2006 Malta established the Central Mediterranean Economic Forum (C-MEF). Frendo explains that this business and economic forum was intended to 'build on the competitive advantages of each country and see how these advantages, for example, Malta's leading role in financial services, could be used as catalysts for economic growth in all the countries of C-MEF'.[34] Bringing together economic stakeholders from Libya, Malta, Sicily, and Tunisia, this was a strategic commercial move designed to reap the rewards of a market of over 20 million people and thereby compensate for Malta's lack of natural resources.

In September 2006, Malta also initiated the first-ever EU-League of Arab States Ministerial Meeting, bringing together 49 states. The Maltese initiative proved so fruitful that meetings are now scheduled every two years. In order to better structure the efforts and increase visibility, the European Commission-League of Arab States Liaison Office (ECLASLO) was set up in Malta in 2009. In 2011, Dr John Paul Grech, then Permanent Secretary to the Ministry of Foreign Affairs, summed up the Maltese approach to foreign policy by explaining that 'geographically we are Mediterranean, but everything about our political identity is European. We wanted

---

[31]Mulqueen et al. (2016).

[32]Patrick Tabone and Veronica Nardelli, "Malta's EU Story: How Ten Years of EU Membership Have Changed the Country."

[33]Michael Frendo, "Diplomats Have an Economic Role to Play Too," *Times of Malta*, November 30, 2006, https://timesofmalta.com/articles/view/diplomats-have-an-economic-role-to-play-too-frendo.33638.

[34]"Central Mediterranean Economic Forum," *Times of Malta*, February 25, 2006, https://www.independent.com.mt/articles/2006-02-25/news/minister-suggests-central-mediterranean-economic-forum-87815.

to be the voice of the Arab world in the European Union . . . At this stage, Malta is being consulted at EU and Arab-world level, which requires acute presence of mind. This is where the credibility of our country comes to the fore.'[35] In this way, institutional membership has extended Malta's reach and provided her with shelter and voice opportunities that enable her to leverage her deep historical and linguistic bond with the Arab population for maximum strategic ends.

Hard security concerns have been more difficult to contend with. Malta supported the development of the Security and Defence Policy as part of the Common Foreign and Security Policy in order to enhance the collective security capabilities of the European Union in preventing and managing crises; however, Malta's support has to be bounded by the limits of neutrality. Therefore, Malta has consistently reiterated that she can only participate within a system of security that is collective, and to date she has not yet joined the Permanent Structured Cooperation in Defence (PESCO), which was instituted by the EU in 2017.

In the interim, the security shelter afforded by the EU treaty grants Malta the certainty that should military or security assistance be required, Malta may invoke the solidarity clause through which other EU countries would be bound to help her. However, as the EU continues to move towards deeper security cooperation, it may become increasingly difficult for Malta to action her strategic neutrality in a way that still enables her to avail of EU security sheltering benefits.

10.10 The Libya Crisis

One success story in regard to finding the right balance was witnessed in 2011. When the revolutionary phenomena known as the Arab Spring flared in 2010 and spread throughout the Arab nations in the Southern Mediterranean, Nationalist Prime Minister Lawrence Gonzi (2004–2013) was propelled into a leading position in engaging with European prime ministers, meeting with Gaddafi's representatives, discussing with the Libyan National Transitional Council, speaking on the subject during European Council Summits, and being actively involved in the work of Malta's newly instituted Government Crisis Centre as delicate rescue operations began to be operated in the Libyan desert.

A government contingency centre was set up for the first time, fully functional within three hours and operating out of the Office of the Prime Minister in Valletta. This served as a 'one-stop shop' to facilitate aid delivery through the Staging Area for Humanitarian Agencies' operation through Malta and for the delivery of aid to

[35]Martina Said, "Foreign Affairs Perm. Sec Says Malta's Foreign Policy 'Has Reached Fruition'," *MaltaToday*, March 17, 2011, https://www.maltatoday.com.mt/news/national/33503/foreign-affairs-perm-sec-says-malta-s-foreign-policy-has-reached-fruition#.XY5DJvZFzn8.

Libya.[36] Humanitarian aid was given in the form of food, water, and medicine, as well as the provision of medical treatment, the evacuation of expatriates, and tending to the injured in Maltese hospitals.

The Maltese government enacted a range of additional measures to optimise the supply chain management of their humanitarian logistics, including waiving costs and expediting the process for the import and export of goods. The speed at which policy change can be pursued in a small state even enabled the national law to be altered in order to implement a fast-track procedure and create a duty-free zone for faster aid delivery through Malta and thereby overcome heavy bureaucratic procedures.

In 2012, Michael Frendo (then Speaker of the House) explained:

> in the recent Libyan conflict Malta played a humanitarian role which is far greater and much more significant than its size proving that it is strategic position and not territory that, at times, is the determining factor in international affairs. Successfully carrying out the function of an interlocutor does not depend on size or population but on positioning and on the cultural versatility characteristic of the Maltese who, for millennia, have navigated along the North-South cultural fault line of the central Mediterranean.[37]

The 2011 Libya crisis typified the utility of Malta for multilateral security cooperation. At the time, NATO's top military commander, American Admiral James Stavridis, commended Malta for providing superb help to NATO with emergency landings, airspace, and response to refugees as Libya operations continued. Malta further provided vital support in the evacuation of third-country nationals and has continued to assist NATO in its capacity-building efforts in Libya in the aftermath of the crisis.

The chain of events in Libya demonstrated Malta's evolution of her strategic calculus: finding a workable *modus operandi* that enables her to fulfil international commitments and the safeguarding of domestic national interests without compromising her constitutional neutrality or becoming paralysed in international affairs. As Malta became the humanitarian hub for the deployment of European humanitarian aid, uncompromised by military involvement, she was able to leverage her strategic location and human resources to assist and project influence whilst still maintaining sovereignty. Former Director of Defence at the Office of the Prime Minister Vanessa Frazier perfectly summed up the island's contribution in her assertion that 'while Malta was neutral, we were not neutralised'.[38]

This is crucial in recognising that strategic neutrality can still be married to a commitment to peacebuilding and the maintenance of international security. Malta's

---

[36]Diana Spiteri, "Malta's Role during the Libya Crisis and Its Impact on UN Humanitarian Affairs," August 2015, https://www.um.edu.mt/library/oar/handle/123456789/6333.

[37]Michael Frendo, "Developing a Vibrant Partnership between China, Europe and the Mediterranean - The Role of Malta and Its Parliament," *Shanghai Institute for International Studies*, September 2012, https://www.parlament.mt/media/82536/siis-speech-speaker-mfrendo.pdf.

[38]Claudia Calleja, "Malta's Admirable Action during the Libyan Crisis," *Times of Malta*, September 13, 2012, https://www.timesofmalta.com/articles/view/20120914/local/Malta-s-admirable-action-during-the-Libyan-crisis.436857.

membership of the EU and NATO's Partnership for Peace gave Malta an amplified voice and platform in responding to the crisis; at the same time, whilst France and the UK opted for military intervention, it was precisely because of her neutral status that Malta could play out an equally essential humanitarian role. Hence, when combined with depth of cultural knowledge and regional connections, Malta was able to continue charting her course as a 'neutral state actively pursuing peace, security and social progress among all nations' by harnessing her small state capabilities and effectively transforming into the so-called 'lifeline to Misurata'.

10.11 Conclusion

When it comes to small states, they have inbuilt structural weaknesses; small states can try to compensate for these weaknesses but cannot ignore them, and any success will be in spite of them. The recent emergence of the shelter seeking theory demonstrates how small states will need external assistance in order to survive (whether bilateral, institutional, or trade). Rather than further constraining the small state, however, this chapter demonstrates how the shelter provided by institutional membership can enable a small state to become more resilient.

Through a case study of Malta, this chapter traced the development of Maltese policymakers' ambitions to accede to the European Union in order to firmly ensconce the small island as a member of the Western community. In so doing, it demonstrated how the economic, political, and societal shelter afforded by membership has proven compatible with the country's strategic culture and constitutional neutrality. Together, these two aspects of Malta's strategic orientation have allowed this small state to not only survive but also thrive as a proactive sovereign actor in the international system.

References

Bull H, Watson A (1984) The expansion of international society. Clarendon Press, Oxford

Caporaso J, Jupille J (1999) Institutionalism and the European Union: beyond international relations and comparative politics. Annu Rev Polit Sci 2:429–444

Cini M (2014) The Europeanization of Malta: adaptation, identity and party politics. Europeanization and the Southern Periphery, December 2014, pp 261–276. https://doi.org/10.4324/9781315039855-12

Fenech D (1997) Malta's external security. GeoJournal 41(2):153–163. https://link.springer.com/article/10.1023/A:1006888926016

Hoffman S (1999) The crisis of liberal internationalism. Foreign Policy 98:159–177

Lee IJH (2016) Differentiating small state foreign policy strategies: drivers and limits of small state strategic choice in selecting multilateral strategies to overcome structural vulnerabilities. The University of Tokyo, p 52. http://www.pp.u-tokyo.ac.jp/wp-content/uploads/2016/02/51158227.pdf

Long T (2017) It's not the size, it's the relationship: from 'small states' to asymmetry. Int Polit 54 (2):144–160. http://centaur.reading.ac.uk/59064/3/Long-IP-It%27s Not the Size-Final.pdf
Mulqueen M, Sanders D, Speller I (2016) Small navies: strategy and policy for small navies in war and peace. Routledge, London
Nohlen D, Stöver P (2010) Elections in Europe: a data handbook. Nomos, Baden-Baden, R.F.A.
Rudolf UJ, Berg W (2010) Historical dictionary of Malta. Scarecrow Press, Lanham, Maryland
Stone D (2008) Global public policy, transnational policy communities, and their networks. Policy Stud J 36(1):19–38. https://doi.org/10.1111/j.1541-0072.2007.00251.x

Hillary Briffa is a Lecturer in Defence Studies at King's College London, working primarily with the Defence Academy of the United Kingdom (the Royal College of Defence Studies and the Joint Services Command and Staff College). She is a founding member of the Centre for Grand Strategy at King's College London, where she read for her Ph.D in War Studies. Previously, she taught at University College London, Birkbeck University of London, and Queen Mary University of London. In 2015 she was appointed an associate fellow of the Royal Commonwealth Society, and in 2016 became a recipient of the U.S. State Department's inaugural Emerging Young Leaders award.

Chapter 11
Friends with Benefits? NATO and the European Neutral/Non-aligned States

Steven Murphy

11.1 Introduction

Far from going it alone, Europe's neutral and non-aligned states—Austria, Finland, Ireland, Sweden and Switzerland (the N-5)—seek economic, political and societal shelter to compensate for their relative weaknesses and smallness. Though they share a history of neutrality in international affairs and none are currently formal members of a military alliance, they maintain nuanced foreign policies aimed at securing shelter through varying degrees of bi- and multilateral cooperation with regional institutions and larger powers. Their membership of NATO's Partnership for Peace (PfP) programme is one way through which those foreign policy objectives are advanced, and the N-5 have been praised for their contributions to the Alliance despite being non-members. The challenges to, and opportunities for, developing deeper cooperation between NATO and the N-5 and the Alliance's suitability as a security provider for them in the current European security environment are assessed here. Though neutral Malta is also a PfP partner and a European Union (EU) Member State, it is excluded from this review as its interactions with NATO are comparably very limited.

At one time in their history, the N-5 were all neutral states or 'neutrals'. Their primary motivation in opting for neutrality was a desire to remain outside wars, but other important drivers included maintaining national cohesion, a desire for and expression of their independence, sovereignty and territorial integrity, and a wish to avoid the entanglements of alliances. Their neutrality policies have had a normative influence on the opinions of the citizens of the N-5 states over time, which can

S. Murphy (✉)
University of Iceland, Reykjavík, Iceland

A.-M. Brady, B. Thorhallsson (eds.), *Small States and the New Security Environment*, The World of Small States 7,
https://doi.org/10.1007/978-3-030-51529-4_11

impose limits on their foreign policy options.[1] However, Sweden and Finland replaced neutrality with a policy of 'military non-alignment' in the 1990s, and the Irish government has long characterised its policy as one of 'military neutrality', which simply involves non-membership of military alliances. Only Austria and Switzerland operate policies of 'permanent neutrality'. These distinctions make grouping these states under a single descriptor problematic and has led some scholars to simply use 'neutrals' as an umbrella term. Here, the European neutral and non-aligned states are categorised as N-states (N-5, N-3 and N-2). These are the European states that currently wish to remain outside military alliances and share a history of neutrality.

The division of the N-5 into the Nordics (N-2) and the rest (N-3) is drawn according to the degree of engagement they have with NATO, but it also reflects the difference in their geo-strategic realities. Finland and Sweden follow similar defence and security strategies, and they hold a reputation for being as closely engaged as, if not more closely engaged than, some of the Alliance's full members. Geographic proximity to a revanchist Russia makes their neighbourhood comparatively less secure than that of the N-3. Ireland has been described as cautious and reluctant in its relations with NATO,[2] but this description could equally fit Switzerland and to a lesser degree Austria. The character of their relations with NATO is more low-key and they participate in fewer initiatives than the N-2. A division can also be drawn between the EU states (Austria, Ireland, Finland and Sweden), hereafter referred to as the EU-4, and Switzerland. These cleavages provide much by way of nuance in how these states approach NATO and European security and defence developments in general.

Domestic public opinion has yet to indicate that any of the N-5 is likely to join NATO soon, though public and political opinion in Sweden is more finely balanced. Nonetheless, Sweden and Finland maintain an enhanced partnership with NATO. Modest opportunities for greater cooperation between the Alliance and the N-3 also exist, but the political will to capitalise on these opportunities is more limited than that of the N-2.

11.2 The N-5, the PfP and Collective Security

Since 1991, the international security environment has become characterised by Western global dominance and resistance to this dominance. With US hegemony secured in the 1990s, the pattern of conflicts shifted from international to intra-national and greater emphasis was placed on the transnational.[3] Europe's failure to

---

[1] See, Tonra (2012), p. 224; Aunesluoma and Rainio-Niemi (2016), pp. 59–60; Reinprecht and Latcheva (2003), p. 439; Wylie (2002), p. 332; Malmberg (2001), pp. 198–199.

[2] Petersson (2011), p. 121.

[3] Cottey (2007), pp. 32–36.

adequately address the break-up of Yugoslavia provided an opportunity for NATO's continued relevance through the implementation of its revised Strategic Concept (1991).[4] The Alliance added concerns for enhancing democratic institutions to a widened concept of security which brought NATO into the conflict resolution and crisis management space as well as economic, political, social and environmental spheres. To further the new Strategic Concept, NATO created the Partnership for Peace (PfP) in the mid-1990s as a framework through which former Soviet states could build trust with NATO via individually tailored programmes. Membership of the PfP was a precursor for many of these states to join NATO as full members, and the programme was seen by some as a waiting room.[5] For the N-5, however, the PfP provided an opportunity to further active elements of their foreign policies, focused on peace support and crisis management missions with United Nations Security Council (UNSC) mandates. Austria, Switzerland, Finland and Sweden joined within 2 years of its establishment, while Ireland joined in 1999, having adopted a wait-and-see approach. The main objectives of the PfP are the following:

1. Transparency in defence planning and budgeting
2. Democratic control of defence forces
3. Non-combat operations under UN (United Nations) or OSCE (Organization for Security and Co-operation in Europe) authority
4. Cooperative military relations with NATO in joint planning, training and exercises and
5. Force interoperability over the longer term with NATO members, including through participation in Combined Joint Task Forces.[6]

The first two objectives comprise the political element, while the rest refer to operational concerns. The political objectives were designed with the Eastern bloc countries in mind;[7] therefore, operational concerns are more pertinent to the N-5.

Following 9/11, the EU adopted a widened security agenda as defined in the 2003 European Security Strategy (ESS). The ESS provided a framework for the Common Foreign and Security Policy (CFSP) (created by the Maastricht Treaty, 1992) and what is now called the Common Security and Defence Policy (CSDP).[8] European states recognised that their national security concerns were intertwined due to increased interconnectivity regionally and globally. Transnational security threats such as terrorism, migration crises, cyberattacks, human trafficking, pandemics, money laundering and propaganda campaigns prompted greater collaboration

[4]NATO, Strategic Concept 1991, https://www.nato.int/cps/ua/natohq/official_texts_23847.htm [accessed 18-05-18].

[5]See Betz (2004), p. 32.

[6]Summary from Petersson, "NATO and the EU "Neutrals," 113. For the original text, see: NATO, *Partnership for Peace: Framework Document* (January 1994), https://www.nato.int/cps/en/natolive/official_texts_24469.htm [accessed 10-05-18].

[7]See, Ferreira-Pereira (2007), p. 207.

[8]EU European Security Strategy (ESS), *A Secure Europe in a Better World*, https://europa.eu/globalstrategy/en/european-security-strategy-secure-europe-better-world [accessed 21-05-18].

between partners to tackle them effectively. Through the PfP, the EU-4 complement their EU security commitments by enhancing interoperability with Member States that are also NATO members. Interoperability entails adherence to NATO standards, rules and procedures, as well as the use of similar equipment by the defence forces of partners. As the security objectives of NATO and the EU overlap, they have developed a partnership to enhance European defence cooperation.

Russian revanchism—exemplified through the annexation of Crimea (2014)—its military reform programme, increased military spending and military war games simulating attacks on EU states have sparked a new spurt of European defence collaboration. Russian actions are of most concern to the N-2 due to their geographic proximity and Russian military manoeuvres in the Nordic/Baltic region; however, Russian aircraft have also overflown Irish airspace.[9] In July 2016, the EU and NATO issued a Joint Declaration in Warsaw, indicating their commitment to deepening their strategic partnership in European defence.[10] NATO's primary focus areas reflect contemporary European security challenges. These are hybrid threats—such as disinformation campaigns and cyberattacks—migration from nearby disadvantaged and conflict-torn regions, lack of European-wide coordination in defence research and development, and interoperability. Anxiety regarding the reliability of the United States' commitment to European security has provided further impetus to EU policymakers seeking deeper and more extensive EU-wide defence and security collaboration. The EU's Permanent Structured Cooperation (PESCO), established under the Lisbon Treaty, was activated in 2017 to address European security frailties, and the EU-4 have all joined this initiative. Switzerland maintains a close dialogue with the EU, collaborates through the European Defence Agency and has contributed to EU-led peace support and security missions in Mali, Kosovo, Bosnia-Herzegovina and Ukraine.[11]

Relations between the N-5 and NATO consequently involve twin-track objectives. Firstly, they further the active or engaged elements of their foreign policies through international collaboration to promote peace and stability. Secondly, as the shelter theory proposes,[12] through NATO they engage in European-wide political and security collaboration, thereby enhancing regional and institutional solidarity which mitigates some of their security weaknesses.

[9]Dan Griffin, "Russian aircraft entered Irish controlled airspace – IAA", *The Irish Times*, 19 February 2015.

[10]Joint Declaration by the President of the European Council, the President of the European Commission, and the Secretary General of the North Atlantic Treaty Organization, 8 July 2016, http://www.consilium.europa.eu/en/press/press-releases/2016/07/08/eu-nato-joint-declaration/ [accessed 09-05-18].

[11]Government of the Swiss Confederation, "Foreign and security policy – a targeted partnership", https://www.eda.admin.ch/missions/mission-eu-brussels/en/home/key-issues/foreign-security-policy.html [accessed 04-02-19].

[12]Alyson et al. (2016), pp. 9–26.

Table 11.1 Character of contributions to NATO-led missions by the N-5

Countries	IFOR/SFOR (ended—now EUFOR)	KFOR (ongoing)	ISAF/RSM (ongoing)	Libya (ended)
Sweden	Infantry battalion	Infantry battalion (2)	Combat troops (29)	Fighter jets
Finland	Infantry battalion	Infantry battalion (20)	Combat troops (29)	
Austria	Transport	Combat troops (450)	Staff officers (18)	
Switzerland		Peacekeepers (235)	Staff officers (0)	
Ireland	Policing + support	Logistics → infantry + support (12)	Staff officers (0)	

Information provided here does not include contributions to the EU-led EUFOR mission. Figures represent 2018 deployment levels

11.3 History of Engagement

The N-5 have had a varied level of engagement with NATO-led missions. In the mid-1990s, Finland, Sweden and Austria contributed to peacekeeping operations in Bosnia and Herzegovina under the NATO-led Implementation/Stabilization Force (IFOR/SFOR). Ireland sent military policing and national support assistance in 1997 despite not yet being a member of the PfP. All of the N-5 contributed to NATO's Kosovo Force (KFOR) operation and the International Security Assistance Force (ISAF) in Afghanistan. Of the N-5, only Sweden contributed to the NATO-led operation in Libya with eight fighter jets. The N-2 have contributed more service personnel to NATO-led missions than the N-3, but in recent years they have heavily reduced the scale of their deployments (Table 11.1).[13]

Outside operational missions, the N-2 participate in other direct NATO initiatives and have increased indirect links. They directly participate in the NATO Response Force (NRF),[14] the Strategic Airlift Capability (SAC),[15] NATO's Centres of Excellence (COEs) and NATO exercises in the Nordic-Baltic region (e.g. BALTOPS and Trident Juncture 18). At the political level, the Alliance invited Finland and Sweden to become Enhanced Opportunities Partners (EOPs) at the 2014 NATO Wales

[13]NATO, KFOR: Key Facts and Figures (February 2018), https://www.nato.int/nato_static_fl2014/assets/pdf/pdf_2018_02/20180213_2018-02-KFOR-Placemat-final.pdf; and NATO, RSM: Key Facts and Figures (December 2018), https://www.nato.int/nato_static_fl2014/assets/pdf/pdf_2018_12/20181203_2018-12-RSM-Placemat.pdf [accessed 04-02-19].

[14]See, NATO, NATO Response Force (NRF), https://www.nato.int/cps/ua/natohq/topics_49755.htm# [accessed 28-05-18].

[15]See, NATO, Strategic Aircraft Capability (SAC), https://www.nato.int/cps/en/natohq/topics_50105.htm [accessed 28-05-18].

Table 11.2 NATO initiatives and N-5 participation - *Accession process under way

Countries	PfP	EOP (PfP+)	COEs	SAC	NRF	BALTOPS	HNS
Finland	X	X	X (4)	X	X	X	X
Sweden	X	X	X (4)	X	X	X	X
Austria	X		X (2)				
Switzerland	X		X (1)*				
Ireland	X		X (1)*				

Summit.[16] This golden circle of partnership status permits the N-2 to deepen dialogue and practical cooperation with the Alliance. Building on their already close partnership through the PfP, they both signed Host Nation Support Agreements with NATO in 2016. These agreements provide for the stationing, operation and transit of NATO forces during exercises or in times of crisis, if mutually agreed. Indirectly, they participate in the Nordic Defence Cooperation (NORDEFCO) structure, which was created in 2009 to boost regional cooperation politically and militarily regarding defence and peace support issues.[17] The Northern Group is another political forum through which the N-2 discuss defence and security issues with European NATO members.[18] In May 2018, Finland and Sweden also signed a Tri-lateral Statement of Intent with the United States to deepen dialogue and bilateral defence relations.[19] The breadth and depth of the N-2's interactions with NATO far exceed that of the N-3 (Table 11.2).

Amongst the N-3, Switzerland deploys over 200 armed forces personnel to the KFOR mission (called Swisscoy) and provides training courses on a wide range of issues from international law to civil protection and medical services. However, Swiss military cooperation has mainly focused on disaster relief in neighbouring countries and training for the Swiss Air Force.[20] Ireland has contributed to a number of NATO-led missions, but its commitment has been comparatively shallow and the relationship can be characterised as low profile.[21] Force interoperability is the main aim of Ireland's membership of the PfP,[22] but Ireland also provides training to NATO members in counterterrorism-related activities, such as countering

[16]NATO, Partnership Interoperability Initiative, https://www.nato.int/cps/ic/natohq/topics_132726.htm [accessed 21-05-18].

[17]NORDEFCO, *The basics about NORDEFCO*, http://www.nordefco.org/the-basics-about-nordefco [accessed 21-05-18].

[18]The Northern Group consists of Denmark, Estonia, Finland, Germany, Iceland, Latvia, Lithuania, the Netherlands, Norway, Poland, the United Kingdom and Sweden.

[19]Finnish Ministry of Defence, Trilateral Statement of Intent among the Department of Defense of the United States of America and the Ministry of Defence of the Republic of Finland and the Ministry of Defence of the Kingdom of Sweden, https://www.defmin.fi/files/4247/Trilateral_Statement_of_Intent.pdf [accessed 29-05-18].

[20]Nünlist (2018), pp. 192–202.

[21]Andrew Cottey, "Ireland and NATO: A Distinctly Low-Profile Partnership", in Cottey, ed., *The European Neutrals and NATO*, 151–180.

[22]Paul Kehoe (Teachta Dála - TD), *Dáil Debates*. 914, no.1 (21 June 2016).

improvised explosive devices (IEDs).[23] Austria's commitment to KFOR was significant, and crisis management is a core focus of the country's engagement with the Alliance. Interoperability and capability enhancement for peacekeeping and peacebuilding operations represent the key concerns of the N-3 in their relations with NATO.

11.4 Domestic Constraints to Deeper Engagement

Domestic-level factors, such as public perceptions of NATO and defence budgets, are important considerations as they can indicate the available space for deeper or broader engagement. Sweden and Finland are the most likely of the N-5 to join NATO at some point in the future, and this possibility has attracted much media comment. Though the time between membership application and acceptance could be 'fast-tracked', it requires strong parallel political and diplomatic coordination as their foreign and security policies are strongly linked.[24] Long-term trends, however, show that public attitudes do not carry sufficient strength to favour the proposition. In the absence of a clear supporting majority, referenda on the issue would be vulnerable to disinformation campaigns and propaganda, would be highly divisive, and the results may differ between the Nordic states.

11.4.1 Finland

Over the course of the last 12 years, Finnish public support for joining NATO has never exceeded 30% of respondents to annual Advisory Board for Defence Information (ABDI) polls (Fig. 11.1) and has been falling since 2014.[25]

Finland's military non-alignment is a product of pragmatism. Preserving neutrality and friendship with the Soviet Union without being drawn into its orbit were key foreign policy goals of successive Finnish governments during the Cold War. The

[23]Former NATO Secretary General Anders Fogh Rasmussen praised these training programmes when he visited Ireland in 2013. See, NATO, *NATO and Ireland: working together for peace* (speech by NATO Secretary General Anders Fogh Rasmussen at the Institute for International and European Affairs (IIEA) in Dublin, 12 February 2013), https://www.nato.int/cps/en/natohq/opinions_98369.htm [accessed 20-05-18].

[24]Finnish Ministry of Foreign Affairs, *The Effects of Finland's Possible NATO Membership: An Assessment* (Government of Finland, April 2016), http://formin.finland.fi/public/default.aspx?contentid=345685 [accessed 06-05-18].

[25]Finnish Ministry of Defence, *Finn's Opinions on Foreign and Security Policy, National Defence and Security* (The Advisory Board for Defence Information, 2018), https://www.defmin.fi/files/4412/ABDI_2018_Finns_opinions_on_foreign_and_security_policy_national_defence_and_security.pdf [accessed 16-01-19].

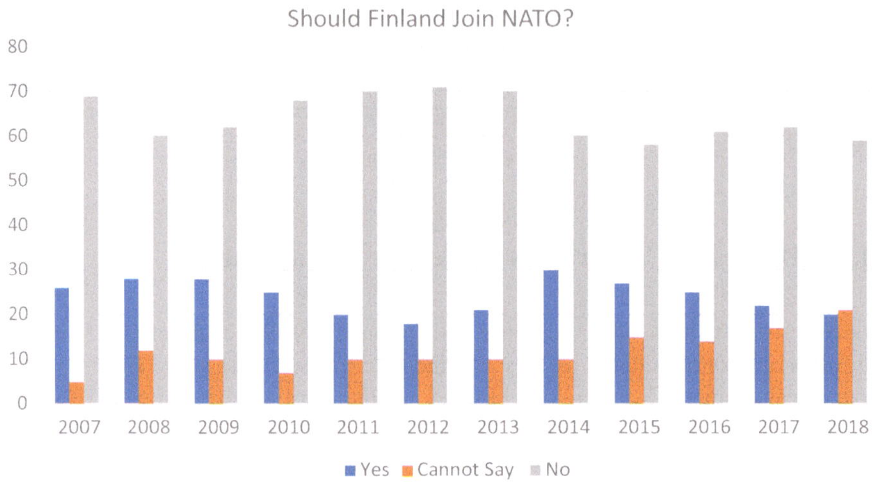

Fig. 11.1 Data based on annual ABDI surveys

success of this approach has enhanced military non-alignment as a concept in the mind of many Finns who cherish the country's role in international conflict mediation.[26] A majority of Finnish politicians are also opposed to NATO membership,[27] but the 2018 ABDI survey does show majority support for the government's policy of multilateral military cooperation (NATO—55%, the US—55% and the EU—90%).

11.4.2 Sweden

Since Russia's annexation of Crimea, the Swedish government has deepened and broadened its cooperation with NATO, issued guidance to all homes on how to prepare for total war,[28] and re-operationalised a Cold War era naval base.[29] Mirroring these defensive measures, Swedish attitudes towards NATO Membership

[26]See Tuomas Forsberg, "Finland and NATO: Strategic Choices and Identity Conceptions," in Cottey, ed., *The European Neutrals and NATO*, 100-102; and Aunesluoma and Rainio-Niemi, "Neutrality as Identity?" 60.

[27]Only the Conservative National Coalition Party (Kokoomus) and the small Swedish's People's Party are actively pro-NATO membership. They command roughly a quarter of the seats in parliament.

[28]John Henley, "Sweden distributes "be prepared for war" leaflet to all 4.8m homes," *The Guardian*, 21 May 2018.

[29]David Crouch, "Swedish navy returns to vast underground HQ amid Russia fears," *The Guardian*, 30 September 2019.

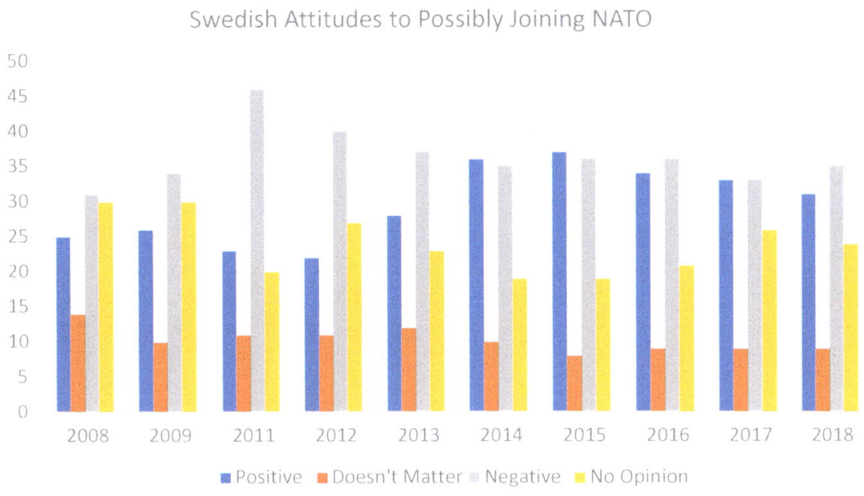

Fig. 11.2 Data based on annual surveys conducted by the Swedish Civil Contingencies Agency (MSB). **No survey in 2010*

have converged, turning the question into a more significant wedge issue (Fig. 11.2).[30]

Though there remains a strong base of opposition, when asked the more direct question of whether Sweden should join NATO, a majority are in favour of eventually joining. However, it must be noted that almost a quarter of respondents express no opinion to both questions. Furthermore, the initial jump in support for immediately joining NATO after Russia's annexation of Crimea may be waning (Fig. 11.3).[31]

Parties in favour of NATO membership command roughly 41% of seats in parliament,[32] while over half, including the Löfven II minority government of the Social Democrats and Greens, oppose full membership. Nonetheless, Swedish political parties generally recognise that the security environment has become more threatening. It remains to be seen what effect increased defence preparedness measures will have on public sentiment, but a recent assessment by Magnus Petersson concludes that it is unlikely that Sweden will join the Alliance, even in the long term.[33]

[30]Swedish Civil Contingencies Agency (2018), https://www.msb.se/RibData/Filer/pdf/28769.pdf [accessed 16-01-19].

[31]Swedish Civil Contingencies Agency, *Opinions 2018.*

[32]The Moderates, Christian Democrats and the Liberals.

[33]Magnus Petersson, "'The Allied Partner': Sweden and NATO Through the Realist-Idealist Lens," in Cottey, ed., *The European Neutrals and NATO*, 90.

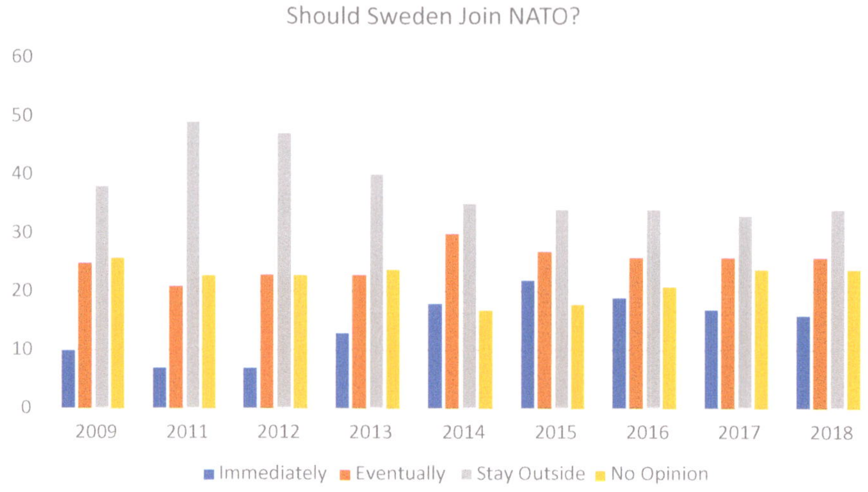

Fig. 11.3 Data based on annual surveys conducted by the Swedish Civil Contingencies Agency (MSB). **No survey in 2010*

11.4.3 Ireland

Surveys and opinion polls since the 1980s have consistently shown that the overwhelming majority of the Irish public want the country to maintain a neutrality policy.[34] The Irish government narrowly defines its policy of 'military neutrality' as non-membership of military alliances, though the Irish public have indicated their preference for an active neutrality policy focused on peacekeeping and maintaining foreign policy independence.[35] Furthermore, a majority favour enshrining neutrality in the Irish constitution.[36] Concern for the protection of Irish neutrality featured prominently during the Nice (2001) and Lisbon (2008) EU treaty debates and was a significant contributor to the Irish electorates' initial rejection of them in referenda.[37]

---

[34]Surveys and opinion polls since the 1980s have also shown a consistently high-level of support for Irish neutrality. A 2013 RED C poll showed that 78% of respondents believe Ireland should have a neutrality policy. See Peace and Neutrality Alliance (PANA) Neutrality Poll conducted by RED C Research and Marketing Ltd., September 2013, https://www.pana.ie/download/Pana-Neutrality-Poll-September-2013-Pie-Charts.pdf [accessed 20-05-18].

[35]Karen Devine, "The difference between Political Neutrality and Military Neutrality" (Address to the Joint Oireachtas Committee on Public Service Oversight and Petitions, 15 July 2015), 4.

[36]Fifty-seven percent of respondents to a poll in 2016 favoured inserting neutrality into the constitution. See Neutrality in Ireland Poll conducted by RED C Research and Marketing Ltd., February 2016, http://www.shannonwatch.org/sites/shannonwatch.org/files/MW_Neutrality_Presentation.pdf [accessed 20-05-18].

[37]See: Devine (2006), pp. 116–117; Laffan and O'Mahony (2008), p. 120; Karen Devine, "Irish Neutrality and the Lisbon Treaty" (Paper presented at "Neutrality: Irish Experience, European Experience" Conference organised by the Irish School of Ecumenics, Trinity College, Dublin and

Despite these concerns, the majority appear to support participation in EU defence and security cooperation, which permits political wiggle room for policymakers seeking to show solidarity with European partners on issues of security.[38] The predominant political consensus between the state's dominant political parties—Fianna Fáil (FF) and Fine Gael (FG)—is that Irish 'military neutrality' in its present form should be maintained. Parties to the political Left have tabled a number of bills to enshrine neutrality in the constitution, but they have been unsuccessful. No major Irish politician has called for the country to join NATO, and hard security issues are far from the minds of the Irish public.[39] Therefore, it is likely that the Irish-NATO relationship will remain low-key so long as the Irish public's conception of neutrality remains popular and parties on the Left remain politically weak.[40]

11.4.4 Austria

Neutrality has been a bedrock of Austrian national identity since 1955 and was necessary for Soviet acceptance of Austrian independence. Neutrality has been emphasised through civic education as a binding agent in opposition to the turbulence of Austria's past.[41] Austrian opinion polls show a strong national attachment to neutrality, with support for the policy ranging between two thirds and three quarters of the population.[42] Austria's new coalition government of the Austrian People's Party and the Greens is highly unlikely to abandon neutrality. During his first administration, Chancellor Sebastian Kurz emphasised neutrality when he refused to expel Russian diplomats in line with EU allies following the Skripal poisoning case in the UK,[43] and he has promoted Austria's stance as an honest broker in the furtherance of peace in Europe.[44] The Greens are firmly committed to neutrality,

---

Dublin Monthly Meeting [Quakers] Peace Committee, 8/9 May 2009), http://doras.dcu.ie/14898/1/Irish_Neutrality_and_the_Lisbon_Treaty.pdf [accessed 20-05-18].

[38]Fifty-nine percent of respondents believe Ireland should be involved in EU defence and security cooperation—see, European Movement Ireland (EMI) Research Poll conducted by RED C Research and Marketing Ltd., March 2018, http://www.redcresearch.ie/wp-content/uploads/2018/05/296918-EU-Movement-Research-Poll-March-2018.pdf [accessed 20-05-18].

[39]The Spring 2017 Eurobarometer survey found that while Irish people were concerned for security in Europe in general, they were amongst the least concerned in Europe about their national security. See, European Union (2017).

[40]Coakley (2010), p. 63.

[41]Reinprecht and Latcheva (2003), p. 439.

[42]Ibid, 441–444; and Gebhard (2013), p. 292.

[43]Stephanie Liechtenstein, "Why Austria's response to the Skripal poisoning wasn't so tough on Russia," *The Washington Post*, April 2018. In 2017, as Chairperson-in-Office of the Organization for Security Co-operation in Europe (OSCE), Kurz was also involved in trying to ease tensions between East and West over the conflict in Eastern Ukraine.

[44]Interview with Sebastian Kurz in *Security Community* (OSCE Magazine, Issue 4, 2016), https://www.osce.org/magazine/292376 [accessed 28-05-18].

while the largest Opposition party—the Social Democratic Party of Austria—is committed to neutrality and European security cooperation, but they are opposed to joining a military alliance.[45] The Freedom Party of Austria—former collation partners under the first Kurz government—is the second largest Opposition party and in favour of distancing the country from NATO.[46] On political grounds, therefore, the scope for wider engagement with NATO is rather limited.

11.4.5 Switzerland

Switzerland is the traditional neutral in the international system, and neutrality is intrinsic to Swiss national identity. The Swiss have been reluctant to compromise neutrality, which explains why they only joined the UN in 2002 and their late decision by referendum to arm Swiss peacekeepers (2001). Through their direct democracy political system, citizens are more capable of shaping Swiss foreign policy than in any other European state. This bottom-up approach does not preclude the government from making foreign policy decisions without citizens' input, as exemplified by its decision to join the PfP without consulting the electorate, but domestic opinion matters greatly.[47] The Swiss Center for Security Studies (CSS) publishes annual reports on Swiss attitudes to security issues, including Switzerland's relations with NATO. The 2017 survey shows that only 19% of the Swiss public favour joining NATO (Fig. 11.4).[48]

Of the seven-seat executive Federal Council, two centrist parties (Christian Democrats and the Liberals), occupying three seats, support continued engagement with NATO through interoperability and crisis management operations. The conservative Swiss People's Party holds two seats, is critical of Swiss involvement in overseas missions, and has made repeated calls for Swiss participation in the PfP to end. The Social Democrats hold the remaining two seats, and they prefer downsizing the army to focus on peacebuilding activities and development aid instead of military peacekeeping. Should KFOR wind down, it is unclear what direction future cooperation would take. However, due to the unusual nature of the Swiss political system, which emphasises compromise in the Federal Council, continued cooperation with NATO, in some form, is likely, but there is little room for greater engagement.[49]

[45]Party Programme of the Social Democratic Party of Austria (SPÖ), https://spoe.at/sites/default/files/das_spoe_parteiprogramm.pdf [accessed 28-05-18].

[46]Party Programme entitled "Austria First", as resolved by the Party Conference of the Freedom Party of Austria on 18 June 2011 in Graz, https://www.fpoe.at/fileadmin/user_upload/www.fpoe.at/dokumente/2015/2011_graz_parteiprogramm_englisch_web.pdf [accessed 28-05-18].

[47]See Nünlist (2018), pp. 194–201.

[48]Tresch and Wenger (2017), p. 146.

[49]See Nünlist (2018), pp. 194–206.

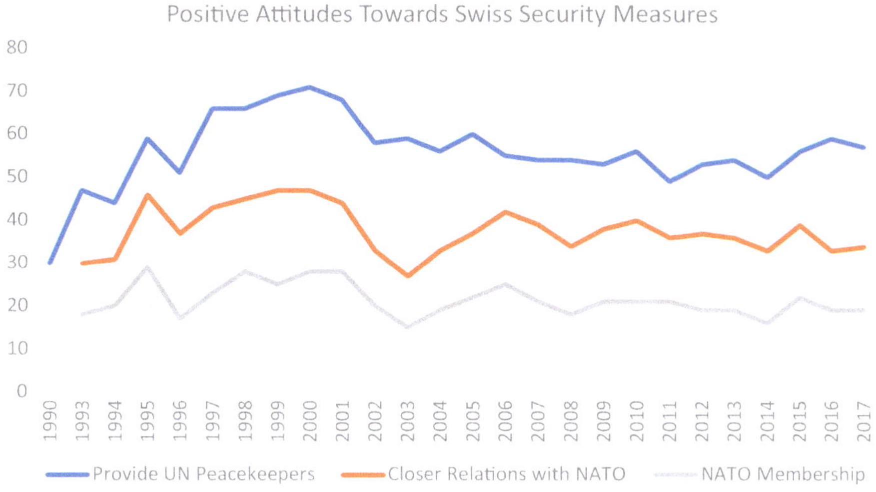

Fig. 11.4 Based on figures from CSS 2017

11.5 Defence Capacity

Defence spending is a crude and inaccurate measurement of a nation's defence capacity, but it can be instructive in highlighting the degree of priority that a government gives to its national defence. None of the N-5 currently meet NATO's 2% of gross domestic product (GDP) target for defence spending amongst its members (Fig. 11.5).[50] Unsurprisingly, the N-2 apportion a higher percentage of GDP to defence. Sweden's defence budget is set to increase under the 2016–2020 Defence Policy,[51] which is framed around the 'Hultqvist doctrine', named after Sweden's defence minister. The doctrine consists of two pillars: (1) boosting Sweden's capacity to defend itself and (2) signing agreements with the United States and NATO which enhance the credibility of Sweden's military deterrence.[52] Finland adopts a similar approach, with a comprehensive and networked national defence across all sectors of society the cornerstone of the policy.[53]

---

[50]Figures derived from the Stockholm International Peace Research Institute (SIPRI) Military Expenditure Database: https://www.sipri.org/sites/default/files/Data%20for%20all%20countries%20from%201988%E2%80%932018%20as%20a%20share%20of%20GDP%20%28pdf%29.pdf [cited 28-01-20].

[51]Government of Sweden, Sweden's Defence Policy 2016 to 2020, https://www.government.se/globalassets/government/dokument/forsvarsdepartementet/sweden_defence_policy_2016_to_2020 [cited 27-05-18].

[52]Barbara Kunz, "Sweden's NATO Workaround: Swedish security and defense policy against the backdrop of Russian revisionism," *Institut français des relations internationals (Ifri)* (Focus Stratégique, No. 64, November 2015), 8.

[53]Ministry of Defence, Finland, *Security Strategy for Society*, 16 December 2010, https://www.defmin.fi/files/1883/PDF.SecurityStrategy.pdf [cited 30-05-18].

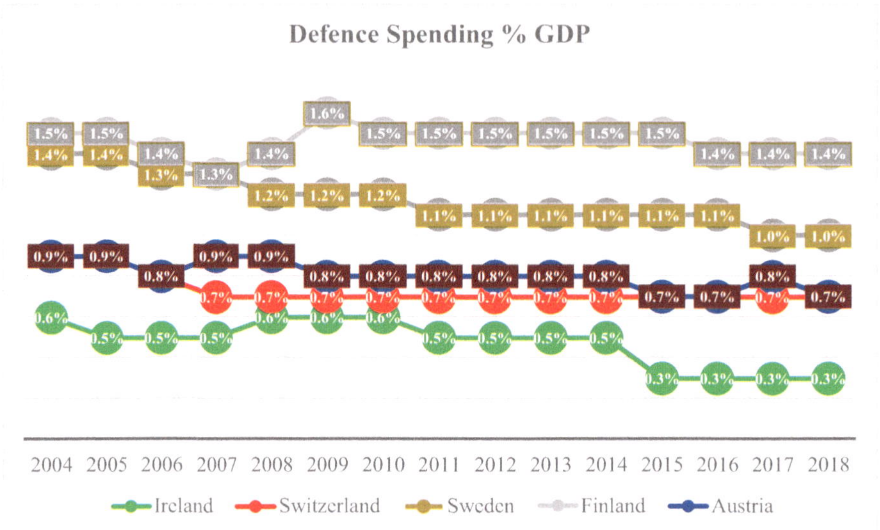

Fig. 11.5 Defence spending by European neutrals 2000–2017

Traditional defence concerns are a lower priority for the N-3 due to their comparatively safe neighbourhoods. Switzerland's current focus is on capability reforms, and the head of the Swiss Armed Forces called for an increase in funding in 2017 to meet the requirements of the ongoing transformation programme.[54] Austrian defence spending has seen a continual decline since the end of the Cold War, and the government is committed to international crisis management tasks more than national defence.[55] Ireland has always economised on defence and has never operated what one would consider an armed neutrality policy.[56] Underinvestment has recently led to problems in recruitment and retention of staff,[57] a weak national security system,[58] and the absence of a credible air defence.[59]

[54]Online news bulletin of Radio Télévision Suisse (RTS), 10 April 2017, https://www.rts.ch/info/suisse/8532695-le-chef-de-l-armee-philippe-rebord-veut-encore-plus-de-moyens.html [cited 21-05-18].

[55]Heinz Gärtner, "Austria: Engaged Neutrality," in Cottey, ed., *The European Neutrals and NATO*, 139.

[56]Ireland's defence forces are primarily concerned with performing civic duties domestically, while their focus internationally is policy-making, peace-keeping and interoperability. See, Irish Department of Defence and Defence Forces, *Statement of Strategy 2016 – 2019*, http://www.defence.ie/website.nsf/strategy2016 [accessed 28-01-19].

[57]Tom Brady, "Urgent bid to increase Defence Forces pay to stop mass exodus", *Independent.ie*, 2 April 2018.

[58]O'Halpin (2016), pp. 184–186.

[59]See, Tom Clonan, "Why it's time to have an open and honest debate about our neutrality", *thejournal.ie*, 15 August 2016; and, Paul Williams, "'Crisis' in the Defence Forces means our Air Corps are effectively working 9-to-5," *Independent.ie*, 19 March 2017.

PESCO entails more financial cost for the EU-4, though the Coordinated Annual Review on Defence (CARD) involves systematic monitoring of spending plans to 'identify opportunities for new collaborative initiatives',[60] and the European Defence Fund (EDF) provides funding and incentives to boost defence cooperation amongst Member States. Reflective of the strong support that the Finnish public have for EU security cooperation, Finland also joined the European Intervention Initiative (E2I) in 2018. This forum, which is designed to be more integrated and ambitious than PESCO, aims to 'develop a shared strategic culture' amongst its members to act in concert 'when and where necessary to protect European security interests'.[61] EU security initiatives foster solidarity amongst participants, but they also reduce available funds and personnel that might otherwise be used for NATO initiatives.

11.6 Future Opportunities and Challenges

The N-2 continue to broaden and deepen their involvement in multilateral security and defence mechanisms. However, they need to carefully manage coordination with NATO and individual NATO members at strategic and political levels. Political coordination between NATO members and the N-2 is currently achieved through various fora such as EU frameworks, the PfP, NORDEFCO, Nordic and Baltic cooperation (NB8), the Northern Group, NATO COEs and bilateral and trilateral consultations with NATO members. However, there is no overarching coordination body with clear policy objectives, and regional meetings have a degree of informality.[62] Strategically, it is important for the N-2 to signal a strong and credible deterrence capability. Participation in various NATO exercises, and exercises with regional NATO members outside Alliance structures, has increased coordination at the operational level, which furthers this aim.[63] Rapid response to hybrid threats (e.g. disinformation campaigns, cyberattacks, sabotage, insurgency support, irregular units) requires specialised units with strong intelligence capabilities and local

[60]European External Action Service (EEAS), PESCO Factsheet, https://eeas.europa.eu/headquarters/headquarters-homepage/34226/permanent-structured-cooperation-pesco-factsheet_en [cited 14-05-18].

[61]Letter of Intent of the European Intervention Initiative (E2I), https://www.defense.gouv.fr/content/download/535740/9215739/file/LOI_IEI%2025%20JUN%202018.pdf [accessed 04-02-19].

[62]See, Tuomas Iso-Markku, "Nordic Foreign and Security Policy Cooperation: The New Strategic Environment as a Catalyst for Greater Unity?" *Finnish Institute of International Affairs (FIIA)* (Briefing Paper, no. 234, March 2018).

[63]See Ann-Sofie Dahl, "NORDEFCO and NATO: "Smart Defence" in the North?", *NATO Defence College Research Division* (Research Paper, no. 101, May 2014), 8; Artur Kacprzyk and Karsten Friis, "Adapting NATO's Conventional Force Posture in the Nordic-Baltic Region", *Polish Institute of International Affairs* (Policy Paper, No. 3 (156), August 2017), 4.

support.[64] Special Operations Forces (SOF) are ideally suited to this task, but to be effective, their position within a larger strategic concept needs to be clear, they need to be adequately resourced and they require a high degree of interconnection with national security structures, personnel and tools pre-crisis.[65]

The utility of SOF as a complement to conventional forces appears to be well recognised in Sweden. Their ability to provide economy of force, act as a force multiplier, create an expansion of choice through flexibility and drive innovation were highlighted as benefits in a recent survey of practitioners.[66] The US Department of Defence (DoD) Directive 3000.07 on Irregular Warfare also notes that 'IW is as strategically important as traditional warfare'.[67] As SOF activities often operate within a legal 'grey zone' below the Article 5 threshold of an 'armed attack' on a NATO member, specialised units capable of countering such threats are valuable.[68] SOF's utility is also supported by research on small state defence strategies, which suggests that irregular warfare (IW) tactics, supported by strong national resilience, can be highly effective against conventional forces.[69] Sweden, Finland and Austria currently participate with NATO members in this field via the NATO Special Operations Headquarters (NSHQ), where enhancing integration and interoperability is a priority, but to be successful, the role of SOF within a wider strategic concept must be clear.[70] In June 2018, Belgium, Denmark and the Netherlands created a Composite Special Operations Component Command (C-SOCC), which the N-2 will no doubt watch with interest.[71]

The N-3 do not face such proximate threats. This does not preclude the possibility that it may become politically inopportune for them not to finance activities that display solidarity with higher spending regional partners in the future. Rather than seeing such contributions as costs, the N-3 should therefore see even minimal

[64]AWE (name anonymised) (2017), pp. 163–164.

[65]Ibid.

[66]See Colonel Ronny Modigs, "The Utility of Special Operations in Small States," in Eriksson and Pettersson, eds., *Special Operations from a Small State Perspective*, 43–64.

[67]US Department of Defense, Directive 3000.07, https://www.hsdl.org/?view&did=800965 [accessed 15-05-18].

[68]Madeleine Moon MP, "NATO Special Operations Forces in the Modern Security Environment" (Sub-Committee on Future Security and Defence Capabilities Report, November 2018), https://www.nato-pa.int/sites/default/files/2018-12/2018%20-%20SPECIAL%20OPERATIONS%20FORCES%20-%20MOON%20REPORT%20-%20169%20DSCFC%2018%20E%20rev.1%20fin.pdf [accessed 04-02-19].

[69]Ivan Arreguín-Toft's examination of 197 conflicts from 1800 to 1998 showed that when small states adopted a different tactical approach to the stronger attacker (typically irregular warfare), they avoided defeat 63% of the time. See Arreguín-Toft (2001), pp. 99–128; Also see, Sandór (2015).

[70]NATO, Special Operations Forces, https://www.nato.int/cps/en/natohq/topics_105950.htm [accessed 14-05-18].

[71]NATO, Three Allies establish Special Forces Command, https://www.nato.int/cps/en/natohq/news_155347.htm?selectedLocale=en [accessed 04-02-19].

participation as a cost-effective means to acquire targeted political shelter over areas of specific weakness. One way to achieve this could be to become sponsoring or contributing nations to NATO's COEs, which cover a wide-range of transnational security concerns.[72] As the COEs are outside of NATO's Command Structure, they may not elicit much domestic political opposition. Austria, Finland and Sweden currently contribute to some NATO COEs. They are all contributing participants to the NATO Cooperative Cyber Defence COE, while Finland and Sweden participate in the joint EU-NATO European COE for Countering Hybrid Threats (Hybrid COE), based in Helsinki, and the NATO Strategic Communications COE. Austria is a participating nation for the COE for Mountain Warfare, Sweden is a contributing partner to the Counter-Improvised Explosive Devices COE and Finland is a contributing partner to the COE for Operations in Confined and Shallow Waters. Ireland and Switzerland only signed up to join the Cooperative Cyber Defence COE in 2019, though they had previously participated in some exercises through the PfP.[73]

Switzerland could also contribute to the COE for Military Medicine as this is an area of Swiss specialty.[74] For Ireland, contributing to the COE for Counter-Improvised Explosive Devices could express solidarity with European partners and ensure that Ireland maintains its status in this field. For both, fielding strong representation at NATO's Cyber Defence Centre could also be prudent, given that Ireland hosts headquarters and data centres for many large American multinational companies and Switzerland hosts many important international financial institutions. Austria, Ireland and Switzerland could also consider joining the EU-NATO Hybrid COE. Its scope is limited to the identification and assessment of hybrid threats (e.g. threats to submarine communication cables, financial threats, security of energy supplies, drones, etc.) from both state and non-state actors,[75] which should not provoke much domestic protest. Regardless, force interoperability through NATO will remain important to their defence forces for some time to come, exemplified by

[72]NATO Centres of Excellence: Analysis and Simulation for Air Operations; Civil-Military Cooperation; Cold Weather Operations; Combined Joint Operations from the Sea; Command and Control; Cooperative Cyber Defence; Counter-Improvised Explosive Devices; Counter Intelligence; Crisis Management and Disaster Response; Defence Against Terrorism; Energy Security; Explosive Ordnance Disposal; Human Intelligence; Joint Air Power; Joint Chemical, Biological, Radiological and Nuclear Defence; Military Engineering; Military Medicine; Military Police; Modelling and Simulation; Mountain Warfare; Naval Mine Warfare; Operations in Confined Shallow Waters; Stability Policing; Strategic Communications; and the joint EU-NATO European COE for Countering Hybrid Threats.

[73]For example, both states participated in NATO's 3-day "Cyber Coalition" exercise in 2013 and 2018 to coordinate responses to cyberattacks.

[74]Switzerland is a significant contributor to the International Committee of Military Medicine (ICMM) through the hosting of workshops and training courses, and via the International Committee of the Red Cross.

[75]See Niklas Helwig, "New Tasks for EU-NATO Cooperation: An Inclusive EU Defence Policy Requires Close Collaboration with NATO," *German Institute for International and Security Affairs* (Stiftung Wissenschaft und Politik Comment 4, January 2018).

the fact that none of the N-3 are members of the EU's interoperability organisation FINABEL.

11.7 Conclusion

Though the prospect of any of the N-5 joining NATO in the short term remains low, their collaboration with NATO and solidarity with NATO members on issues of international peace and stability continue to provide a degree of political shelter. For the EU-4, NATO collaboration also supplements the political shelter provided by the EU. The N-2 continue to expand their cooperation with the Alliance, and they are increasing their overall defence spend in line with GDP growth. Coordinating their cooperative security arrangements is a significant strategic challenge. Balancing desires to exhibit solidarity at the EU level through participation in security and defence initiatives, deepening cooperation with NATO and NATO members to further their deterrence strategy and ensuring a strong national defence may lead to policy incoherence and departmental conflict over budgetary issues. Operationally, leveraging SOF capabilities within a clear strategic concept provides an opportunity for the N-2 to enhance deterrence at low cost and address 'grey zone' threats.

The N-3 have little political and financial room to expand their current relations with NATO. Austria and Switzerland remain constitutionally bound by neutrality. Though Irish neutrality is not codified in law, the majority of the Irish electorate appear to support enshrining neutrality in the constitution. Furthermore, security and defence issues remain a low priority for the general populace outside of EU treaty referenda, and the defence forces remain underfunded. Opportunities exist for the N-3 to enhance cooperation and knowledge transfer and display solidarity with European partners via NATO's COEs. However, budget constraints and a lack of domestic support will likely limit ambitions for any further and deeper engagement.

References

Alyson J, Bailes K, Thayer BA, Thorhallsson B (2016) Alliance theory and alliance "Shelter": the complexities of small state alliance behaviour. Third World Thematics TWQ J 1:9–26

Arreguín-Toft I (2001) How the weak win wars: a theory of asymmetric conflict. Int Secur 26 (1):99–128

Aunesluoma J, Rainio-Niemi J (2016) Neutrality as identity?: Finland's quest for security in the Cold War. J Cold War Stud 18(4):59–60

AWE (name anonymised) (2017) Framing SOF intelligence. In: Eriksson G, Pettersson U (eds) Special operations from a small state perspective: future security challenges. Palgrave Macmillan, London, pp 163–164

Betz D (2004) Civil-military military relations in Russia and Eastern Europe. Routledge-Curzon, Abingdon-on-Thame, p 32

Coakley J (2010) Society and political culture. In: Coakley J, Gallagher M (eds) Politics in the Republic of Ireland, 5th edn. Routledge, Abingdon, p 63

Cottey A (2007) Security in the New Europe. Palgrave Macmillan, London, pp 32–36

Devine K (2006) 'The Myth of Irish Neutrality': deconstructing concepts of Irish neutrality using international relations theories. Irish Stud Int Aff 17:116–117

European Union (2017) Standard Eurobarometer 87: first results. European Commission, Brussels

Ferreira-Pereira LC (2007) Inside the fence, but outside the walls: the militarily non-allied states in the security architecture of post-cold war Europe (Peter Lang AG). International Academic Publishers, Bern, p 207

Gebhard C (2013) Is small still beautiful? The case of Austria. Swiss Polit Sci Rev 19(3):292

Laffan B, O'Mahony J (2008) Ireland and the European Union. Palgrave Macmillan, London, p 120

Malmberg MA (2001) Neutrality and state-building in Sweden. Palgrave, London, pp 198–199

Nünlist C (2018) Switzerland and NATO: from non-relationship to cautious partnership. In: Cottey A (ed) The European neutrals and NATO: non-alignment, partnership, membership? Palgrave Macmillan, London, pp 192–202

O'Halpin E (2016) Ireland: Plus Ça Change, 1945–2015. In: de Graaff B, Nyce JM, Locke C (eds) Handbook of European intelligence cultures. Rowan & Littlefield, Lanham, pp 184–186

Petersson M (2011) NATO and the EU "Neutrals" – instrumental or value-oriented utility? In: Edström H, Matlary JH, Petersson M (eds) NATO: the power of partnerships. Palgrave Macmillan, London, p 121, New Security Challenges Series

Reinprecht C, Latcheva R (2003) Neutrality and Austrian identity: discourse on NATO and neutrality as reflected in public opinion. In: Kovács A, Wodak R (eds) NATO, neutrality and national identity: the case of Austria and Hungary. Böhlau Verlag, Wien, p 439

Sandór F (2015) Irregular warfare: the future military strategy for small states. CreateSpace Independent Publishing Platform, Scotts Valley

Tonra B (2012) Security, defence and neutrality: the Irish dilemma. In: Tonra B, Kennedy M, Doyle J, Dorr N (eds) Irish foreign policy. Gill and Macmillan, Dublin, p 224

Tresch TS, Wenger A (eds) (2017) Sicherheit 2017: Aussen-, Sicherheits- und Verteidigungspolitische Meinungsbildung im Trend. Center for Security Studies, ETH Zürich, Zürich, p 146

Wylie N (2002) Switzerland: a neutral of distinction? In: Wylie N (ed) European Neutrals and non-Belligerents during the Second World War. Cambridge University Press, Cambridge, p 332

Steven Murphy holds a PhD from the School of History at University College Cork, Ireland, where he focused on historical analysis of Irish foreign policy. As a post-doctoral researcher at the University of Iceland, he was a member of the Small States and the New Security Environment (SSANSE) project team. He has held various positions in academia, private industry and government service.

Chapter 12
One Region, Different Strategies: Slovakia and the V4 in the Euro-Atlantic Security Environment

Andrea Figulová and Kristína Janková

12.1 Introduction

The theoretical approaches to small states have mostly been drawn from great power studies relying on core international relations (IR) theories. Classical and traditional IR literature assumes in the main that small states do not possess the power to influence international relations. Compared to large states or great powers, small states are more vulnerable. To manage their position in the international arena, small states apply different strategies in their foreign and security policy. One of the fundamental strategies is to create alliance(s). The traditional approach to alliance theory includes balancing (a joint coalition against a powerful state) and bandwagoning (a weaker state aligning with a more powerful state).[1,2] Bátora[3] claims that small states have a foreign policy instinct that helps them develop a joint position on international issues more readily than many large states. Small states benefit from the protective umbrella of international institutions. Small states can pursue and promote their security concerns and interests through their engagement with other states and other relevant non-actors in international institutions. In this light, the concept of shelter or alliance shelter is of greater utility in the study of small states. The shelter theory distinguishes three types of vulnerabilities—

This work was supported by the Slovak Research and Development Agency under contract No. APVV-16-0540.

[1]Thorhallsson and Bailes (2017), pp. 51–52.

[2]Bailes et al. (2016), p. 11.

[3]Bátora (2015), p. 73.

A. Figulová · K. Janková (✉)
Comenius University, Bratislava, Slovakia
e-mail: andrea.figulova@fses.uniba.sk; kristina.jankova@fses.uniba.sk

A.-M. Brady, B. Thorhallsson (eds.), *Small States and the New Security Environment*, The World of Small States 7,
https://doi.org/10.1007/978-3-030-51529-4_12

political, economic and societal. Each type seeks a shelter in the form of larger states or international and regional organizations.[4]

The literature on small states consists of rather empirical works and tends to over-rely on case studies from the Nordic countries due to the high level of cooperation among them. The research on the Visegrad group (V4), on the other hand, has focused in particular on why and how the V4 was formed and works.[5] The V4 is an interesting case study as it consists of three small states and one medium-sized country. Poland has the largest territory and population, and traditionally it has been most concerned about its security. At the same time, Poland has also been developing its relations within other formations, such as the Weimar Triangle, the Normandy format and the Baltic Council.

The V4 is an appropriate grouping for illustrating differences between small states and medium-sized countries not only in their security policies but also among the small states themselves, as small states are not a homogenous group and their foreign and security policy strategies can differ based on the external as well as the domestic environment. The V4 has not been the subject of many investigations in alliance theory despite representing a suitable case study as "the Visegrad cooperation focused on economic, cultural and security issues but its chief task was helping member states in the transformation path".[6] Thus, one might expect that the V4 would seek political, economic as well as societal shelter not only outside the region but also inside the regional cooperation. The chapter analyzes NATO as a shelter for the V4 countries, emphasizing the reciprocal relationship building mainly on policies towards Russia and migration as the most current issues in security and defence. Moreover, the chapter explores whether the V4 represents a new, alternative shelter for its member states as in the case of Nordic Cooperation.

12.2 The Visegrad Group

The Visegrad group is cooperation between four Central European countries—the Czech Republic, Hungary, Slovakia and Poland. It was established in February 1991 after the fall of the communist regimes in the four countries with the aim of closer cooperation and mutual support in integration into Euro-Atlantic structures. There were several motivations behind the establishment of the V4. As the initial purpose was to enter the European Union (EU) and NATO, the countries (at that time Czechoslovakia, Hungary and Poland) wanted to prove that they were capable of integration and cooperation. However, the level of integration should not give a sign

[4]Thorhallson (2018), p. 62, Institute for Public Administration and Politics, Iceland.

[5]See special issue of *Politics in Central Europe*, 14, no.2 (2018).

[6]Schmidt (2016), p. 119.

of any alternative formation opposing the EU or NATO.[7] Therefore, in the beginning, cooperation was limited. A more pragmatic reason for the development of Visegrad cooperation was mutual support and help on the path towards integration.

Unlike other regional arrangements within Europe (i.e. Nordic cooperation), the history of theV4 cannot be characterized by deeply rooted friendly relationships. Over time, the V4 countries were able to develop a narrative based on common historical roots like the meeting of the Polish, Hungarian and Czech kings in 1335,[8] which aims to connect the countries through a common identity in an "imagined Visegrad regional community".[9] Moreover, as Fawn[10] argues, especially after 1999, the V4 has been characterized by deeper governmental as well as societal communication and cooperation with a crucial role played by the International Visegrad Fund (IVF) set up in 2000, which "facilitated grassroot activities... allowing a popular, organic sense of common Visegrad identity to develop".[11] Despite this, the V4 does not consider itself an institutionalized organization. However, in view of the increase in cooperation and the constant development of formal and informal rules, the V4 has become institutionalized, even though it does not have a set of bodies such as a Secretariat that would be responsible for the organization of meetings and communication on V4 issues.[12]

During its existence, the Visegrad group has had its ups and downs and several times it was considered to be dead. At the beginning of its existence, following the dissolution of Czechoslovakia, cooperation was interrupted by the non-supportive position of the Czech Republic and by the semi-authoritarian regime of Vladimir Mečiar in Slovakia. That slowed down its progress, and Slovakia did not join the rest in entering NATO in 1999. However, after a centre-right government led by Mikuláš Dzurinda replaced Mečiar, the V4 was reborn.[13] Slovakia was provided with a lot of support in catching up from the rest of the V4 and subsequently entered NATO and the EU in 2004. The V4, similarly to NATO after the end of the Cold War, suffered from a lack of purpose after the countries became members of the EU and NATO. Their response was to broaden the areas of common interest and construct a leadership position within the whole Central and Eastern European region. It is not

---

[7]Marek Madej, 2013. "Visegrad Group defence cooperation: what added value for the European capabilities?" *Note de la FRS No. 19/13* (2013):2, NORDIKA Programme, Foundation pur la Recherche Strategique, https://www.frstrategie.org/web/documents/publications/notes/2013/201319.pdf (accessed December 12, 2018).

[8]Rácz (2009), http://www.visegradgroup.eu/congress-of-visegrad/gyorgy-racz-the-congress (accessed January 4, 2019).

[9]Bátora and Matlary (2012).

[10]Fawn (2013), p. 342.

[11]Ibid, 342.

[12]Ibid, 343.

[13]Handl (2001).

a crucial player within the EU, but it has some power to influence EU policies, especially the Eastern Partnership.[14,15]

The V4 started to meet before European Council meetings to harmonize their positions, to act with one voice and to push for policies that would benefit the region and to oppose those that went against V4 interests, thus serving as a lobby for its own regional interests. The meetings of the V4 also extend to other partners in different V4+ formats, including Ukraine, Slovenia or recently Croatia. The V4 is broadening its areas of cooperation and establishes its future aims pragmatically, although this does not necessarily imply deeper integration and mostly utilizes the current structures and capabilities of its members.[16] The constant cooperation and broader scope are also a result of the changing international security environment that caused an institutional crisis in NATO.[17] Fawn argues that the V4 can be considered a successful project as a sense of regionness is present in the region, while at the same time the "Visegrad targets well" with the aims it has.[18] The importance of regional cooperation was underlined by the first foreign visits (summer 2019) of the new Slovak President, Zuzana Čaputová, which took her to the V4 countries, Brussels and Germany.

12.3 Security and Defence Cooperation in the V4

The V4 agenda is broadening to include the field of security and defence. The security strategies of the V4 countries, however, do not reflect this tendency to a high degree. There are still relatively few references to the V4 in documents. But where these aspects do appear, they tend to underline the importance of the strategic partnership among the countries for more effective and harmonized activities in the security and defence area aiming at the development of strategic capabilities.[19]

Security and defence should play a significant role in the V4 agenda, but the integration of the area is still in process, and the current state of affairs is far from being a deep cooperation. The field of security and defence mostly comprises words rather than deeds. Morawiec[20] and Madej[21] argue that cooperation grew "in circles". The most active phase came after 1997, before the first three Visegrad countries

---

[14]Fawn (2013), p. 348.

[15]Madej, "Visegrad Group defence cooperation," 3.

[16]Madej, "Visegrad Group defence cooperation," 6–9.

[17]Bátora and Matlary (2012).

[18]Fawn (2013), p. 348.

[19]Bezpečnostní strategie České republiky (2015) (Security Strategy of Czech Republic – translated by authors), https://www.vlada.cz/assets/ppov/brs/dokumenty/bezpecnostni-strategie-2015.pdf (accessed February 6, 2019).

[20]Rafal (2010). http://www.pism.pl/zalaczniki/Report_V4.pdf (accessed December 12, 2018).

[21]Madej, "Visegrad Group defence cooperation".

entered NATO structures, and later continued to speed up Slovakia's membership as well. After Slovakia entered NATO, the purpose of the V4 shifted to being a political forum for its members and a platform for common positions.[22] Later on, closer V4 cooperation was generated by three "momentums": the security environment in Europe has changed, and NATO's institutional crisis has caused its decreased importance; the V4 governments were constituted by similar political leanings based on common visions and identities; energy security challenges were caused by a gas crisis in early 2009.[23] However, the significant impact of the financial crisis pushed countries to austerity regimes that contributed to a rapid decrease in the defence budgets in Slovakia and Hungary in particular and partially in the Czech Republic.[24] For Slovakia and Hungary, the financial crisis represented a window of opportunity to deepen cooperation in the V4 in terms of further cuts in national defence budgets and the possible "outsourcing" of some tasks.[25] However, the long-term underfinancing of defence budgets cannot be "solved" either by the EU's "Pooling and Sharing" concept[26] or by the Permanent Structured Cooperation (PESCO) and NATO's "Smart Defence". Kufčák also argues that not only inadequate funding but also ineffective spending of the budget (such as high expenditure on personnel) causes structural problems that hinder some V4 countries from modernization and investment in the defence field. Such modernization is crucial for fulfilling NATO's requirements and foreign operation tasks.[27]

Based on security strategies, the affiliation of the V4 countries to the EU and NATO is clear.[28] The V4 countries consider NATO as the crucial institution in terms of security and defence cooperation, with the EU playing more complementary role. Deeper EU integration in this area has not yet made the EU the main party that V4 countries rely on. Even though NATO is primarily a military organization, not all V4 countries perceive NATO as a military shelter. In this respect, Poland as the "natural leader" of the region is also a most reliable partner for NATO as its defence budget has been balanced since 2008, with a slight increase after 2014.[29] Despite not being a small state, the shelter theory provides a useful insight into Poland's foreign and security policy. Poland is the only V4 country where there is a strong public as well as governmental perception of Russia as a threat to their sovereignty and integrity in a military sense. This feeling grew even stronger after the illegal annexation of

[22]Ibid, 3.

[23]Bátora and Matlary (2012), pp. 32–33.

[24]Kufčák (2015).

[25]Madej, "Visegrad Group defence cooperation," 7.

[26]Valášek (2011).

[27]Kufčák (2015).

[28]National Security Strategy of the Republic of Poland (2014), Bezpečnostní strategie České republiky/Security Strategy of the Czech Republic (2015), Hungary's National Security Strategy 2012, Hungary's National Military strategy 2012, Bezpečnostná stratégia Slovenskej republiky (2005)/Security Strategy of the Slovak Republic Bezpečnostná stratégia Slovenskej republiky—návrh (2017)/Security Strategy of the Slovak Republic—draft.

[29]SIPRI - Stockholm International Peace Research Institute (2018).

Crimea, which demonstrated Russia's will to regain crucial territories and restore its faded glory. After the fall of communism, Poland's comeback to Europe was accompanied by a fear of Russia's ambitions, and membership in NATO and the EU played a crucial role in protecting not only Poland's newly established democratic institutions but also the fundamental conditions for a state's existence—borders and population. Hence, NATO as the "main guarantor of security"[30] represents primarily a military shelter for Poland due to Article 5 of the Washington Treaty. That does not mean that societal and economic shelters are not present as well, but their role is marginalized compared to the military shelter, or political shelter.

The Czech Republic, according to its security strategy, also considers NATO as the main guarantor of security, with the EU playing a less important role in this field. Unlike Poland, the Czech Republic does not suffer from a direct threat from Russia as there are no common borders and the discourse of a military threat is not strong. Moreover, Czech President Zeman is more pro-Russian with the tendency to soften critique of Moscow. Membership in NATO triggered closer cooperation particularly with the USA, which established a missile-defence radar system in the Czech Republic that should protect Europe against a possible threat coming from Iran. This topic was politicized and became an issue of conflict not only between politicians but also among the general public. There were voices saying that it would make the Czech Republic a target for US enemies.[31] Therefore, the military shelter is not a primary motivation for the Czech Republic. Rather, it wanted to get back on to Western Europe's cognitive map as well as to trigger interstate cooperation.

A draft for the new Slovak security strategy used different words for NATO to emphasize its crucial role for the state—"security and defence pillar".[32] "Pillar" represents something that holds everything else together and provides support for other things that can be built on it. Thus, NATO became a crucial institution for the future existence of Slovakia in several areas. One must keep in mind that at the time of EU and NATO integration, Slovakia was not threatened by any direct military danger, so seeking a military shelter was not a primary motivation behind the candidacy. It was rather the idea of a democratic community providing help and assistance in various areas and the vision of a prosperous economy and standard of living that stood behind it. One might argue that after the annexation of Crimea, the military shelter became an issue in Slovakia too, but direct military conflict between Russia and Slovakia is considered improbable. Therefore, other types of shelter prevail over the military one, especially the societal and economic ones. Slovakia's

---

[30]*National Security Strategy of the Republic of Poland* (Warsaw, 2014).

[31]"Many Czechs Love U.S. but Say "Hold the Radar,"" *New York Times*, October 1, 2007, https://www.nytimes.com/2007/10/01/world/europe/01czech.html (accessed September 28, 2019).

[32]*Bezpečnostná stratégia Slovenskej republiky – návrh* (2017) (Security Strategy of Slovak republic – draft - translated by authors), https://www.slov-lex.sk/legislativne-procesy/SK/LP/2017/627 (accessed January 6, 2019).

defence has been problematic for a long time. The decreasing tendency of the defence budget (which has been evident since 2003 but even more rapid after 2009 due to the financial crisis) and low investment have made Slovakia's capabilities unreliable, even *de facto* non-existent. Several critical articles[33] have been written by the State Secretary of the Ministry of Defence, Róbert Ondrejcsák, calling for an increase in the defence budget and the modernization of the armed forces in order to comply fully with NATO requirements and fulfil the role of a NATO member and responsible partner. As a response to this criticism and the call from US President Trump to comply with NATO's budget requirements, Slovakia has recently conducted several big purchases in the defence field (e.g. F-16 fighter aircraft), but they have lacked transparency and have been subject to public criticism and the refusal of the deal by the Prime Minister.[34] So the Ministry of Defence shows a will to improve the armed forces and improve the capabilities of the Slovak Republic, but that is accompanied by corruption scandals and a lack of transparency that leads to deeper distrust of the government among the public. Nevertheless, the Slovak case is an interesting one as Ondrejcsák puts emphasis on Slovakia's "belonging" to the West, thereby denying the possibility of its being a "bridge" due to Russia's aggression on Ukraine. In his articles, he clearly recognized NATO not only as a military shelter for Slovakia but also as a societal shelter based on the "democratic security community" that the NATO is.[35] In this light, the violation of international law by Russia in 2014 after the annexation of Crimea represents another key point in analyzing V4 cooperation and its contribution to NATO. During her visits, President Čaputová stressed that the main goal of the V4 is to contribute to the further unification of Europe and to global cooperation, which should be based on accepting the rules.[36]

Last but not least, Hungarian security and military strategy did not assign any particular role to NATO, unlike Poland, Czech Republic or Slovakia (e.g. "guarantor of security" or "defence and security pillar"). If we also take into account the high level of populism and Euroscepticism in Hungary and the almost unlimited power possessed by Prime Minister Orbán, one might expect a very critical relationship with the USA. However, under President Trump, the USA has had a completely different position from the EU in Orbán's domestic political campaigning. Hungary confirmed the relationship of a close ally with the USA before the visit by Secretary

[33]More on Ondrejcsák's blog on https://dennikn.sk/autor/robert-ondrejcsak.

[34]SITA. "Zmluvy na nákup stíhačiek F-16 považuje Pellegrini za neplatné, opozícia žiada demisiu Gajdoša", *Financial Report*, December 1, 2018, http://www.finreport.sk/agenturne-spravy/zmluvy-na-nakup-stihaciek-f-16-povazuje-pellegrini-za-neplatne-opozicia-ziada-demisiu-gajdosa/ (accessed January 3, 2019).

[35]Williams and Neumann (2000).

[36]"Čaputová: Jednota NATO je potrebná aj vzhľadom na vzťahy s Ruskom," *Trend*, July 15, 2018, www.etrend.sk/ekonomika/caputova-pricestovala-do-polska-s-dudom-chce-hovorit-medzi-styrmi-ocami.html (accessed September 28, 2019).

of State Michael Richard Pompeo in early 2019.[37] Neither has Hungary's sceptical position towards the EU been transferred into its relationship with NATO. Hungary will apply for the command of the Kosovo Force (KFOR) mission after Italy's command finishes in mid-2019, and it plans to deploy 40 more troops to Afghanistan and provide financial support for Afghan defence forces.[38] Moreover, during the V4's defence ministers meeting in late 2018, Hungary proclaimed its intention to spend 20% of its defence budget on modernization.[39] This might look as if Hungary is a reliable partner. Yet on the other hand, Orbán stated in May 2017 that after successful reforms of domestic politics, the government would focus on national security and defence as it has not been paid enough attention.[40] He said that "a nation that is incapable of defending itself does not deserve to be one",[41] stressing the crucial role of the state itself in its own protection and refusing the use of NATO or the EU as a military shelter. Despite this refusal, international and regional cooperation continues.

Russia is an issue on which the V4 countries are not united. Poland considers Russia to be its main security threat, and this is clearly demonstrated in its security strategy, which includes nine references to Russia, and emphasizes the difficulties arising from the illegal annexation of Crimea.[42] Poland, due to a shared border with Russia, has concerns about its own territorial sovereignty and integrity and relies on NATO as a crucial ally against Russia. Slovakia's new security strategy draft possesses seven references to Russia, also highlighting Ukraine as a challenge. Slovakia supports sanctions but is more moderate in relation to Russia, calling for dialogue and further negotiations.[43] Doubts are raised due to the attitude of the Chairman of Parliament, Andrej Danko, who has several times suggested cancelling sanctions and made a speech in the Russian Parliament. Such divided positions

---

[37] "Hungary is an ally of the United States," Ministry of Foreign Affairs and Trade, Website of the Hungarian Government, last modified January 29, 2019, http://www.kormany.hu/en/the-prime-minister/news/viktor-orban-hungary-is-an-ally-of-the-united-states (accessed February 1, 2019).

[38] "Hungary is increasing its involvement in Afghanistan and Kosovo", Ministry of Foreign Affairs and Trade, Website of the Hungarian Government, last modified December 5, 2018, http://www.kormany.hu/en/ministry-of-foreign-affairs-and-trade/news/hungary-is-increasing-its-involvement-in-afghanistan-and-kosovo (accessed February 1, 2019).

[39] "V4 cooperation reinforces both the European Union and NATO", Ministry of Foreign Affairs and Trade, Website of the Hungarian Government, last modified November 16, 2018, http://www.kormany.hu/en/ministry-of-defence/news/v4-cooperation-reinforces-both-the-european-union-and-nato (accessed January 4, 2019).

[40] "PM Orbán says Hungary's defence is "not the task of NATO or the European Union but our task,"" *About Hungary*, last modified May 17, 2018. http://abouthungary.hu/news-in-brief/pm-orban-says-hungarys-defence-is-not-the-task-of-nato-or-the-european-union-but-our-task/ (accessed January 3, 2019).

[41] ibid.

[42] *National Security Strategy of the Republic of Poland* (Warsaw, 2014).

[43] "Slovensko ako člen EÚ uznáva sankcie voči Rusku." *SME*. October 10, 2018. https://domov.sme.sk/c/20934029/danko-volodin-slovensko-ako-clen-eu-uznava-sankcie-voci-rusku.html (accessed January 3, 2019).

domestically are not exceptional for the V4 countries. The Czech Republic's political leaders are divided as well. With Prime Minister Babiš, who supports EU and NATO membership, and President Zeman, a convinced supporter of Putin, the Czech public is confused by unclear directions. Lastly, Hungary represents in this respect an interesting case as neither the security nor the military strategy refers to Russia at all. The security strategy only mentions the need to diversify energy supplies to provide sufficient energy security for the country.[44] Moreover, Orbán has over past years developed a close relationship with Putin and criticized EU sanctions. It is remarkable how Orbán manages to distinguish between EU and NATO issues. That differs from the discourse in Slovakia, where the EU and NATO come in one package, in the "Euro-Atlantic" discourse.

The Russian annexation of Crimea is also crucial because Ukraine is a bordering country for three of the V4 countries. These borders are also the eastern border of NATO and the EU. Russia's aggression was the moment that the V4 could have utilized the NATO shelter. The NATO response was not robust and relied in particular on reinforcing the Baltic airspace and increasing the number of marines in the Black Sea, where two more vessels were also sent.[45] The response of the V4 was strong support of Ukraine's territorial sovereignty and integrity. Schmidt[46] argues that this triggered not only the idea of the V4 Battlegroup but also a stronger commitment to the EU's Eastern Partnership. Poland was incorporated into the Normandy format negotiating with Russia as well. After 2014, we may also observe a gradual but modest increase in the defence budgets of all the V4 countries (see Fig. 12.1). By 2017, the increase was 0.2% of gross domestic product (GDP) in Slovakia, 0.018% of GDP in Hungary, 0.08% in the Czech Republic and 0.06% of GDP in Poland. In Poland, there was, however, an immediate budget increase of 0.242% of GDP between 2014 and 2015.

From what has been stated above, we can argue that the V4 has been struggling to reach the status of a security community[47] as the countries have had different perceptions of threat and have not had identical approaches towards other international actors. This has been overshadowed from 2015 onwards by the migration crisis, where the V4 have very similar perceptions and policies and have been staunch opponents of EU quotas for redistributing asylum seekers. As former Slovak Prime Minister Robert Fico claimed, "The V4, including Slovakia, will never ever agree with obligatory quotas, never ever will it agree with the fact that somebody will tell a sovereign country what shall be done in this area".[48] Migration has become

[44]Ministry of Defence. *Hungary's National Military Strategy*. (2012), https://www.files.ethz.ch/isn/167317/Hungary%202012%20national_military_strategy.pdf (accessed January 6, 2019).

[45]Belkin et al. (2014), p. 286.

[46]Schmidt. "Friends forever?".

[47]For more on security communities see Deutsch et al. (1957) or Adler and Barnett (1998).

[48]TASR. "Fico: V4 vrátane Slovenska nikdy nebude súhlasiť s povinnými kvótami" *Teraz.sk*, last modified February 23, 2018, http://www.teraz.sk/slovensko/fico-v4-vratane-slovenska-nikdy-nebude-s/310359-clanok.html (accessed January 4, 2019).

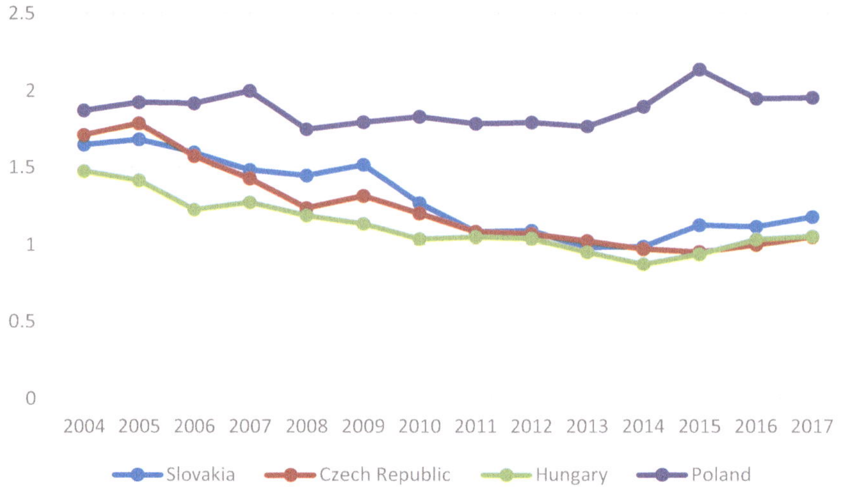

Fig. 12.1 The development of defence budgets in the V4 from 2004 to 2017 (in % of GDP). Source: Based on SIPRI (2018)

the issue of the moment for the Visegrad group. With regard to security strategies, migration is approached from a pragmatic point of view and can be linked to organized crime and drug trafficking (Hungary), demographic security (Poland) or economic benefits (Czech Republic).

All of the V4 countries have a clear stance on illegal migration, and at the peak of the crisis the political elites misused the issue for increasing their popularity and election votes. All of them realize that the roots of illegal migration need to be tackled. This moderate approach is not to be found in the speeches of the political leaders of the V4's small states. Poland claims that "we cannot accept migrants",[49] referring to the inability of the state (and society) to accept it as it would threaten the security and identity of the Polish people. A similar perspective can be seen in Orbán's statements: "for us migration is not a solution but a problem... not medicine but a poison, we don't need it and won't swallow it".[50] Andrej Babiš stressed the consequences of migrant quotas, that they are dividing Europe and are ineffective.[51]

The shelter theory argues that small states enter alliances to provide them with political, societal and economic shelter. For that, the small states must act as a

[49]"Polish PM: We cannot accept refugees." *Radio Poland*, last modified May 16, 2017, http://www.thenews.pl/1/9/Artykul/307247,Polish-PM-We-cannot-accept-refugees (accessed January 3, 2019).

[50]"Hungarian prime minister says migrants are "poison" and "not needed."". *The Guardian*, last modified July 27, 2016, https://www.theguardian.com/world/2016/jul/26/hungarian-prime-minister-viktor-orban-praises-donald-trump (accessed January 4, 2019).

[51]Siegfired Mortkowitz, Andrew Gray, "Babiš to EU: If you think I'm bad, Czech out the other guy," Politico, last modified February 2, 2018, https://www.politico.eu/article/andrej-babis-to-eu-if-you-think-im-bad-czech-out-the-other-guy-migration-quotas-euroskepticism/ (accessed January 4, 2019).

credible partner and provide what is required for the alliance. In the case of the V4, seeking shelter was not the only motivation for entering the Euro-Atlantic structures, especially NATO. Some argue that the V4 small states did not contribute much to the Alliance operations and are more like freeriders or bystanders than credible partners.[52,53] The only reliable state in this respect is Poland, mainly because it feels the Russian threat the most, and this triggers its compliance in ensuring application of NATO's Article 5. The rest of the group take it more as a matter of international presence and image, thereby seeking diplomatic shelter, but do not take their contribution to NATO that seriously, especially in financial terms. These countries were for most of their history states that were given assistance, not those that provided assistance. In Slovakia, membership in the EU is presented as an economically beneficial agreement where we get more than we give, so it is a good thing to stay in the EU. Economy is thus an essential part of the discourse related to membership in international organizations, despite the lack of expertise and staff. The countries are more prone to take the risk of low active participation than to risk the membership itself.

In case of NATO, it is also due to the lack of direct threat. Compared to the V4 countries, the Baltic states do take their membership seriously because their motivation is similar to that of Poland—a direct threat from Russia. Estonia followed NATO guidelines and developed an area of specialization that guarantees Estonia a stable and important place among NATO members: it is a leader in digitalization and cybersecurity.

When considering the contribution of small states, we cannot expect them to provide thousands of troops to operations or a huge amount of military equipment, but we can expect them to do as much as possible to contribute and to improve their future capacity.[54] There were several occasions when the V4 countries did not perform with a united approach. The Czech Republic struggled to support the NATO intervention in Kosovo in 1999 as the Prime Minister had a different opinion from the President. It acted similarly in the case of Libya, when statements indicated an unclear position. The Czech Republic did not contribute militarily to the mission but released an anti-chemical unit for deployment if necessary. Hungary also hesitated in Kosovo due to the large Hungarian minority on Yugoslav territory and did not contribute to the operation in Libya in 2012. Slovakia was not a NATO member in 1999, but to prove its commitment to becoming a member, it opened its airspace for NATO. Similar to the other three Visegrad states, Slovakia contributed only humanitarian assistance in Libya. On the other hand, all the Visegrad states actively participated in Afghanistan (see Table 12.1).

As Bell and Hendrickson state, the major powers were not able to persuade the small states to follow them in Libya.[55] They also argue that due to divided attitudes

---

[52]Hendrickson (2000).

[53]Bell and Hendrickson (2012).

[54]Hendrickson (2000), p. 28.

[55]Bell and Hendrickson (2012), p. 160.

Table 12.1 Military personnel contribution to NATO missions 2004–2018

Operation/mission	Slovakia	Czech Republic	Hungary	Poland
ISAF (2003–2014)[a]	19 (2004)/ 626 (2011)	16 (2004)/ 329 (2011)	90 (2004)/ 413 (2011)	120 (2004)/ 2475 (2011)
Resolute Support Afghanistan (2015–current)	36 (2018)	364 (2018)	93 (2018)	315(2018)
KFOR	0[b] (2018)	10 (2018)	385 (2018)	260 (2018)
Enhanced Forward Presence Baltic (in operation since 2019)[c]	152	60	0	200

Sources: The Secretary General's Annual Report 2018, NATO's Enhanced Forward Presence Factsheet (December 2018), NATO in Afghanistan Factsheet (April 22, 2004), International Security Assistance Force (ISAF): Facts and Figures, Operations and Missions: Past and Present

[a]ISAF as a NATO mission operated from 2003 till 2006/2014 in Afghanistan. Numbers express highest and lowest participation of the V4countries during the mission

[b]Slovakia's troops were deployed during 1999-2011, and currently Slovakia does not have any military personnel present in KFOR

[c]The numbers provided in this table are based on initial agreement and may not be operationalized during operational phase

and performance, the V4 have become less politically significant as an actor within NATO. We can thus say that the motivations and the participation of the various V4 countries differ. Slovakia, the Czech Republic and Hungary contribute only to the extent that it is safe for them and not much political effort is needed. On the other hand, after the experiences with Afghanistan and Iraq, they are much more careful about where to send soldiers and for what reasons. In this respect, these are the countries that are not willing to risk the lives of their soldiers in very unsafe areas.

Although the countries were not always united, the will to continue in the V4 format has been always present. The deepening of common positions and the enhancement of the region's strength is witnessed by the establishment of the V4 Battlegroup within the EU Common Security and Defence Policy. The idea of creating a common battlegroup emerged in 2011, and in 2014 it was officially formed within the EU structures.[56] The leader of the group is Poland, and each of the countries provides specific skills: Slovakia contributes specialists on protection against weapons of mass destruction, the Czech Republic is responsible for logistics and medical provisions; apart from the headquarters, Poland provides also special forces; and Hungary looks after civil-military cooperation. Despite its first standby in 2016, the V4 Battlegroup has been not deployed yet. Such a deployment could test the level of cooperation and might also serve as a learning process. Analysts argue

[56]Klára Mrázková, Alžbeta Neuschlová, Milan Puchoň. "Dosavadní působení a otazníky nad V4 Battle Group", *CBAP*, December 10, 2017, http://www.cbap.cz/archiv/3695 (accessed January 3, 2019).

that no deployment of the battlegroups makes it useless.[57] The next standby has been taking place since summer 2019. The latest development of V4 defence cooperation is the signing of the Memorandum of Understanding on the establishment of the V4 Joint Military Logistics Support Group Headquarters (V4 JLSG HQ),[58] which has been one of the priorities of the recent Slovak presidency of the V4.[59]

12.4 Conclusion: One Region, Different Strategies?

This chapter provided a comprehensive perspective on the V4 in the area of security and defence. It analyzed the security strategies of the V4 countries and the contribution of the V4 countries to NATO. The V4 countries work hard on their agenda in order to increase their influence not only in the Central and Eastern European region but also in the EU, but they suffer from various obstacles holding them back from more comprehensive actions. These impediments include different positions on Russia, ineffective financial management of the defence budget and the construction of threats that are utilized on the domestic rather than the international level. The main motivation behind the V4 countries' membership in NATO as well as the EU was to return to the cognitive map of "the West", hence seeking societal and diplomatic shelter, in order to institutionalize democracy and improve their international image. Being part of a democratic security community is still a dominant discourse on NATO membership. Poland's motivation was complemented by the fear of Russia's threat, which got stronger after the annexation of Crimea, so the military shelter has a strong position as well. Nowadays, we can observe multiple strategies in the region. Hungary's alignment with Russia and confrontational statements on NATO relate to strategic hedging rather than to alliance shelter. Poland pushes for stronger military cooperation. Slovakia and the Czech Republic are still using NATO as a nice visual of their international presence. NATO thus serves as a diplomatic and societal shelter. Despite NATO being the crucial guarantor of security and hence an alliance shelter, the V4 meeting before the Council of the EU is a traditional alliance that should balance the great powers within the EU. However, the current diversion from democratic values prevents the V4 from undertaking deeper integration and becoming a democratic security community itself.

[57] "V4 battlegroup is on standby," *The Slovak Spectator*, last modified January 5, 2016, http://abouthungary.hu/news-in-brief/pm-orban-says-hungarys-defence-is-not-the-task-of-nato-or-the-european-union-but-our-task/ (accessed January 3, 2019).

[58] "V4 cooperation reinforces both the European Union and NATO".

[59] MOSR-KOd. "Prioritami v oblasti obrany počas slovenského predsedníctva vo V4 bude príprava Bojovej skupiny EÚ, spoločná ochrana vzdušného priestoru, či spolupráca v rámci PESCO", *Ministry of Defence of Slovak Republic*, last modified July 1, 2018, https://www.mod.gov.sk/42219-en/prioritami-v-oblasti-obrany-pocas-slovenskeho-predsednictva-vo-v4-bude-priprava-bojovej-skupiny-eu-spolocna-ochrana-vzdusneho-priestoru-ci-spolupraca-v-ramci-pesco/ (accessed January 3, 2019).

References

Adler E, Barnett M (eds) (1998) Security communities. Cambridge University Press, Cambridge
Bailes AJK, Bradley T, Thorhallsson B (2016) Alliance theory and alliance 'Shelter': the complexities of small state alliance behavior. Third World Thematics TWQ J 1(1):11
Bátora J (2015) Small if needed, big if necessary: small member states and the EU's diplomatic system in Kiev. In: Baldersheim H, Keating M (eds) Small states in the modern World vulnerabilities and opportunities. Edward Elgar Publishing Ltd, Cheltenham, p 73
Bátora J, Matlary HJ (2012) Regional security integration: Nordic and visegrad approaches. In: Baldersheim H, Bátora J (eds) The Governance of small states in turbulent times. Barbara Budrich Publishers, Berlin
Belkin P, Mix DE, Woehrel S (2014) NATO response to the crisis in Ukraine and security concerns in Central and Eastern Europe. Curr Polit Econ Russia 29(2):286
Bell JP, Hendrickson RC (2012) NATO's Visegrad Allies and the Bombing of Qaddafi: the consequence of alliance free-riders. J Slavic Military Stud 25(2):149–161
Deutsch KW et al (1957) Political community and the North Atlantic Area: international organization in the light of historical experience. Princeton, Princeton University Press
Fawn R (2013) Visegrad: fit for purpose? Communist Post-Communist Stud 46:342, Special Issue: Reconfiguration in Central and Eastern Europe: International Security, Foreign Policy, and Political Economy
Handl V (2001) Visegrad - chances for recovery? In: Dangerfield M, Goryunov V (eds) Subregional dimensions of European Union enlargement. Russian and East European Research Centre, University of Wolverhampton, Wolverhampton
Hendrickson RC (2000) NATO's Visegrad allies: the first test in Kosovo. J Slavic Military Stud 13 (2):25–38
Kufčák J (2015) The V4 Countries and the impacts of the Austerity cuts on their defence spending and armed forces. Obrana a strategie (Defence Strategy) 14(2):35–48
Rácz G (2009) The congress of Visegrád. In: Rácz G (ed) Visegrád 1335. International Visegrand Fund, Bratislava, http://www.visegradgroup.eu/congress-of-visegrad/gyorgy-racz-the-congress. Accessed 4 Jan 2019
Rafal M (2010) Military cooperation in Visegrád Group. In: Madej M (ed) Cooperation on security in Central Europe: sharing V4 experience with the neighboring regions. The Polish Institute of International Affairs and Visegrad Fund, Warsaw. V4 Papers, No. 1, http://www.pism.pl/zalaczniki/Report_V4.pdf. Accessed 12 Dec 2018
Schmidt A (2016) Friends forever? The role of the Visegrad Group and European integration. Polit Central Eur 12(3):119
SIPRI - Stockholm International Peace Research Institute (2018) SIPRI yearbook. Armaments, disarmament and international security. Oxford University Press, Oxford
Thorhallson B (2018) A small state in world politics: Icelands's search for shelter. Icelandic Rev Polit Adm 14(1):62, Institute for Public Administration and Politics, Iceland
Thorhallsson B, Bailes AJK (2017) Do small states need 'Alliance Shelter'? Scotland and the Nordic Nations. In: Neil AW (ed) Security in a small nation: Scotland, democracy, politics. Open Book Publishers, Cambridge, pp 51–52
Valášek T (2011) Surviving austerity: the case for a new approach to EU military collaboration. Centre for European Reform, London
Williams MC, Neumann IB (2000) From alliance to security community: NATO, Russia, and the power of identity. Millennium 29(2):35–48

Andrea Figulová is an assistant professor at the Institute of European Studies and International Relations of the Faculty of Economic and Social Sciences, Comenius University in Bratislava, Slovakia, where she lectures on general political science courses for bachelor students. In her research, she focuses mainly on domestic issues in the Slovak political environment and on energy and security issues in international relations.

Kristína Janková is an assistant professor at the Institute of European Studies and International Relations of the Faculty of Economic and Social Sciences, Comenius University in Bratislava, Slovakia. Her research interests include EU foreign and security policy in a broader context of international law, especially the EU as an international actor and human rights protector. She did her PhD on the EU and Responsibility to Protect. She is also interested in nationalist and gender perspectives of football fans.

Chapter 13
Shelter and Strategic Hedging in the Gulf Cooperation Council

Imad K. Harb

13.1 Introduction

Several strategic challenges and threats face the small states of the Gulf Cooperation Council (GCC), necessitating serious attempts to find committed partners and allies that would provide security and other assistance. Bahrain, Kuwait, Oman, Qatar, and the United Arab Emirates need to address concentric circles of such challenges originating in an unbalanced relationship with Saudi Arabia, the largest state within the GCC, and extending outward to neighboring Iran and Iraq, which also boast larger areas and populations. They all have tried several strategies of alliance building, sheltering, bandwagoning, and hedging—strategies that need constant reevaluation for efficacy and assurance. Generally speaking, they have arrived at mixtures of these strategies that their leaders see as sustaining their rule and providing the necessary security for their well-being and domestic peace.

Importantly, the GCC's smaller states have serious concerns about preserving their sovereignty from Saudi and Iranian interference. Both have large populations and areas and stronger militaries. To ameliorate their concerns, they sought shelter from the United States (which also is shelter to Saudi Arabia) but also applied alternative strategies that partly insure their freedom from the limits of their size. Qatar and the UAE have shown more determination than Bahrain, Kuwait, and Oman to chart ambitious policies that make them project power despite their fear from the domineering neighbors.

This chapter argues that although some small states can bandwagon with larger and more powerful states and seek shelter with the latter for protection, their strategic location and financial resources can help them find alternative and complementary

I. K. Harb (✉)
Arab Center Washington, Washington, DC, USA
e-mail: iharb@arabcentredc.org

A.-M. Brady, B. Thorhallsson (eds.), *Small States and the New Security Environment*, The World of Small States 7,
https://doi.org/10.1007/978-3-030-51529-4_13

strategies for self-preservation. Some in the GCC have succeeded in using their financial resources to broaden their foreign policy choices, while others have judged that it is in their interest to shelter and hedge. In general, however, all have on different occasions used shelter, strategic hedging strategies, and influence, which make them appear stronger than their small size would otherwise allow.

13.2 Shelter Theory and GCC States

The basic outlines of the shelter theory assume that small states try to compensate for their size and limited capabilities by seeking protection by, patronage of, and relationships with larger and more endowed states. The specific concern for small states is to address their inherent vulnerabilities in an unstable and unpredictable international environment so they can seek assistance in political, economic, and societal matters important to them.[1] In other words, small states are realist-oriented entities that understand the rigorous requirements for their survival and act accordingly, arguably without venturing out on their own lest their adventurism increase the possibility of harm.

Although Saudi Arabia is not considered a small state because of its relatively large population, size, and economic endowments, it has always sought and developed a sheltering relationship with the United States that combines bandwagoning and alliance dynamics. At different times in its political existence, it has feared threats and intimidation from Iraq, Egypt, and Iran, and its royal family wants to assure its stable rule by relying on the premier international power. Indeed, it and the other GCC states have considered the United States to be their international shelter, most importantly since the dramatic strategic developments of the 1970s, especially the success of the Islamic revolution in Iran in 1979, and, later, the Iraqi invasion of Kuwait in 1990. As Guzansky argues, "The GCC's security is closely connected to the dependence of the Gulf states on outside protection and the necessity for foreign actors to have access to the Gulf economy."[2] Overwhelmingly, all six states are largely dependent for their military and security needs on American arms and ammunition.[3]

The GCC states have extensive economic relations whereby they import the latest American technology and services and invest large sums of capital in American enterprises. The United States also provides social services related to education, healthcare, and entertainment. All GCC states rely on Washington in their strategic

---

[1]Thorhallsson (2018), p. 64.

[2]Guzansky (2015), http://www.mepc.org/foreign-policy-tools-small-powers-strategic-hedging-persian-gulf.

[3]Anthony (2016), pp. 23–43. See also Clayton Thomas, "Arms Sales in the Middle East: Trends and Perspectives for U.S. Policy," Congressional Research Service, R44984, October 11, 2017, https://fas.org/sgp/crs/mideast/R44984.pdf.

thinking and posturing to the point that it is hard not to see the United States as a protector against any and all threats from Iran.[4] This, however, does not obscure some trepidation that GCC states have about American commitment to their security and well-being, which was most obvious during the last few years of the Obama administration.[5]

Lately, however, one serious development has negatively impacted the Saudi sheltering relationship with the United States. As the Saudi-led Yemen war becomes a humanitarian calamity and as accusations increase about Saudi Crown Prince Mohammad bin Salman's (MbS) responsibility in the killing of *The Washington Post* columnist Jamal Khashoggi, the American Congress is showing opposition to general Saudi policy. The American Senate in December 2018 sent a symbolic message to MbS and the Trump administration by voting 56-41 to cut off assistance in the Yemen war and unanimously to hold the Crown Prince responsible for Khashoggi's killing.[6]

13.3 Shelter and Tempered Hedging in Bahrain and Kuwait

Bahrain and Kuwait have had their concerns about Saudi Arabia and Iran. But Bahrain's less-endowed financial situation has prompted it to adhere more closely to Saudi policy, especially on facing Iran. Bahrain's royal family's main concern has been the fact that the Shia constitute the majority of the population, making Iran a natural element in the country's domestic security and regional alignments. The Sunni Al Khalifa rulers not only always bandwagon with Saudi Arabia, but they also side with whatever American policy is directed toward containing the Islamic Republic, as is happening today with the Trump administration. During Bahrain's

[4]Kenneth Katzman, "Bahrain: Unrest, Security, and U.S. Policy," Congressional Research Service, 95–1013, October 11, 2018, https://fas.org/sgp/crs/mideast/95-1013.pdf; Kenneth Katzman, "Kuwait: Governance, Security, and U.S. Policy," Congressional Research Service, RS21513, December 4, 2018, https://fas.org/sgp/crs/mideast/RS21513.pdf; Kenneth Katzman, "Oman: Reform, Security, and U.S. Policy" Congressional Research Service, RS21534, May 8, 2018, https://fas.org/sgp/crs/mideast/RS21534.pdf; Kenneth Katzman, "Qatar: Governance, Security, and U.S. Policy," Congressional Research Service, R44533, March 1, 2018, https://fas.org/sgp/crs/mideast/R44533.pdf; Kenneth Katzman, "The United Arab Emirates (UAE): Issues for U.S. Policy," Congressional Research Service, RS21852, April 10, 2018, https://fas.org/sgp/crs/mideast/RS21852.pdf. See also Christopher Blanchard, "Saudi Arabia: Background and U.S. Relations," Congressional Research Service, RL33533, December 19, 2018, https://fas.org/sgp/crs/mideast/RL33533.pdf.

[5]Ilan Goldenberg and Melissa Dalton, "Bridging the Gulf," *Foreign Affairs*, November/December 2015, https://www.foreignaffairs.com/articles/middle-east/bridging-gulf.

[6]"US Senate votes to end military support for Saudi coalition in Yemen," *France24*, December 14, 2018, https://www.france24.com/en/20181214-usa-senate-votes-end-military-support-saudi-arabia-coalition-yemen-khashoggi-mbs.

2011 Arab Spring protests, seen by its leaders as Iran instigated, the Al Khalifas called for and received military assistance from Saudi Arabia and the UAE.[7] Bahrain also bandwagoned with Saudi Arabia on Gulf affairs such as relations with Iran and sanctioning Qatar.[8]

Kuwait, on the other hand, has striven to be nonaligned in GCC and other disputes and has generally acted as a mediator. Since 2014, it twice engaged in mediating disputes between Bahrain, Saudi Arabia, and the UAE on one side and Qatar on the other, succeeding in 2014 and failing in 2017.[9] Still, Kuwait has supported Saudi Arabia's policy toward Egypt since the 2011 Arab Spring and in fact joined the kingdom and the UAE in supporting the new military regime after the 2013 coup.[10] On relations with Iran, Kuwait has hedged. It has shown openness to the moderate Iranian President Hassan Rouhani but also dealt harshly with attempts by Iran's Islamic Revolutionary Guards Corps to destabilize its security.[11]

In summary, Bahrain and Kuwait have been more accommodating to Saudi Arabia and have avoided clashing with its policy preferences, while Bahrain has been adversarial with Iran. Bahrain has simply bandwagoned with its larger sister, while Kuwait has avoided fully distancing itself from the kingdom. Both have been different in their policies and strategies from Oman, Qatar, and the UAE.

[7]Ethan Bronner and Michael Slackman, "Saudi Troops Enter Bahrain to Help Put Down Unrest," *New York Times,* March 14, 2011, https://www.nytimes.com/2011/03/15/world/middleeast/15bahrain.html.

[8]"Saudi Arabia's allies Bahrain, Sudan, and UAE act against Iran," *BBC News,* January 4, 2016, https://www.bbc.com/news/world-middle-east-35222365; Ian Black, "Arab states withdraw ambassadors from Qatar in protest at 'interference'," *Guardian*, March 5, 2014, https://www.theguardian.com/world/2014/mar/05/arab-states-qatar-withdraw-ambassadors-protest; Ishaan Tharoor, "The Persian Gulf crisis over Qatar, explained," *Washington Post,* June 6, 2017, https://www.washingtonpost.com/news/worldviews/wp/2017/06/06/the-persian-gulf-crisis-over-qatar-explained/?utm_term=.ebb807463f73.

[9]Sylvia Westfall, "Kuwait hopes for remedy to Gulf row over Qatar soon," Reuters, April 9, 2014, https://www.reuters.com/article/us-qatar-gulf-kuwait/kuwait-hopes-for-remedy-to-gulf-row-over-qatar-soon-idUSBREA381VE20140409; Aarti Nagraj, "Kuwait's emir tells US President he is hoping for 'an early end' to the GCC crisis," *Gulf Business*, September 6, 2018, https://gulfbusiness.com/kuwaits-emir-tells-us-president-hoping-early-end-gcc-crisis/.

[10]"Gulf states offer $12.5 billion aid to Egypt," *Al-Arabiya,* March 13, 2015, https://english.alarabiya.net/en/business/economy/2015/03/13/Saudi-announces-4-billion-aid-package-to-Egypt.html.

[11]Kristian Coates Ulrichsen, "Walking the Tightrope: Kuwaiti-Iranian Relations in the aftermath of the Abdali Affair," *International Policy Digest,* August 10, 2017, https://intpolicydigest.org/2017/08/10/kuwait-iran-relations-aftermath-of-abdali-affair/.

13.4 Oman: Hedging As Historical Trend

The sultanate has always nursed a good degree of skepticism about Saudi Arabian intentions. While active in GCC institutions, it has rejected the council's scheme of a monetary union and a common currency. It also vehemently rejected the idea of a full GCC union that was proposed by the late Saudi King, Abdullah bin Abdulaziz.[12] It has combined neutrality in GCC and regional affairs with what approaches on defiance are needed in handling Iran. Oman guards its freedom to decide on relations with Iran, with which it shares sovereignty over the Hormuz Strait.[13] Any Iranian threat to close the strait is enough to throw the region and the international security order into disarray, negatively affecting Oman first and foremost.

Noticeably, Oman's relations with Iran have been leader directed and business supported. Sultan Qaboos remembers that the late Shah of Iran Mohammad Reza Pahlavi helped him (after Qaboos staged a palace coup against his father in 1970) and the Omani state to defeat the leftist Dhofar Rebellion of the 1960s and 1970s.[14] While it is obvious that the current Iranian leadership is nothing like the late shah, it is unquestionable that today's Tehran sees much efficacy and benefit in staying on Qaboos' good side. In fact, Oman has not behaved as if there is any change in Tehran after the revolution of 1979. Despite very poor health, Sultan Qaboos was the first Gulf monarch to visit Iran's President, Hassan Rouhani, upon his first election in 2013, a visit that was reciprocated by Rouhani, who saw that there could be a good role for Oman to play in arranging a less contentious relation with the GCC.[15] Omani business relations with Iran are also lucrative for both sides, with hopes to increase trade between them to $1 billion per year.[16] Despite American sanctions against Iran, Tehran and Muscat are planning for an undersea pipeline at a cost of $1.2 billion that would carry Iranian natural gas to Oman's Sohar for use or reexport as liquified natural gas.[17]

Perhaps the most jarring Omani "singing outside the flock" regarding Iran was its secret mediation between Washington and Tehran in the lead-up to the signing of the Joint Comprehensive Plan of Action (JCPOA). Between 2009 and 2015, Muscat mediated between the two capitals to arrange for the release of American hikers and to close gaps in nuclear talks between American and Iranian officials. This mediation

[12]Katzman, "Oman," op. cit.

[13]Ahmad Ghaddar, "Factbox: Strait of Hormuz: the world's most important oil artery," Reuters, May 13, 2019, https://www.reuters.com/article/us-saudi-oil-emirates-tanker/factbox-strait-of-hormuz-the-worlds-most-important-oil-artery-idUSKCN1SJ0PS.

[14]Paul et al. (2013), pp. 274–286.

[15]"UAE runs Aden as protectorate, while Hadi hides in the shadows," *Middle East Eye*, November 28, 2017, https://www.middleeasteye.net/news/uae-runs-aden-protectorate-while-hadi-hides-shadows.

[16]"Iran, Oman seek to boost trade to $1 billion," *Iran Daily*, October 28, 2018, http://www.iran-daily.com/News/233500.html.

[17]Jonathan Gorvett, "Oman plans pipeline to Iran as US sanctions loom," *Asia Times*, October 2, 2018, http://www.atimes.com/article/oman-plans-pipeline-to-iran-as-us-sanctions-loom/.

was essential for the talks between Iran and the P5+1 (China, France, Russia, United Kingdom, and the United States plus Germany).[18] Needless to say, this could not be seen except as a snub to Saudi Arabia, Bahrain, and the UAE, which are interested in preventing Iran from having a nuclear program.

On intra-Arab affairs, Oman continues to strike different positions from those by Saudi Arabia. For instance, Oman remained on good terms with the regime of Syrian President Bashar al-Assad and refused to suspend diplomatic relations with Damascus.[19] The sultanate also refused to participate in the Saudi-led Arab coalition against the Houthi rebels in Yemen and in fact continued to play a mediator role in the ongoing war in that country. Just as importantly, Oman refused to take sides with Saudi Arabia, Bahrain, and the UAE in their 2017 siege and blockade of Qatar[20] and actually helped the latter circumvent them.[21]

13.5 Qatar: Audacious Hedging and Soft Power

Within the GCC, Qatar has interestingly shown deference and agreement with most Saudi wishes and policy recommendations. It has agreed to participate in the GCC's monetary union and common currency[22] and refrained from dismissing outright the Saudi call for more integration in the council. It also joined the Saudi-led coalition to fight the Houthi insurgency in Yemen, until it was expelled from the military alliance following the start of the 2017 GCC crisis.[23] It participates in the GCC-wide Peninsula Shield for desired common defense. Despite its somewhat different understanding of the Arab Spring uprisings, it joined Kuwait, Saudi Arabia, and the UAE in 2011 in providing Bahrain and Oman, the poorest among the GCC states, with $10 billion each to help them ameliorate the causes for their protests.[24]

[18]Guzansky, "The Foreign Policy Tools," op. cit.

[19]"Syria's foreign minister hails 'brotherly' ties during rare Oman visit," *New Arab*, March 27, 2018, https://www.alaraby.co.uk/english/news/2018/3/27/syrias-foreign-minister-hails-brotherly-ties-during-oman-visit.

[20]Camille Lons, "Oman: between Iran and a hard place," European Council on Foreign Relations, May 3, 2018, https://www.ecfr.eu/article/commentary_oman_between_iran_and_a_hard_place1.

[21]Imad Harb, "Determinants of Oman's Strategic Position on the Gulf Crisis," Arab Center Washington DC, January 23, 2018, http://arabcenterdc.org/policy_analyses/determinants-of-omans-strategic-position-on-the-gulf-crisis/.

[22]"Gulf single currency inevitable – Oman c. bank chief quoted," Reuters, October 31, 2016, https://www.reuters.com/article/oman-gulf-currency-idUSL8N1D11O1.

[23]Ali Abdelaty, "Qatari forces in Saudi coalition return home," Reuters, June 7, 2017, https://www.reuters.com/article/us-gulf-qatar-alliance/qatari-forces-in-saudi-led-coalition-return-home-idUSKBN18Y2YH.

[24]Ulf Laesing and Cynthia Johnson, "Gulf states launch $20 billion fund for Oman and Bahrain," Reuters, March 10, 2011, https://www.reuters.com/article/us-gulf-fund/gulf-states-launch-20-billion-fund-for-oman-and-bahrain-idUSTRE7294B120110310.

Still, Qatar may be the most audacious among the GCC states in its efforts to escape Saudi pressure and influence and has extensively and aggressively used strategic hedging tools to assert its foreign policy independence. Kamrava argues that what has defined Qatar's foreign policy over the years has been a combination of domestic and external dimensions: the geopolitical considerations of regional and international conditions, the emphasis on internal stability and the autonomy of the state from social groups, and the need to assure security, protection, and self-preservation.[25]

Two important events in the 1990s contributed as triggers for Qatar's striking out on its own. The first was what can be called a loss of confidence in Saudi Arabia's ability to act as a protector of the small GCC states when Iraq invaded Kuwait unimpeded in 1990.[26] The second was the animosity that developed between the Saudi leadership and Qatar's former ruler, Sheikh Hamad bin Khalifa Al Thani, who accused the kingdom of sponsoring a coup against him in 1996.[27] Interestingly, 1996 was also the year the pan-Arab Al Jazeera news channel was established in Doha to be an element among Qatar's soft power tools, but it has been the cause of many dustups and problems between Qatar and its GCC neighbors.[28]

Qatar's most egregious fault is its good relationship with the Muslim Brotherhood (MB) and its offshoots. In fact, Al Jazeera has long been accused of being the MB's mouthpiece since the organization's spiritual guide, Sheikh Yusuf al-Qaradawi, has resided in Doha for decades and had a religious program on the network about the Islamic Sharia and jurisprudence.[29] During the Arab Spring, Al Jazeera was at the forefront of covering protests and demonstrations against the regimes in Tunisia, Egypt, Libya, Yemen, Syria, and elsewhere. As Khatib argues, Qatar saw an opportunity during this time to advance its position and interests, despite the negative impact it had on its relations with its GCC sisters.[30]

An important indication of its relationship with the MB has been Qatar's steadfast support for the Egyptian revolution of January 2011 against the Hosni Mubarak regime and for the Brotherhood until 2013. Qatar was arguably the Arab world's

---

[25]Kamrava (2014), p. 159.

[26]Sultan Barakat, "Qatari Mediation: Between Ambition and Achievement," Brookings Doha Center, Analysis Paper no. 12, June 2016, https://www.brookings.edu/wp-content/uploads/2016/06/Final-PDF-English.pdf.

[27]Randeep Ramesh, "The long-running family rivalries behind the Qatar crisis," *Guardian*, July 21, 2017, https://www.theguardian.com/world/2017/jul/21/qatar-crisis-may-be-rooted-in-old-family-rivalries.

[28]Gregg Carlstrom, "What's the Problem with Al Jazeera?" *Atlantic*, June 24, 2017, https://www.theatlantic.com/international/archive/2017/06/al-jazeera-qatar-saudi-arabia-muslim-brotherhood/531471/.

[29]Sudarsan Ragavan and Joby Warrick, "How a 91-year-old imam came to symbolize the feud between Qatar and its neighbors," *Washington Post*, June 27, 2017, https://www.washingtonpost.com/world/middle_east/how-a-91-year-old-imam-came-to-symbolize-feud-between-qatar-and-its-neighbors/2017/06/26/601d41b4-5157-11e7-91eb-9611861a988f_story.html.

[30]Lina Khatib, "Qatar and the Recalibration of Power in the Gulf," Carnegie Middle East Center, September 2014, https://carnegieendowment.org/files/qatar_recalibration.pdf.

most enthusiastic and ardent supporter of MB President Mohammad Morsi, who narrowly defeated a former general, Ahmad Shafiq, in the 2012 presidential election. During his presidency (2012–2013), which was cut short by a military coup led by then Defense Minister now President Abdel Fattah el-Sisi, Qatar contributed some $7.5 billion to Egypt's economy.[31] Upon Morsi's election in June 2012, Qatar pledged to invest $18 billion over 5 years in Egypt's tourism infrastructure ($10 billion) and industrial projects ($8 billion) in "gas, power and iron and steel plants."[32]

By contrast, Saudi Arabia and the UAE immediately supported the coup. Saudi Arabia announced that it will support Egypt's interim government with $5 billion, as the UAE provided $4.9 billion. In 2014, they were preparing an aid package amounting to $20 billion,[33] indicating that they have achieved victory against Qatar.

Another practice in Qatari foreign policy that showed it overcoming its small size in the GCC was its mediation in disputes in regional states. Between 2004 and 2009, Qatar attempted to mediate between the Yemeni government of late President Ali Abdullah Saleh and the Houthi rebels. Another was a mediation effort between the Sudanese government and rebels in the Darfur region. Both of these did not bear much fruit. A third mediation attempt, done in consultation with Saudi Arabia, was between Lebanese factions in 2008, which ended a constitutional crisis and paved the way for the election of a new president.[34]

Qatar's striking out on its own has helped trigger the decision by Saudi Arabia, Bahrain, and the UAE to cut diplomatic relations with Doha, impose a blockade on it, and demand a set of policy changes that no sovereign state can accept.[35] If anything, the crisis has resulted in Qatar's increasing its push for more independence in its foreign policy. It started a serious strategic dialogue with the United States—held twice, in 2018[36] and 2019[37]—which gave it more freedom of action. It also opened itself up to military assistance from Turkey despite Saudi trepidation.[38] And

---

[31]Sara Aggour, "Tracking financial assistance to Egypt," *Daily News Egypt*, November 25, 2014, https://ww.dailynewssegypt.com/2014/11/25/tracking-financial-assistance-egypt/.

[32]Marwa Awad, "Qatar says to invest $18 billion in Egypt's economy," Reuters, September 6, 2012, https://www.reuters.com/article/us-egypt-qatar-investment/qatar-says-to-invest-18-billion-in-egypt-economy-idUSBRE8850YK20120906.

[33]Andrew Critchlow, "Saudi and UAE ready $20 billion boost for Egypt's El-Sisi," *Telegraph*, June 1, 2014, telegraph.co.uk/finance/newsbysector/banksandfinance/10868522/Saudi-and-UAE-ready-20bn-boost-for-Egypts-El-Sisi.html.

[34]Barakat, "Qatari Mediation," op. cit.

[35]"Arab states issue 13 demands to end Qatar-Gulf crisis," *Al Jazeera*, June 11, 2017, https://www.aljazeera.com/news/2017/06/arab-states-issue-list-demands-qatar-crisis-170623022133024.html.

[36]Kabalan (2018), http://arabcenterdc.org/policy_analyses/the-us-qatar-strategic-dialogue-messages-and-implications/.

[37]"Join Statement of the Second United States-Qatar Strategic Dialogue: Forward Together," US Department of State, Office of the Spokesman, Media Note, January 13, 2019, https://www.state.gov/joint-statement-of-the-second-united-states-qatar-strategic-dialogue-forward-together/.

[38]"Turkey and Qatar: Behind the strategic alliance," *Al Jazeera*, August 16, 2018, https://www.aljazeera.com/news/2017/10/turkey-qatar-strategic-alliance-171024133518768.html.

it recently provided financial assistance to Lebanon, prompting Saudi Arabia to also pledge help for the country.[39] Finally, Doha has for years hosted an office for the Afghani Taliban movement to facilitate negotiations with the United States about the future of that country.[40]

13.6 The UAE: Hedging Augmented by Strategic Expansion

The UAE's challenge to Saudi Arabia is qualitatively different from those of Oman and Qatar. Abu Dhabi steers close to Riyadh on certain policy choices—Iran, the Arab Spring, Yemen—but it has asserted its freedom to oppose Saudi dictates on intra-GCC issues important to its leadership and to chart an aggressive military policy in the region.

The UAE has been as strident in its anti-Iran stance as Saudi Arabia. What fuels this position is the reality that Iran has occupied three of its islands in the Gulf, Abu Musa and the Greater and Lesser Tunbs, since a few days before the UAE's independence from Britain in 1971. Negotiations over the islands' fate have led nowhere as Iran has rejected any attempts at compromise, including a UAE proposal for international arbitration.[41]

Interestingly, however, the UAE's Emirate of Dubai remains Iran's best venue for imports of different kinds of materials, a fact that puts it and its ruler, Sheikh Mohammed bin Rashid Al Maktoum, who is also UAE prime minister, in an awkward position. It also weakens the UAE government's claims on Iran in the eyes of Saudi Arabia. In 2018, trade between Iran and Dubai—mostly reexports from the latter to the former because of restrictions on Iranian direct imports—totaled $17 billion, which was a drop from $20 billion in 2013.[42]

The UAE has also been opposed to the Arab Spring uprisings. Two specific concerns united it with Saudi Arabia. The first was the challenge that the Arab Spring revolutions represented to the GCC monarchies and the second was the fear of the Muslim Brotherhood as a pan-Islamic organization claiming religious credentials. The UAE and Saudi Arabia designated the Brotherhood a terrorist organization in

[39]"Saudi claim will support Lebanon after Qatar's bond investment," *New Arab*, January 24, 2019, https://www.alaraby.co.uk/english/news/2019/1/24/saudis-claim-will-support-lebanon-after-qatars-bond-investment.

[40]Craig Nelson, "U.S., Taliban Show Optimism in Afghan Peace Talks," *Wall Street Journal*, January 27, 2019, https://www.wsj.com/articles/u-s-taliban-show-optimism-in-afghan-peace-talks-11548622334.

[41]For a historical rundown of the islands dispute, see Mattair (1995). See also, Al-Mazrouei (2015), http://gulfresearchmeeting.net/publication_pdf/Noura%20paper.pdf.

[42]Alexander Cornwell, "UAE fully complying with U.S. sanctions on Iran: official," Reuters, November 19, 2018, https://www.reuters.com/article/us-iran-emirates-sanctions/uae-fully-complying-with-u-s-sanctions-on-iran-official-idUSKCN1NO1IV.

2014, and that was after they supported the July 2013 coup by the Egyptian military against President Mohammad Morsi.[43]

On the other hand, the UAE has asserted its independence from Saudi wishes on many issues, of which two stand out. The first is Abu Dhabi's 2009 rejection of the GCC's monetary union because Riyadh insisted on hosting the GCC Central Bank.[44] As the second largest economy in the GCC, the UAE felt that it had the right to host the bank and be a deciding actor in how the GCC manages its financial affairs. Practically, the UAE and Oman have put the scheme of a GCC common currency in jeopardy.

The second issue has been the UAE's wish to become a military power that could expand its strategic landscape, a prospect not many small states can aspire for or sustain were it not for its favorable financial status. Long before former US Secretary of Defense James Mattis called it "Little Sparta" when he was Commander of US Central Command,[45] the UAE had begun building up its military forces, acquiring advanced weapons from the United States, France, and others. It also has launched its own arms industry.[46] The UAE also used mercenaries in its military adventures, a tactic that may have brought it unwarranted attention regionally and internationally.[47]

Currently, the UAE is involved alongside Saudi Arabia in the bloody war in Yemen. But it is not its involvement in the war that is in question but its seemingly independent actions there. While UAE forces have participated in 2015 in the actual battles to regain southern Yemen from the rebellious Houthis, they have set up local forces that are challenging the legitimate authority of Yemeni President Abdrabbuh Mansour Hadi.[48] In fact, the southern city of Aden and its environs are under the control of Emirati forces, while Hadi continues to avoid his country's second largest city.[49] The UAE has further forced Hadi to agree to the assault on the seaport city of

[43]Adam Schreck, "UAE brands Muslim Brotherhood terrorists," *Times of Israel*, November 16, 2014, https://www.timesofisrael.com/uae-brands-muslim-brotherhood-terrorists/.

[44]Robin Wigglesworth, "UAE quits Gulf monetary union," *Financial Times*, May 20, 2009, https://www.ft.com/content/822cab2e-4534-11de-b6c8-00144feabdc0.

[45]Rajiv Chandrasekaran, "In the UAE, the United States has a quiet, little ally nicknamed 'Little Sparta'," *Washington Post*, November 9, 2014, https://www.washingtonpost.com/world/national-security/in-the-uae-the-united-states-has-a-quiet-potent-ally-nicknamed-little-sparta/2014/11/08/3fc6a50c-643a-11e4-836c-83bc4f26eb67_story.html.

[46]Dania Saadi, "UAE well positioned to create own defense industry," *National* (UAE), December 6, 2017, https://www.thenational.ae/business/economy/uae-well-positioned-to-build-own-defence-industry-experts-says-1.682127.

[47]Mark Mazzetti and Emily Hager, "Secret Desert Force Set Up by Blackwater's Founder," *New York Times*, May 14, 2011, https://www.nytimes.com/2011/05/15/world/middleeast/15prince.html.

[48]Harb (2017), http://arabcenterdc.org/policy_analyses/troubling-ambiguities-in-the-uaes-role-in-yemen/.

[49]"UAE runs Aden as protectorate," *Middle East Eye*, op. cit.

Hodeida in June 2018.[50] Reports have also surfaced that the UAE is using mercenaries as death squads in Yemen.[51]

Finally, the UAE acts as an expanding maritime power whose economic and military influence extends from the Indian Ocean to the Mediterranean Sea. It has a military presence on the Yemeni island of Socotra in the Arabian Sea, which caused a crisis in its relationship with the Yemeni government in 2018.[52] It has signed economic agreements with the Horn of Africa countries of Djibouti and Eritrea and has great influence over the Bab al-Mandab waterway near the Gulf of Aden and overall maritime trade in the Red Sea.[53] Importantly, it is instrumental in propping up Libyan renegade General Khalifa Haftar, leader of the so-called Libyan National Army, who challenges the United Nations supported Government of National Unity in Tripoli.[54]

13.7 Conclusion

Discussing shelter, bandwagoning, alliance strategies, and hedging is a multi-layered process when dealing with the countries of the GCC. While the shelter theory in its broad outlines applies to the small states of the GCC in addition to Saudi Arabia despite its large size, population, and resources, it does not necessarily fit the patterns of small states' foreign policies in general. Indeed, discussing how the GCC's small states assure their security and peace adds important elements that may not have received sufficient attention.

First, if financially endowed, as Kuwait, Qatar, and the UAE are, small states can afford to hedge their bets and seek to stray outside the confines of a supposed sheltering state, be it the United States or Saudi Arabia. In other words, if small states have something strategically valuable to "trade in," they may be at a slightly better advantage than other unendowed small states. Being able to use their ample financial resources to invest in larger economies, small states have leverage they can

[50] "Exclusive: UAE forced Hadi to support Hodeidah assault against his will," *Middle East Eye*, June 13, 2018, https://www.middleeasteye.net/news/exclusive-uae-forced-hadi-support-hodeidah-assault-against-his-will.

[51] Aram Rostom, "American Mercenaries," *BuzzFeed News*, October 16, 2018, https://www.buzzfeednews.com/article/aramroston/mercenaries-assassination-us-yemen-uae-spear-golan-dahlan.

[52] "UAE forces 'occupy' sea and airports on Yemen's Socotra," *Al Jazeera*, May 4, 2018, https://www.aljazeera.com/news/2018/05/uae-forces-occupy-sea-airports-yemen-socotra-180504181423573.html.

[53] "The United Arab Emirates in the Horn of Africa," International Crisis Group, Briefing No. 65, November 6, 2018, https://www.crisisgroup.org/middle-east-north-africa/gulf-and-arabian-peninsula/united-arab-emirates/b65-united-arab-emirates-horn-africa.

[54] "Supported by the UAE, Haftar seeks to control south Libya," *Middle East Monitor*, January 2, 2019, https://www.middleeastmonitor.com/20190102-supported-by-the-uae-haftar-seeks-to-control-south-libya/.

use to convince any other that can provide shelter to do so and be economically rewarded. To be sure, GCC small states have many security arrangements with the United States, France, Great Britain, South Korea, India, and Turkey, in large part because of their importance to the world economy.

Second, historical relations that a small state has with a supposed adversary may trump the conditions for that adversarial relationship, as Oman has shown in its continuance of old relations with Iran. Oman does not show the same degree of apprehension from Iran as Bahrain and the UAE, for instance, because Sultan Qaboos basically owes his throne to Iran's assistance during the rule of the former Shah Mohammad Reza Pahlavi. Although the current religious regime in Tehran is antithetical to the Pahlavi regime, Muscat still has a cordial relationship with the Iranian nation and people.

Third, ambitious leaderships such as those in Qatar and the UAE may exploit their financial resources to chart an adventurous foreign policy despite their small size and continued threat from a larger neighboring state such as Saudi Arabia or Iran. The element of leadership type and style adds a personalist angle to the study of small states whereby leaders' proclivities expand their options and possibilities. In the Gulf's current geostrategic environment, this element becomes decisive because Iran is under tremendous international and American pressure and Saudi Arabia feels threatened by several unsettling conditions around it. Qatari and Emirati leaders thus feel that they can be daring and adventurous.

Fourth, all small states are interested in preserving their sovereignty and the stability of their governments. Those of the GCC prove the point that a combination of some sheltering strategies—like their relationship with the United States—and an active search for disparate allies is best suited to help their self-preservation and strategic interests. Indeed, the GCC's small states could not simply choose only one unchanging strategy to help secure themselves specifically because of the constantly changing conditions of the international order.

References

Al-Mazrouei NS (2015) Disputed Islands between UAE and Iran: Abu Musa, Greater Tunb, and Lesser Tunb in the Strait of Hormuz. Gulf Research Center, Cambridge, http://gulfresearchmeeting.net/publication_pdf/Noura%20paper.pdf

Anthony JD (2016) GCC arms imports: strategic assessment and economic benefits to the United States. In: Roches DD, Thafer D (eds) The arms trade, military services and the security market in the Gulf States. Gerlach, Berlin, pp 23–43

Guzansky Y (2015) The foreign policy tools of small powers: strategic hedging in the Persian Gulf. Middle East Policy 22(1):112–122, http://www.mepc.org/foreign-policy-tools-small-powers-strategic-hedging-persian-gulf

Harb I (2017) Troubling ambiguities in the UAE's role in Yemen. Arab Center Washington, Washington DC, http://arabcenterdc.org/policy_analyses/troubling-ambiguities-in-the-uaes-role-in-yemen/

Kabalan M (2018) The US-Qatar strategic dialogue: messages and implications. Arab Center Washington, Washington DC, http://arabcenterdc.org/policy_analyses/the-us-qatar-strategic-dialogue-messages-and-implications/

Kamrava M (2014) The foreign policy of Qatar. In: Hinnebusch R, Ihtishami A (eds) The foreign policies of Middle East states, 2nd edn. Lynne Rienner, Boulder, p 159

Mattair T (1995) The three occupied UAE Islands: the Tunbs and Abu Musa. Emirates Center for Strategic Studies and Research, Abu Dhabi

Paul C et al (2013) Oman (Dhofar Rebellion): 1965–1975, case outcome: COIN Win. In: Paul C et al (eds) Paths to victory: detailed insurgency case studies. Rand, Washington, DC, pp 274–286

Thorhallsson B (2018) A small state in world politics: Iceland's search for shelter. Icelandic Rev Polit Adm 14(1):64

Imad K. Harb is the director of research and analysis at the Arab Center Washington DC (ACW). Previously, he taught as an Adjunct Professor of Middle East Studies at the Center for Contemporary Arab Studies, Georgetown University, and as a Lecturer in Political Science and Comparative Politics at the University of Utah and San Francisco State University. Harb earned his PhD in Political Science from the University of Utah. He writes on Middle East and Arab current affairs.

Chapter 14
The Conduct of Armenian Foreign Policy: Limits of the Precarious Balance

Vahram Ter-Matevosyan and Narek Mkrtchyan

14.1 Introduction

Since regaining its independence in 1991, Armenia's security dilemmas have been put in an unflattering spotlight. It has encountered an overabundance of challenges that seemed well over its weight. In addition to the collapse of the economy, societal structures, and ensuing widespread poverty, Armenia had to deal with the consequences of the 1988 devastating earthquake in the northern regions and the widespread emigration. Regional conflicts and rivalry in the early1990s have exacerbated Armenia's precarious situation. Two major foreign policy issues have particularly shaped Armenia's security agenda since the early days of independence—the conflict around Nagorny Karabakh and the Turkish-Azerbaijani blockade of Armenia. In the 2000s, the stand-off between Russia and the Western powers has visibly affected Armenia, especially when the latter had to determine the strategy of cooperation with the EU. The increasing tensions between the parties have overshadowed the concerns and aspirations of other small states, too. Some of them (for instance, Ukraine, Georgia, and Moldova) deepened relations with the EU at the expense of confrontation with Russia, while Armenia favored the "both . . . and" formula. Being a member of Russian-led integration projects and simultaneously expanding the cooperation with the EU make Armenia a rare case in the post-Soviet space.

Situated in a volatile region, Armenia remains in a geopolitically challenging situation. Two of Armenia's four land borders are hermetically sealed, visibly limiting Armenia's communication, transport routes, and development prospects. Since the early days, Turkey has refused to establish diplomatic relations with

V. Ter-Matevosyan (✉) · N. Mkrtchyan
American University of Armenia, Yerevan, Armenia
e-mail: termatevosyan@aua.am; nmkrtchyan@aua.am

A.-M. Brady, B. Thorhallsson (eds.), *Small States and the New Security Environment*, The World of Small States 7,
https://doi.org/10.1007/978-3-030-51529-4_14

Armenia, nor was it eager to open the border. In addition to waging a war against the Nagorno Karabakh Republic, Azerbaijan has also stopped all communication and transit routes that connected Soviet Armenia to the Union republics. The 30-year-long Karabakh conflict has made Armenia readjust its regional priorities according to the new geopolitical security architecture. As a result, Iran and Georgia became Armenia's key partners as they were the only gateways to the outer world. Georgia became the only land corridor connecting to Russia, Armenia's only strategic ally. It is against this background that many foreign and security policy choices of Armenia can be understood and analyzed.

At the outset, the chapter will discuss theoretical aspects of small states and sheltering and their applicability to the Armenian context. The second part of the chapter will concentrate on these problems and discuss their impact on Armenia's development prospects; it will then discuss Armenia's relations with Russia and the EU.

14.2 Contextualizing the Small States Theory: The Armenian Case

Despite the interest in small state studies since the eighteenth century, it is considered one of the youngest categories in international relations. Smallness is a concept that mostly causes misunderstandings, equating it with deficiency of power or capabilities.[1] In this regard, the examination of capabilities and institutions can provide a new insight into the nature of small states. The concept of smallness is often wrongly used in many academic and political settings, assuming it to mean weakness and inability. There are some authors who define small states by their capabilities, such as Rothstein, who categorizes small state as one that recognizes its inability to obtain security and hence should depend on other powers (great), international organizations, etc.[2] Thorhallsson's small state definition relies on its capabilities shaped by material resources and commonly used four criteria, like population, territory, gross domestic product (GDP), and military capacity.[3] The position of the small state in the international system can be described by the shelter theory, which defines small states' vulnerabilities through three categories: political, economic, and societal. The mentioned vulnerabilities push small states to find alliances and patrons, which can be found through the providence of political, economic, and societal shelters via large states and international organizations.[4]

The shelter theory is widely used to describe the role of small Nordic states in the international system; however, in the case of Armenia, the shelter theory can be

[1]Browning (2006), pp. 669–684.

[2]Rothstein (1968).

[3]Thorhallsson (2006), pp. 7–31.

[4]Thorhallsson and Bailes (2017), p. 52.

applied only partly. According to the shelter theory, small states seek political shelter both for military and diplomatic backing because states with "smaller populations, less absolute wealth and less territory, small states lack the self-sufficiency, resources and strategic depth needed to defend themselves, including the maintenance of adequate armed forces."[5]

Considering the fact that Armenia is a strategic ally of Russia and a member of the Collective Security Treaty Organization (CSTO), one could argue that Armenia found a political shelter in Russia-led organizations. The same shelter theory argues that alliances deter conflict, reduce the likelihood that allies are targeted, and guarantee military assistance to allies in case they are attacked;[6] however, when in April 2016 Azerbaijan launched a large scale military aggression against Nagorny Karabakh, the defense and security of Armenia were maintained by the armed forces of Armenia, not by the "shelter providers".

The political, economic, or societal shelters provided by larger powers cannot be accomplished without costs, which can be the limitation of the small partner's freedom of maneuver and choice.[7] Nevertheless, some small states have the potential to play quite unique roles in international relations "[...] because they have been able to carve out for themselves a special niche in the strategic conceptions, political doctrines, and domestic opinions of their chief ally."[8] In the Armenian case, the lack of resources and the small size of population and territory should not be considered as the sole determinants of its international engagement or integration preferences. The problem here is grounded in the political institutions of a certain state shaped by leaders or the ruling political elite, who can have some power over their state's foreign policy choices, but only if the same leaders of small states express willingness to take advantage of opportunities present in the international system.[9] Sometimes Armenia's integration preferences or the level of international engagement is derived from the interests of the ruling elite or domestic policies. For example, among other factors behind Armenia's 2013 decision to join the Customs Union (CU) and participate in the processes of formation of the Eurasian Economic Union (EAEU) were oligarchical and corrupt practices and the question of Serzh Sargsyan's regime survival, which steadily increased Armenia's dependence on Russia and limited Armenia's foreign policy choices.[10]

In the small state theory, there is another approach, according to which small states, despite various security risks, can in certain situations "act against great powers" if the territory of a certain small state is geostrategically important for the great power.[11] Laura Neack claims "small powers without such an economic

[5]Ibid, 53.

[6]Thorhallsson and Sverrir (2018).

[7]Thorhallsson and Bailes (2017), p. 54.

[8]Bobrow and Chan (1988), pp. 56–57.

[9]Maria and Harvey (1978).

[10]Ter-Matevosyan et al. (2017), p. 341.

[11]Barston (1973).

resource need to look elsewhere for ways to exploit the system and gain greater independence and they can draw on their geostrategic location for such leverage."[12] However, in the case of Armenia, the situation is quite complicated in terms of gaining greater independence. It would not be an exaggeration to argue that Armenia is the only European small state facing multidimensional security threats related to complicated regional security architecture and dependence on Russia in economic and energy sectors.

Another form of shelter is economic shelter. According to Thorhallsson, small states need economic shelter to compensate for their small domestic markets and, in some cases, resource-poor economies. The cost of economic shelter may be economic dependence on larger states.[13] If we apply the concept of economic shelter to the Armenian context, then we can argue that Armenia found economic shelter in the Russia-led Eurasian Economic Union (EAEU), which has the potential to turn into a real economic shelter if Armenia as a small state expresses its willingness to take advantage of the common market opportunities. Armenia is the only EAEU member state that simultaneously signed a new strategic document, the Comprehensive and Enhanced Partnership Agreement (CEPA), with the EU in November 2017. After ratification of the CEPA by EU member states, Armenia's access to Western markets has expanded. Thus, Armenia's economic shelter is not only strengthened, but Armenia is also sheltered by the norms and rules of the international system.

The third form of shelter is societal shelter, which is associated with innovation and the ideas of the larger states. Small states need societal shelter to diminish cultural, educational, and technological stagnation and import new technological practices from larger states.[14] Armenia's uniqueness as a small state concerns its powerful diaspora widespread around the world. The Armenian societal shelter can be provided by its own diaspora, which has started to introduce and implement of innovative projects in Armenia. The Armenian diaspora has long complimented Armenia's smallness in the international system. The social capital of the Armenian nation comes to redefine its physical and economical smallness. The existence of around eight million Armenians in diaspora across the continents can be economic, social and even diplomatic *shelter* for Armenia. The Armenian diaspora institutions with powerful lobbying capabilities provide diplomatic and soft-power support. Some components of the economic shelter are provided by the Armenian diaspora too, that is, the establishment of diaspora-based business companies in Armenia, investments in education and public health, and, of course, economic assistance and remittances sent from different diaspora centers. However, even for the engagement of the resources of diaspora, the Armenian government should create an incentive-based investment environment in Armenia which in turn may overcome the demographic challenges in the country through facilitation of repatriation. The societal shelter of a small state can also define its international status and identity. In

---

[12]Neack (2008), p. 169.

[13]Thorhallsson and Bailes (2017), p. 53.

[14]Ibid, 54.

the case of Armenia, the social capital, diaspora capabilities, and continuing growth of innovative and high technologies define Armenia's identity as "small but smart"—another powerful force capable of compensating the smallness of Armenia in the international system.

14.3 Geopolitical Opportunities and Constraints: The Nagorny Karabakh Conflict and the Blockade of Turkey and Azerbaijan

The violent conflict between Armenia and Azerbaijan over the Nagorny Karabakh, which since the Soviet Union's twilight had two active phases, from 1988 to 1994 and since 2008 till present, has visibly limited Armenia's development perspectives and constrained its strategic choices. Coined as "the most worrying unresolved conflicts in the Caucasus region," a conflict that "has polarized countries and their allies, and has also created a security vacuum that encourages the proliferation of trans-national security challenges,"[15] framed as an "enduring rivalry"[16] or "the Gordian knot preventing the transformation of this region,"[17] the conflict around Nagorny Karabakh has become one of the complex conflicts in the world.

On December 1, 1989, the Supreme Soviet of the Armenian Soviet Socialist Republic (SSR) and the Artsakh National Council adopted a joint decision on the reunification of the Armenian SSR and the mountainous region of Karabakh. In the May 1990 parliamentary elections, the Pan-Armenian National Movement came to power in Armenia, ousting the Communists from power. In August 1990, Armenia adopted its Declaration of Independence,[18] which reconfirmed the reunification decision adopted in December 1989. After a year, in September 1991, more than 98% of Armenians voted for the independence of Armenia in the referendum. The Supreme Soviet of the Azerbaijan SSR, which adopted a Declaration of Independence on August 31, 1991, based it on the idea of restoration of the "People's Republic of Azerbaijan," which existed in 1918–1920. During its short existence, Karabakh (as well as Nakhijevan) was never a constituent part of it and was a disputed territory. After some 50 days, on October 18, 1991, the constitutional act was adopted on the State Independence of the Republic of Azerbaijan.

The initial years of post-Soviet transformation in Azerbaijan were particularly impactful. From 1991 to 1993, Azerbaijan had three presidents, two interim presidents, and a number of military revolts. Each time, the removal of the president in Azerbaijan was either followed or succeeded by domestic instability and substantial territorial losses in Karabakh or in the surrounding regions.[19] Even the arrival of

[15]German (2012), pp. 216–229.

[16]Broers (2015), pp. 556–576.

[17]Oskanian (2013).

[18]Armenian Declaration of Independence, http://www.gov.am/en/independence/.

[19]Bolukbaşi (2011), pp. 179–212.

Heydar Aliyev, former leader of Soviet Azerbaijan, did not stop the territorial losses of Azerbaijan. In fact, most of the territories that Azerbaijan has lost was during his tenure. In May 1994, the military leadership of Armenia and Nagorny Karabakh agreed to Azerbaijani's requests for a ceasefire,[20] which, aside from a handful of relatively minor violations, was held until the late 2000s. The Karabakh conflict in the 1990s demonstrated that Armenia, as a small country, being surrounded by Azerbaijan and Turkey, had to possess more than weapons to win the war. Being able to find supporters and sympathizers in Russian power structures (presidential administration, parliament, and executive) and especially with security institutions—ministries of defence and national security, army generals, commanders of Russian army units stationed in Armenia and Georgia—played a crucial role in changing the power asymmetry in the Karabakh conflict. Unlike Azerbaijan, which changed the leadership frequently, Armenia was able to ensure domestic stability between 1991 and 1994—until the ceasefire agreement was signed. No less instrumental were institutional, organizational, infrastructural, human, and financial resources that the Armenian diaspora has invested in promoting Armenia's position in different countries. Acting as a societal shelter, the diaspora institutions have slowly developed *modus operandi* with Armenia's state institutions. The newly created Armenian embassies around the world received invaluable support from the diaspora institutions, which opened the power corridors of the host countries for the newly established republic. Armenian diplomatic missions in different countries and organizations were intensively engaged in a process where they had no prior experience or institutional traditions. Of course, Armenia's Ministry of Foreign Affairs (MFA) invited many ethnic Armenians around the world, especially from the Russian MFA, to join the newly created ministry; however, most of the diplomats posted aboard were recruited from the Armenian academia and universities.

Since 1992, in parallel with the intensification of the conflict in Nagorny Karabakh, the international community has started to play an intensive role in finding a solution to the conflict. The Organization for Security and Co-operation in Europe (OSCE) Minsk Group was set up, and until now it serves as the only format for negotiations. In 1997, the OSCE Minsk Group cochairmanship was established, composed of Russia, France, and the US. In 1997, the OSCE Minsk Group presented two conflict settlement options to the parties, which were coined "Package" and "Step-by-Step" solutions. Neither of them gained necessary support from the conflicting parties. Levon Ter-Petrosyan, Armenia's first president, who was opting for the "Step-by-step" solution, resigned in February 1998. Robert Kocharyan, the former president of Nagorny Karabakh, was elected president of Armenia, and he served in that position until 2008. In 2003, Heydar Aliyev died, and his son Ilham replaced him. During the initial years of his presidency, Ilham Aliyev was busy with the consolidation of his power in the country and balancing the needs of different stakeholders. The situation has changed starting from 2006–2007, with the completion of two pipelines and with the final consolidation of his power. The

[20]Croissant (1998), p. 97.

arrival of first vast revenues from the export of energy resources coincided with the frequent violations of ceasefire in the line of contact between Nagorny Karabakh and Azerbaijan. Since 2008, the Nagorny Karabakh conflict, which until then was dubbed as frozen, has ceased to be such. It was transformed into a low-intensity conflict with frequent phases of high-intensity escalation. The most violent outbreak occurred in April 2016, when the Armenian side suffered around 100 causalities, including civilians. Because of a massive attack, Karabakh lost 8 km^2 of its territory. Even though since September 2014 Azerbaijan has kept the information on combat causalities under strict control, analysis of a number of statements reveals that Azerbaijan's minor territorial gain came with a high price—between 250 and 350 deaths. The April escalation, which Armenians coined as a "Four-day war," was widely interpreted as a watershed in the modern phase of the Karabakh conflict.

The period from 2007 and 2008 was also significant for the negotiation process and for the role that international mediators started to play. In November 2007, the Madrid principles were introduced to the conflicting parties, but they were not made public. Between 2008 and 2013, three presidents of the OSCE Minsk cochairmanship have adopted five joint statements (in L'Aquilla, Muskoka, Deauville, Los Cabos, and Enniskillen,) urging the leaders of Armenia and Azerbaijan to demonstrate political will and move forward with the signing of the basic principles of the conflict settlement. The joint statements also revealed a part of the basic principles that were at the core of Madrid proposals. They included a) the return of the occupied territories surrounding Nagorny Karabakh, b) the interim status for Nagorny Karabakh guaranteeing security and self-governance, c) a corridor linking Armenia to Nagorny Karabakh, d) the final status of Nagorny Karabakh to be determined in the future by a legally binding expression of will, d) the right of all internally displaced persons and refugees to return, e) international security guarantees, including (which would include) a peacekeeping operation.[21]

In the same period, Russia was intensively involved in the negotiations. Between 2008 and 2001, Russian President Dmitrij Medvedev invested a substantial amount of time and resources to hold trilateral meetings with Aliyev and Serzh Sargsyan, who was elected as Armenia's president in February 2008. During three years, nine trilateral summits were held. Thanks to Medvedev's efforts, for the first time since 1994, Sargsyan and Aliyev adopted a joint declaration in the Meyendorff Castle, not far from Moscow, in November 2008.[22] It aimed to initiate a number of confidence-building measures to improve the security in the region. Medvedev's active involvement in the negotiation process was meant to yield tangible results in June 2011, when he invited two presidents to Kazan to sign the document on the basic principles. However, despite Medvedev's hopes and assurances and the pressure of the international community, the leaders failed to agree on the previously

[21] Statement by the OSCE Minsk Group Co-Chair countries, *L'Aquila*, 10 July 2009, https://www.osce.org/mg/51152. Accessed 20 Jan 2020.

[22] The Presidents of Armenia, Azerbaijan, and Russia signed a declaration on the resolution of the Nagorny Karabakh conflict, President of Armenia, https://goo.gl/ptsQRR. Accessed 20 Jan 2020.

negotiated principles.[23] According to different accounts, during the meeting, Aliyev presented around ten reservations and conditions to resume the negotiations and sign the basic principles.[24] The process came to a halt, and the international community became deeply skeptical about the conflict-resolution prospects.

Since the failure in Kazan in 2011 until April 2016, the presidents of the two countries had met only a few times. The meetings were held in the atmosphere of mutual distrust and lack of confidence. The Armenian side insists on the principles of international law, particularly the nonuse of force or the threat of force, equal rights and self-determination of peoples, and territorial integrity.[25] The Azerbaijani size, instead, prefers only the territorial integrity principle, downplaying other core principles of international law.[26] The Armenian side has also repeatedly endorsed the confidence-building measures proposed by the cochairs on the consolidation of ceasefire, withdrawal of the snipers from the line of contact, and establishment of a mechanism for investigation of the ceasefire violations.[27] However, periodical obstructing of the confidence-building measures by Azerbaijan and frequent provocations on the line of contact with Nagorny Karabakh and on the border with Armenia, which resulted in new casualties, have visibly limited the possibility of finding a working consensus on the most basic principles of joint work. No less exacerbating is the fact of the drastic increase of Azerbaijan's military budget, which has changed the conflict dynamics. The military buildup in Azerbaijan initiated unparalleled arms race with Armenia. Armenia's security policy became containment and keeping the military balance in check.[28]

The change of government in Armenia through public protests in April–May 2018, which the leaders have coined "peaceful, non-violent, velvet revolution," created a new hope among the members of the international community that the new government of Armenia will provide new stimulus to the peace talks between conflicting states over Nagorny Karabakh. The change of power has somehow influenced the negotiation processes as Armenia's new Prime Minister Pashinyan resurrected a claim to bring back the representatives of Nagorno Karabakh to the negotiation process. On various platforms he has reiterated the final solution of the

---

[23]Russia's Medvedev 'Frustrated' with Karabakh, Radio Liberty, https://www.azatutyun.am/a/24247967.html. Accessed 20 Jan 2020.

[24]V MID Armenii raz'jasnili slova Lavrova: rech' shla o kazanskom dokumente [Armenia MFA clarified the words of Lavrov: He was referring to the Kazan documents], https://regnum.ru/news/2113938.html. Accessed 20 Jan 2020.

[25]Statement by H.E. Mr. Edward Nalbandian, Minister of Foreign Affairs of the Republic of Armenia at the 24th Meeting of the OSCE Ministerial Council, Vienna, December 2017, https://goo.gl/iKjXsA. Accessed 20 Jan 2020.

[26]Ilham Aliyev: Azerbaijan's territorial integrity supported by whole world, https://goo.gl/PxDVcw. Accessed 20 Jan 2020.

[27]Address of Foreign Minister of Armenia Edward Nalbandian at the Stockholm International Peace Research Institute (SIPRI), 26 November 2014, MFA of Armenia, https://goo.gl/R3qDh1. Accessed 20 Jan 2020.

[28]Minasyan (2016).

Karabakh conflict should be acceptable to the people of Armenia, Artsakh as well as Azerbaijan. He has also been sending signals to the Azerbaijani society urging to build peace. His wife has been no less vocal to demonstrate the desire for peace. However, he has also made several other statements that were not consistent with his previous positions.

It bears mentioning that Azerbaijan's strategic partner, Turkey, has also exacerbated the situation by unreservedly supporting Azerbaijan. For the last 27 years, numerous initiatives have tried to find ways of normalization of bilateral relations between Armenia and Turkey, but the two countries still have no diplomatic relations, and the border remains hermetically sealed.[30] The closed border and the nonexistence of diplomatic relations, which are widely seen as the last reminders of the Cold War era in Europe, significantly hinder the development of Armenia. With closed border in the west and mined borders in the east, Armenia is one of the rare states in the world that has more than 80% of its borders sealed. Armenia has only two open borders—Georgia (219 km) in the north and Iran (44 km) in the south.

14.4 Relations with Russia and the EU

In parallel with the stand-off in the Karabakh conflict, Armenia chose to deepen its strategic partnership with Russia, which has also become an important trade partner and political ally in major international organizations and policy forums. Being a strategic ally of Russia and a CSTO member state, Armenia continues to rely heavily on military assistance from Moscow. Russia provides Armenia credits to purchase weapons, and Armenia buys weapons mainly from Russia at discount prices. In addition, Armenia and Russia have worked to create the Caucasus Unified Air Defense System as well as a joint Russian and Armenia military group. The 102nd Russian military base (around 5000 personnel) in Gyumri, the lease of which Russia extended to 2044, and its air-force component, the 3624th airbase (squadron size) in Erebuni Airport in Yerevan, belong to the Southern Military District of the Russian Federation. The border control division of the Federal Security Service (FSS) of the Russian Federation, together with Armenian partners, protects Armenia's borders with Turkey and Iran. Armenia, in its turn, helped Russia in its military operation in Syria by deploying humanitarian mission in Aleppo. The Aleppo mission, is composed of doctors and 83 *deminers, and the personnel ensuring their safety (military police) was sent in February 2019. The mission will conduct its activities in the Armenian*-populated areas and the territory adjacent to the group's base.[31] It needs to be added that since 2004, Armenia has deployed peacekeepers in Kosovo, Afghanistan, and Lebanon.

---

[30]Grigoryan et al. (2019), pp. 25–43.

[31]"The Aleppo Mission: Armenian Experts' First Week," *Mediamax*, February 19, 2019, https://bit.ly/2T7miUO.

Meanwhile, Armenia has intensified its relations with Europe, too. One of the central initiatives of the last ten years started in 2009, when the EU and Armenia, along with five other Eastern European countries (Azerbaijan, Belarus, Moldova, Georgia, and Ukraine), launched the Eastern Partnership (EaP) with the main goal of creating necessary conditions to accelerate political association and further economic integration between the EU and participant states. For the next four years, following the objectives of the EaP declaration, the Armenian government carried out a series of political and socioeconomic reforms aimed to facilitate approximation toward the EU.

However, on September 3, 2013, the president of Armenia shifted the long-praised process of initialing political association and economic integration with the European Union and announced Armenia's decision to join the Russia-led Customs Union and participate in the processes of formation of the EAEU. Practitioners and observers interpreted it either as a U-turn or as a surprise move, mainly assuming that what happened was the result of Russian pressure on Armenia. However, when tensions and uncertainty eased, it became obvious that what happened was a result of complex reasons. Geopolitical constraints and sociopolitical problems that had accumulated in Armenia during recent years coincided with an assertive expansion of Russia's foreign policy.[32] The EAEU came to be formally operative on January 1, 2015. The next day, Armenia became a member of the EAEU, which is currently comprised of five states from the post-Soviet era (Russia, Belarus, Armenia, Kazakhstan, and Kyrgyzstan).

In this context, any observer would assume that Armenia lost its interest in the European Union. However, the Armenian government hardly abandoned the idea of finding a working deal with the European Union; the latter also was not interested in letting Armenia go. After years of negotiations, Armenia and the EU signed a new strategic document, Comprehensive and Enhanced Partnership Agreement (CEPA), in November 2017, which many interpreted as the tailor-made version of the Association Agreement that Armenia and the EU were planning to sign in Vilnius in 2013. In the following months, both Russia and the EU praised Armenia for carefully maneuvering between different power centers and for successfully completing the partnership agreement with the EU. After signing the deal, the Armenian government officials often emphasized that unlike Georgia, Ukraine, and Moldova, Armenia was able to expand its relations with the EU without harming its relations with Russia.

In addition to foreign policy determinants, the Armenian domestic politics had also impacted its integration preferences. To understand Armenia's decision to side with the Eurasian Economic Union, the socioeconomic consequences of the global financial-economic crisis in 2008 and 2009 should also be considered. Experiencing one of the dramatic declines in the world, it took several years for Armenia to recover from the economic downturn. Substantial decline of foreign direct investment (FDI) since 2008, heavy taxation policy on small and medium enterprises, the size of the

[32]Ter-Matevosyan et al. (2017), pp. 340–360.

shadow economy, abundant monopolies in various import and export sectors, and many other factors (dependence on a limited number of commodity exports, a difficult external economic environment, etc.) caused Armenia's economy to be both fragile and sensitive to external instabilities. These trends intensified the labor migration, which headed mainly to Russia. According to the Federal State Statistics Service of the Russian Federation, 200,000 Armenian citizens went to Russia between 2008 and 2013. Chronically, the Armenian economy has been heavily dependent on remittances coming mostly from Russia, equal to USD 1.5 billion, or 15% of Armenia's GDP. The purchasing power of the population, trade turnover, and service sectors have dramatically suffered. As the Russian economy entered into a decline, private money transfers to Armenia declined by 30%, or USD 520 million, in 2014. Private remittances received from Russia reduced by another 36% in 2015 (USD 916 million), though still comprising 76% of the total noncommercial money transfers to Armenia. Naturally, the slowdown in domestic demand also affected unemployment in the respective countries, which grew to 18.5% in Armenia in 2015. Meanwhile, many Armenians working in Russia lost their jobs or earned less because of the devaluation of the ruble. Armenia's slow recovery from the 2008–2009 economic crisis and a number of sluggish economic, structural, and social reforms increased the poverty rate in the country. As a result, the percentage of the population living below the poverty line reached 35.4% in 2011, up from 27.6% in 2008. In 2017, according to the most recent data revealed by the Statistical Committee, the poverty rate was down to 25.7%.[33] In other words, in 2017, around 766,000 people (out of 2.8 mln) in Armenia earned less than 41,162 Armenian dram per month (78 EUR).

Armenian export volumes have increased after Armenia joined the EAEU in 2015. In 2016, Armenian exports to EAEU countries increased by 53%, compared to the previous year, equaling USD 392.1 million, of which USD 371 million went to Russia. The latter remained the principal foreign trade partner for Armenia. The export volumes to that country has increased even further in 2017 and 2018: USD 557 million and USD 666 million respectively.[34] Armenia's export to Russia was composed of beverages, spirits, textile, clothes, food, cigarettes, precious stones, metals, etc.

[33]Statistical Committee of the Republic of Armenia, 2018, https://www.armstat.am/file/article/poverty_2017_a_2.pdf. Accessed 20 Jan 2020.

[34]Statistics Committee of the Republic of Armenia. Foreign Trade Volumes. https://www.armstat.am/am/?nid=717&thid%5B%5D=643&years%5B%5D=2017&submit=%D5%93%D5%B6%D5%BF%D6%80%D5%A5%D5%AC. Accessed 20 Jan 2020.

14.5 Conclusions

Traditionally, smallness has usually been perceived as a major disadvantage for Armenia. For a long time, physical size, geopolitical volatility, and conflicts have limited Armenia's "manoeuvring front" and specter of alternatives. The chapter discussed how the protracted conflict in Nagorny Karabakh and the blockade imposed by Turkey and Azerbaijan have visibly constrained Armenia's foreign and security policy choices. These limitations have also shaped Armenia's regional and transregional perceptions viewing the existing reality as an insurmountable challenge. Poor democratic practices and underdeveloped institutions made them even more vulnerable to foreign policy influences.

The chapter also examined the applicability of the shelter theory to the Armenian context. Political, economic, and societal vulnerabilities of small states push them to find alliances and shelters with large states and international organizations. The theory, the chapter argued, can be applied to Armenia; however, it requires certain efforts of elaboration. Armenia's experience of state building since the early 1990s demonstrated a heavy reliance on the discourse of securitization, which shaped both domestic and foreign policy orientations. The political-military shelter provided by Russia was instrumental, but certain peculiarities were attached to it. Russia's chaotic and impactful transformation in the 1990s made Armenia look for parallel shelters, especially for economic and societal ones. Thus, diversifying political and economic shelters became necessity rather than a policy choice. The benefits it received complemented the Russian shelter. By the mid-2000s, when Russia regained its international status and started to reposition itself as a global player, Armenia's geopolitical challenges and regional hostile environment did not change much. Turkey and Azerbaijan continued Armenia's blockade, leaving it out from regional energy and transportation projects. The Karabakh conflict also remained unresolved; moreover, since 2008, it has gradually escalated. In addition to these, because of mismanagement of institutional and economic reforms, Armenia's development showed obvious signs of weakness and sluggishness. Against these drawbacks and realities, Armenia started to narrow down its "shelter search perimeter." Because Russia started to promote its regional and global integration agendas, Armenia's leadership felt more secure to return to the same political and economic shelter. Russia, in essence, provided both. The societal shelter, however, differed as the Armenian diaspora institutions in different countries have provided alternative platforms against the Russian Armenian diaspora. Competition and various levels of engagement have changed the power dynamics among different diaspora institutions. The Russian Armenian diaspora, albeit influential, was not the only one to cope with.

References

Barston RP (1973) The other powers: studies in the foreign policies of small states. George Allen and Unwin Ltd, London

Bobrow DB, Chan S (1988) Simple labels and complex realities: national security for the third world. In: Azar EE, Chung-in M (eds) National security in the third world: the management of internal and external threats. Edward Elgar, Aldershot, pp 56–57

Bolukbaşi S (2011) Azerbaijan: a political history. I. B. Tauris, London & New York, pp 179–212

Broers L (2015) From "frozen conflict" to enduring rivalry: reassessing the Nagorny Karabakh conflict. Nationalities Pap 43(4):556–576

Browning C (2006) Small, smart and salient? Rethinking identity in the small states literature. Camb Rev Int Aff 19(4):669–684

Croissant M (1998) The Armenia-Azerbaijan Conflict: causes and implications. Praeger, Westport, p 97

German T (2012) The Nagorny-Karabakh Conflict between Azerbaijan and Armenia: security issues in the Caucasus. J Muslim Minority Aff 32(2):216–229

Grigoryan A, Khachatryan K, Ter-Matevosyan V (2019) Armenia-Turkey border opening: what determines the attitude of Armenians? Caucasus Survey 7(1):25–43

Maria P, Harvey S (1978) Opportunity, willingness, and small states: the relationship between environment and foreign policy. In: Hermann CF, Kegley CW, Rosenau JN (eds) New directions in the study of foreign policy. Unwin Hyman, Winchester

Minasyan S (2016) Sderzhivanie v karabahskom konflikte [Containment in the Karabakh conflict]. Caucasus Institute, Yerevan

Neack L (2008) The new foreign policy: power seeking in a globalized era. Rowman & Littlefield Publishers, p 169

Oskanian K (2013) Fear, weakness and power in the post-Soviet South Caucasus. Palgrave Macmillan, Basingstoke

Rothstein RL (1968) Alliances and small powers. Columbia University Press, New York and London

Ter-Matevosyan V, Drnoian A, Mkrtchyan M, Yepremyan T (2017) Armenia in the Eurasian Economic Union: reasons for joining and its consequences. Eurasian Geogr Econ 58(3):341

Thorhallsson B (2006) The size of states in the European Union: theoretical and conceptual perspectives. J Eur Integr 28(1):7–31

Thorhallsson B, Bailes AJK (2017) Do small states need 'alliance shelter'? Scotland and the Nordic nations. In: Andrew WN (ed) Security in a small nation: Scotland, democracy, politics. Open Book Publishers, Cambridge, p 52

Thorhallsson B, Sverrir St (2018) The theory of shelter. Paper presented at the Conference 'Small States and the New Security Environment'. University of Iceland, Reykjavik, 26 June 2018, SSANSE Project policy briefs

Vahram Ter-Matevosyan holds a Dr. Phil. in History, University of Bergen, Norway. He is associate professor and program chair of the Political Science and International Affairs Program at the American University of Armenia. His research interests cover Armenia's foreign and security policy and Turkish domestic and foreign policy issues.

Narek Mkrtchyan has a Ph.D in World History, Yerevan State University. Narek Mkrtchyan is an adjunct lecturer at the American University of Armenia. His research interests are in post-Soviet (Central Asian) nation and state building, as well as small state studies. Narek Mkrtchyan is a member of the National Assembly of the Republic of Armenia.

Chapter 15
Qatar's Military Power and Diplomacy: The Emerging Roles of Small States in International Relations

Brahim Saidy

15.1 Introduction

Qatar, a small country in the Arabian Gulf, comprises an area of 11,437 sq km with a population of 2.7 million. It holds the third-largest natural gas reserves in the world, and its population enjoys the world's highest per capita income. It is regarded as the most advanced state in terms of human development among Arab countries. Although Qatar is identified as a small state, size was not a potential constraint to find a way to position itself internationally. Qatar has attracted considerable regional and international attention within the past two decades. It has been able to punch above its weight through its aligned interests and gained freedom of action within a geopolitical environment dominated by regional and global actors. Qatar does not break the tradition of the small state when it comes to military power. Its strategy is focused on self-defense and sheltering and not neutrality. In the context of Middle East conflicts, it is not possible for Qatar to choose to stay neutral because such status could be not recognized by neighboring states and powers in the region and would not provide it with guarantees to deter aggression and avoid access to its territory.

This chapter investigates Qatar's strategy of resilience as a relevant foreign policy tool. Resilience is a common concept, useful for identifying how a state deals with political, economic, and social challenges and threats. How does Qatar deal with its vulnerabilities and maintain its national interests? To what extent can it handle various security and diplomatic challenges? To answer these questions, this chapter will look at Qatar's defense strategy with a focus on self-defense capabilities, bandwagoning, and military shelter. The chapter will also examine Qatar's use of mechanisms of soft power as a tool for foreign policy, specifically the use of

B. Saidy (✉)
Qatar University, Doha, Qatar
e-mail: brahim.saidy@qu.edu.qa

A.-M. Brady, B. Thorhallsson (eds.), *Small States and the New Security Environment*, The World of Small States 7,
https://doi.org/10.1007/978-3-030-51529-4_15

mediation, multilateral cooperation, and public diplomacy to enhance its global reputation.

15.2 Counterbalancing Smallness

Smallness weighs heavily on the defense policy choices of any small state. It explains small state security behavior, which most often ranges from balancing and bandwagoning to participation in military alliances. Small states tend to rely on self-defense capability, superpowers for protection and security partnerships and employ diplomatic and economic resources to ensure their survival. Being small "has been viewed as a handicap to state action and even state survival."[1] Beyond the differences or even disagreements between scholars regarding "what a small state is and how to conceptualise it analytically,"[2] the criteria commonly used in the discipline of international relations to categorize small state is fundamentally derived from the "concept of size." This concept refers to quantitative criteria and qualitative criteria. The first is the state's physical size, which includes the geographic size, population size, economic development size, and military capability size.[3] The second relies on foreign policy behavior and the abilities of the small state to show involvement in international affairs. In this regard, Matthias Maass notes that this definition based on behavior patterns introduces a normative element into the conceptualization of small states. For Maass, the characteristics of this behavior are "the support for International Law, working multilaterally and through international organisations, the reliance on diplomacy and the rejection of the use of force."[4] In fact, the quantitative approach and the qualitative one are interconnected and complementary.[5] In the words of Máté Szalai, "the quantitative approach – in which a small state's primary attribute is its scarcity of resources – translates the notion of size as a measurable variable, while the qualitative approach basically puts an equality sign between smallness and weakness."[6]

The criteria used by these two approaches have a direct impact on the defense policy of the small state. For example, the indicator of population size means that a country with a small population would lack the necessary manpower for its armed forces. Small states will have trouble competing with those that have a large army. A small state is condemned to have a modest military, which creates a recruitment problem and requires a specific policy to deal with military conscription. The issue is to find the appropriate way to "maximize almost all its potential manpower, and thus

[1]Browning (2006), p. 669.

[2]Maass (2009), p. 65.

[3]Ólafsson (1998).

[4]Maass (2009), p. 79.

[5]Ibid, 80.

[6]Szalai (2015), p. 2.

to deploy forces of a size which might compensate for their inherent demographic inferiority."[7] In addition, the small state's geographic size may affect the strategic thinking of the small state government and is one of the most important element to constrain military operations. It puts the small state at risk of lack of strategic depth and imposes limitations on addressing direct threats. It also has implications for organizing the structure of the army in accordance with a specific concept of territorial defence and military commandment. Obviously, space limitations affect a small state's defense policy objectives, including the ways in which the small state feels constrained by such limitations in seeking to adapt to its environment, and it may hinder or limit attempts to obtain some degree of security guaranties through the mechanisms of alliances and defense diplomacy.

The small state is more vulnerable compared with the large state. Robert Rothstein notes: "A small power is a state which recognizes that it cannot obtain security primarily by use of its own capabilities and that it must rely fundamentally on the aid of other states, institutions, processes or developments to do so."[8] In the same vein, Annette Fox wrote: "We can think of small states as those whose leaders recognize that their own stat's political weight is limited to a local arena rather than a global one, that they are dependent upon outside political forces for much of their security, and that their particular state's interest may be dispensable in the eyes of one or more great powers."[9]

In order to overcome the challenges imposed by vulnerability, a small state generally considers four things. First, a small state attempts to take as many measures as possible for self-reliance, which is reflected in a strategy to maximize whatever internal resources may be available to maintain an army capable of defending the country from the enemies. Second, the most obvious survival strategy is to find one or more stronger states capable of providing shelter and to join a military alliance that consists of direct and visible diplomatic and military backing "at any time of need by another state or by an international or regional organization."[10] Bailes calls this strategy "bandwagoning": "requiring the protégé to align its behavior with the sponsor's and perhaps to pay more concretely, for example by accepting bases on its territory."[11] In that sense, Qatar's relations with Turkey and the USA are the result of "bandwagoning." Third, a small state, motivated by its desire for survival, considers the option of "balancing" to avoid being dominated or threatened by a hostile neighbor and also to reduce overdependence on a single ally.[12] Fourth, a small state has another alternative: to declare neutrality, nonalignment, or nonallied status between competing power blocs. However, Bailes says that

[7]Cohen (1995), p. 89.
[8]Rothstein (1968), p. 29.
[9]Fox (1969), pp. 751–752.
[10]Bailes et al. (2006), p. 14.
[11]Bailes (2015), p. 23.
[12]Ibid, 24.

the cost of this option is high in terms of "building an independent defense capabilities to deter violations of neutrality."[13]

It follows from the above that Qatar is in a process of modernization in order to counterbalance its "smallness" by maximizing its resources for military and diplomatic purposes. Qatar's resilience strategy[14] has proved to be very adaptive to the changing of international system and developed mechanisms to defend the country's sovereignty and territorial integrity in every situation. As a small state, Qatar's military power is on the defensive and is entirely focused on its own survival; likewise, its diplomacy is operating to balance and counterbalance threats and challenges generated by the regional and international system (Table 15.1).

15.3 Military Power

For an analytical perspective, smallness is implicit in the many differences in the way that Qatar sees its military power relative to other countries and its strategy of resilience. Qatar is involved in a number of bilateral and multilateral military partnerships. It has a close real-world military cooperation with the US, along with Britain and France. Military links with Russia, while not negligible, remain limited. Like other Gulf monarchies, Qatar looks primarily to the US for security guarantees. In 1992, Qatar and the United States concluded a Defense Pact, which is reviewed and renewed every ten years.[15] Qatar relies heavily on the assistance of Western powers for its security and defense as regional organizations such as the Arab League and Gulf Cooperation Council (GCC) have failed to establish a mechanism of collective defense for its members. In fact, the absence of a real regional military integration pushed Qatar to seek other security options provided by external power through bilateral security agreements. The credibility and efficiency of this option were proven during the Gulf War (August 2, 1990–February 28, 1991) when the United States of America formed a coalition force from 35 nations to liberate Kuwait against the Iraqi invasion.

This choice is useful for defense preparedness because it has positive impacts on Qatari armed forces in terms of training, interoperability, and access to military advanced technology. For any strategy of resilience, defense preparedness refers to programs of joint military exercises to achieve interoperability, which allows forces, units, or systems to operate together and improve the ability of different armies to conduct joint operations. The programs of training, education, and joint exercises have brought Qatari officers very close to many Western armed forces. This interaction is carried out through three mechanisms: bilateral military exercises, GCC-US

[13]Ibid, 24.

[14]Abdullah Baabood, "Qatar's Resilience Strategy and Implications for State-Society Relations," IAI Working Papers, Roma, December 2017.

[15]Saidy (2017), pp. 286–299.

Table 15.1 Characteristics of Qatar as a small state

Criteria	Vulnerability	Resilience
Military power	• Cannot defend itself against external threats, i.e., based on its own power • High reliance on external support • High dependence on arms acquisition from foreign suppliers • Small standing army, combined with low war potential	– Alliance shelter relationships with Turkey – Military agreement with the United States of America (signed in 1992, renewed twice each time for a decade: Dec. 2002 and Dec. 2013) – Military cooperation with Western countries (namely, France, the United Kingdom ...) and NATO – Program of joint military exercises to achieve interoperability and enhance effectiveness of the Qatari army – Presence of foreign military bases on Qatari soil – Ambitious plan to develop a Qatari military industry – Defense procurement policy based on the acquisition of advanced military technology – Mandatory military service: Law n.5 (2014)
Diplomacy	• Little influence on the balance of power • Chronic regional instability and uncertainty in the Gulf due to succession issues, internal politics, regional conflicts, terrorism, lack of democracy and human rights... • Intra-Gulf tensions (e.g., blockade imposed on Qatar in 2017 by Saudi Arabia, the United Arab Emirates, Bahrain, and Egypt)	– Dynamic and active diplomacy: Qatar has mediated a number of regional conflicts in Africa and the Middle East – Strong public diplomacy: Qatar relies on public diplomacy as a tool for its foreign policy in order to build its regional and international profiles through, especially, media, culture, and sport – Large scopes of interests and relations beyond neighboring and regional areas – Active presence and participation in international organizations and strong support for international law – Qatar's diplomacy tends to maximize gains rather than to minimize risks

Source: The author

military exercises, US military exercises in the Middle East in which the Qatari army takes part; and military cooperation with the North Atlantic Treaty Organization (NATO).[16] Qatar's objectives in conducting these combined military exercises are in

[16]Qatar has joined NATO's Istanbul Cooperation Initiative (ICI), launched at the Alliance's Summit in the Turkish city in June 2004. The ICI is framework for practical cooperation in the security field addressed to the countries of the Gulf Cooperation Council. On 16 January 2018,

harmony with its defense policy, seeking close partnership with the armed forces of Western countries. It aims to maintain modern equipment, well-trained and motivated personnel with enough capabilities to provide minimal border defense, and air and maritime security. In general, the Qatari army as a small army has made interoperability an important strategic goal in all its military partnerships to enable it to operate successfully and enhance its effectiveness.

The strategy of resilience in Qatar's experience as a small state also includes the presence of foreign military bases on Qatari soil, which are used to deter or repel a direct attack and maintain regional balance. This dates back to the aftermath of the Gulf War in 1991, when Qatar granted US forces substantial access to military facilities. Qatar hosts two US military bases: the As Sayliyah, which houses the prepositioned equipment of the US Central Command (CENTCOM), and the Al Udeid Air Base, which is estimated to accommodate a total of 10,000 troops and 140 aircraft. Qatar invested $1 billion in the 1990s to expand Al Udeid Air Base. The US Army uses this base as an important store of war reserve materials in the Middle East, and it is a critical logistical hub for regional operations. In parallel, Qatar also hosts a Turkish military base, which was activated following the blockade imposed on Qatar on June 5, 2017, by Saudi Arabia, the United Arab Emirates (UAE), Bahrain, Mauritania, Maldives, Djibouti, Comoros, Jordan, Senegal, and Egypt, citing allegations of Qatari government support for terrorism. After two days of this blockade, Turkey's Parliament approved an agreement to establish a military base in Qatar. The agreement is reciprocal, allowing for Qatari army personnel and aircraft to be stationed in Turkey.[17] Currently, there are more than 30,000 Turkish soldiers stationed in Qatar. In 2018, the two countries signed an agreement to establish a naval base. The Turkish military presence was crucial to avoid military aggression against Qatar. This is why the withdrawal of Turkish troops from Qatar was drafted in the list of demands by the blockading countries as a step toward ending the Gulf crisis. In general, the presence of these military facilities on Qatari soil is an important power projection, and it is welcomed by the local population due to the protection it could afford in case of war and its role to act as a response to any incitement to attack. The facilities contribute to the external and internal security of its host. It is used as a security shield and to send a message from Doha to its powerful near neighbors in the Gulf, especially Saudi Arabia and the UAE.

In addition, the other aspect of this strategy of resilience relates to the way by which Qatar acquires the necessary equipment (military items such as weapon systems and nonmilitary items) and services that allow its armed forces to fulfill their missions. The strategy adopted by Qatar to meet its needs in terms of defense procurement was and is still based on acquisition of advanced military technology with special procedures for choosing suppliers. Over the last 20 years, Qatar has

---

Qatar has signed individual security agreements with NATO for exchange of classified information and for deeper bilateral cooperation focusing on interoperability and building capacity, and supporting defence and security reform.

[17]Aras and Akpınar (2017), p. 4.

spent massively on advanced military systems and infrastructure, but sometimes beyond the operational capacity of the national forces. Qatar is planning to spend billions of dollars to increase its military power, particularly its air force capabilities, but it faces a staffing shortage. Amid the ongoing Gulf crisis, Doha had signed on June 14, 2017, a $12-billion deal to purchase 36 F-15 fighter jets from Washington. The F-15 is one the most powerful fighter jets in the world, designed to gain and maintain air superiority in aerial confrontation. In addition, Qatar concluded a contract with BAE Systems valued at around 5 billion pounds ($6.7 billion) to buy 24 Typhoon combat aircraft, and another deal was reached with France to buy 12 Dassault Rafale.

Qatari weapon systems are very dependent on French, US, and British suppliers. Qatar has built up its defence capabilities over time to acquire an adequate defense adapted to the size of its army and territory. Its procurement policy has evolved many times since the country gained independence in 1971; it has been shaped by relationships with three major suppliers: the UK, France, and the US. The country kept up high defense spending for sophisticated and extremely costly weapon systems. In addition, Qatari's military procurement is deeply related to the question of interoperability. Given that Qatar is wholly dependent on Western countries to provide it with weapons, training, and equipment, it is in its interest to keep a more unified defense capability in order not to impede interoperability and not undermine cooperation with suppliers. This variation allows for greater interoperability in the event of conflict and for joint military exercises. The main concern for Qatar is to find a way to absorb advanced military technology that it is going to acquire in the coming years into an effective armed forces in order to complete its military modernization.

The Qatari defense industry is still underdeveloped. It relies on OEMs (original equipment manufacturers) to enhance its capabilities. In 2018, the country established Barzan Holdings as the first defense company for investment in the military industry. This company acts also as an advisor for the Ministry of Defense with respect to military procurement by providing research and development as well as knowledge transfer for this purpose. Qatar needs to create the right environment for a national defense industry that should be embedded in a knowledge economy.

Finally, the smallness also affects the size of the army and creates particular challenges for military recruitment. In this regard, the size of the Qatari army—in terms of number of personnel—represented a critical issue. Qatar maintains a small but professional army of approximately 27,500 men, including active-duty troops and reserves. It maintains its status as a major Gulf military power by keeping modern equipment and well-trained and motivated personnel with enough capabilities to achieve the missions of border defense, air, and maritime security. The modest size of the military poses a recruitment problem, and there are difficulties in attracting the local population to join the army, and for that reason mandatory service was implemented. In 2014, Qatar's government approved Law No. 5, which introduces mandatory military service for male Qataris between the ages of 18 and 35 years. The legislation aims to enhance the country's defense preparedness by mobilizing Qataris for the defense of the country and to ensure a regular army that could be backed up, if necessary, by reservists. The Qatari army, which received substantial British support from its inception after the independence in 1971, has long engaged national officers and expatriates from Sunni Muslim countries (especially Sudan, Pakistan, and Yemen). The current Qatari military doctrine aims to achieve a significant change in the military balance in the Gulf. This decision is part of a strategy of defense modernization and reflects the idea that the major advantage of mandatory military service is that it can serve as a powerful agent of socialization by bringing together young men from disparate socioeconomic background and helping to integrate them into a real community through training and shared experiences.

15.4 Diplomacy

Qatar has become "the poster illustration of how a small state can upgrade its diplomatic reputation" by using a set of conventional and unconventional techniques to rebrand itself.[18] Since the 1995 peaceful coup ending his father's reign, Sheik Hamad bin Khalifa Al Thani has attempted to follow an innovative diplomatic role for his country, shifting Qatar's foreign policy agenda away from the hegemony and the influence of its much larger neighbor, Saudi Arabia, and to place it on the world map. Sheikh Hamad has adopted a strategy of modernization with wide-sweeping political, economic, social, and media reforms. In mid-2013, he abdicated power to his son, the current Emir Tamim bin Hamad, who continued his father's policy with a pragmatic attitude toward regional and global powers. Taking advantage of its enormous wealth from natural resources, Qatar's diplomacy relies on mediation, conflict resolution, peacemaking, and public diplomacy.

Over the last two decades, mediation took on a prominent role in Qatar's foreign policy. According to Article 7 of Qatar's 2003 Constitution, Qatari foreign policy "is based on the principle of strengthening international peace and security by means of encouraging peaceful resolution of international disputes." Mediation is "a process whereby a third party assists two or more parties, with their consent, to prevent, manage or resolve a conflict by helping them to develop mutually acceptable agreements."[19] Akpinar notes that "an ideal mediator is a neutral entity that lacks any prior interest in the outcome of a mediation process. As such, neutrality is a primary principle in mediation. However, the literature largely ignores the fact that when the mediator is a state, mediation often becomes a tool of foreign policy, if not the foreign policy itself."[20] In this regard, Qatar's ultimate goal as a mediator was not always solely altruism or to end conflict but to counterbalance its smallness and to

---

[18]Cooper and Momani (2011), p. 117.

[19]United Nations, United Nations Guidance for Effective Mediation, September 2012, http://peacemaker.un.org/sites/peacemaker.un.org/files/GuidanceEffectiveMediation_UNDPA2012%28english%29_0.pdf (accessed 15 February 2019).

[20]Akpınar (2015), p. 253.

develop soft power. Mediation is used as a resilience strategy to enhance Qatar's reputation, legitimacy, and prestige in the regional and international arena.

Qatar took a number of mediator roles, some of which have been successful, while others have proved ineffective. Recently, in January 2019, Doha hosted peace negotiations between the United States and the Taliban in order to put an end to the 17-year Afghanistan war and engage in intra-Afghan dialogue. This mediation led to a "draft peace deal," stipulating the withdrawal of foreign forces from Afghanistan within 18 months of the agreement being signed.

US special envoy Zalmay Khalilzad thanked the government of Qatar for "their constructive engagement and their facilitation of this round of talks."[21] Qatar has long had close contacts with the Taliban, who consider Doha as a "neutral" place to meet with Washington. In June 2013, the Taliban officially opened their office in Doha, one year after the role of Qatar in arranging a prisoner exchange in which five Taliban detainees were released from the US in return for the freedom of captured US Army Sgt. Bowe Bergdahl. At that moment, US Secretary of State John Kerry said that the deal "exemplifies how vital our partnership with Qatar is and will remain."[22]

Qatar has mediated a number of conflicts in Lebanon, Syria, Yemen, Sudan, and Libya and between Israel and Palestine. In September 2014, following Qatar's mediation, a group of 45 peacekeepers held hostage by Syrian Al-Nusra Front was released. They were part of the UN's Disengagement Observer Force, which has been monitoring the demarcation line between Syria and the Israeli-occupied Golan Heights since 1974. The Qatari Foreign Ministry maintained that its mediation "came out of Qatar's belief in the principles of humanity," and "Qatar will spare no effort to harness all its potential and diplomatic mechanisms to maintain life."[23] Additionally, in March 2014, Qatar successfully negotiated the release of a group of 13 nuns and three maids held by rebels in Syria for more than three months. They were kidnapped from the Christian town of Maaloula north of Damascus by al-Qaeda affiliate Jabhat al-Nusra. Qatar also paid ransom money as part of the deal.

In Sudan, Qatar has put considerable resources into the resolution of the conflict in Darfur. Doha hosted negotiations between the Sudanese government and Darfur's Justice and Equality Movement, which resulted in a peace agreement in 2011. The Darfur conflict erupted in March 2003 with armed attacks by the Sudan Liberation Movement and the Justice and Equality Movement against the government of Sudan, which they accused of negligence of this region and oppression of Darfur's non-Arab population. The counterattacks by government forces and their militia allies, called Janjaweed, further escalated the conflict, resulting in huge human

---

[21] See: https://twitter.com/US4AfghanPeace/status/1089194662789869570 (accessed 15 February 2019).

[22] US Department of State, 'Sergeant Bowe Bergdahl', 31 May 2014, http://www.state.gov/secretary/remarks/2014/05/227013.htm.

[23] "Qatar's mediation helps free Fiji soldiers," *The Peninsula*, 12 September 2014, http://thepeninsulaqatar.com/news/qatar/299785/qatar-s-mediation-helps-free-fiji-soldiers.

casualties that range up to several hundred thousand dead from either war or starvation, disease, and mass displacements. In March 2005, the UN Security Council referred the situation in Darfur to the prosecutor of the International Criminal Court (ICC), which charged Omar al-Bashir, President of Sudan, with three counts of genocide in July 2010. The situation in Darfur led the neighboring countries, the Arab League, the African Union, and the United Nations to find ways to resolve the conflict. In 2008, Qatar undertook mediation by establishing contacts with the Sudanese government and Darfuri armed groups in concert with regional and international actors involved in the conflict.[24] This led in 2011 to the conclusion of the Doha Document for Peace in Darfur (DDPD), which is still the framework for the comprehensive peace process in Darfur. The DDPD addresses the root causes of the conflict and the key issues of the peace process, particularly power sharing and wealth sharing, as well as human rights, justice and reconciliation, permanent ceasefire, compensation and return, and internal dialogue.[25]

Qatar has been an active peace-broker in Yemen as well. In 2007, Qatar succeeded in negotiating first a ceasefire deal between the government and the Houthi rebels and then in 2008 a peace agreement, supported by a Qatari pledge to invest up to 500 million in aid for the development of Houthi areas. However, the conflict reerupted in 2009 due to Yemeni President Ali Abdullah Saleh's denouncement of the agreement. Qatar's diplomatic approach to Yemen was fairly limited and became complicated in 2011, when the revolutions began in Yemen during the period of the Arab Spring, because Qatar sided with the opposition and called on President Ali Abdullah Saleh to step down. Qatar even helped fund the revolution. In addition, Qatar's involvement in the military coalition in 2015 led by Saudi Arabia against the Houthis marked a major failure of its mediation.

Similarly, Qatar also has an extensive history of involvement in the Arab-Israeli conflict. For instance, Qatar hosted a regional conference of some Arab states, Iran, and Hamas, which urged all Arab states to cut ties with Israel following the Gaza War (December 27, 2008–January 18, 2009), which resulted in a humanitarian crisis, more than 1000 Palestinian deaths, and the deterioration of infrastructure and basic services in Gaza. In July 2014, the Qatari government mediated between Israel and Hamas to discuss a possible five-year ceasefire. Its mediation came from a US request following the failure of Egyptian mediation, because Qatar was the only actor that had good ties with Hamas and was able to facilitate communication. Qatar's role as a mediator had come onto the table in the ceasefire talks during the Israel-Gaza crisis in 2014. This was an asset for the conclusion of the ceasefire agreement. Furthermore, Qatar was very active in Palestinian dialogue, particularly between Hamas and Fatah. In Lebanon, Qatar succeeded in negotiating a 2018 agreement to end the political crisis between Shiite Hezbollah and the Sunni-led government and to build confidence among the country's multiple sectarian

[24]Kamrava (2011), p. 540.

[25]See, "Doha Document for Peace in Darfur" at: https://unamid.unmissions.org/sites/default/files/ddpd_english.pdf.

communities. By getting involved in Lebanon and Palestine, Qatar placed itself alongside larger countries with a history of negotiation in the region, such as Egypt and Saudi Arabia.

Qatar has repeatedly offered to broker peace in Africa and the Middle East region over the two past decades and proved its ability and efficiency to bring parties to the table for negotiations. Qatar's financial resource—the highest GDP (gross domestic product) per capita among rentier states—enables it to foster change, finance talks, and implement peace agreements. In other words, it relies on its "financial capacity when mediating conflicts by promising huge sums of money after a peaceful settlement to build up infrastructure and so on."[26] Nuruzzaman says that Qatari mediatory interventions in these conflicts were based on "...realities and the strategies of communication facilitation and manipulation. Like any other mediator, Qatari mediators have worked with their own mediation frameworks, they have attempted to manipulate the mediation outcomes by promising financial benefits. [...] In general, Qatari mediation strategies can be classified under two broad categories: (1) get to know all and act strategy; and (2) personalized diplomacy and intervention strategy."[27]

Qatari mediation has succeeded in reducing violence and hostilities with empirical observations of change in the behaviors of the disputants. It has taken the lead in many conflicts in signing peace agreements. As a typical small state with a lack of military power, Qatar used mediation as a tool for survival for ensuring its national security in a volatile region. This illustrates the potential of small states to project discourse power and challenge the traditional assumption of an automatic link between size and power. They only need to learn how to use to their advantage the important sources of strength that they have,[28] which is the method of exercising soft power. According to Joseph Nye, soft power is an "indirect way to get what you want... (and) set the agenda and attract others in world politics... This soft power – getting others to want the outcomes that you want – co-opts people rather than coerces them."[29]

Qatar has also managed to find an important diplomatic presence in international organizations. It assumed the chairmanship of the Organization of Islamic Cooperation in 2000 and was elected chair of the G77+China group at the UN in 2004. On 22 June 2011, Qatari Ambassador Nasser Abdulaziz Al-Nasser was elected President of the UN General Assembly during the 66th Session. Qatar was elected in most of the key UN committees and forums, including the Human Rights Council, the Commission on Sustainable Development, and the Economic and Social Council. It sat on the United Nations Security Council for a two-year term (2006–2007) as a nonpermanent member. Qatar invited former Iranian President Mahmoud Ahmadinejad to the 2007 GCC Doha summit.

[26]Antwi-Boateng (2013), p. 357.

[27]Nuruzzaman (2015), p. 8.

[28]Dorsey (2015), pp. 422–439.

[29]Nye Jr. (2004), p. 5.

Furthermore, Qatar hosted many important multilateral conferences, such as the World Trade Organization Doha Round in November 2001, which was aimed to achieve major reform in the international trading system through the introduction of lower trade barriers and revised trade rules regarding open agricultural and manufacturing markets and intellectual property rights protection. It also hosted the conference on the United Nations Convention on Climate Change from November 26 to December 8, 2012, with about 17,000 participants. These facts illustrate the influence that small states can make on the regional and international system through participation in international organizations. In general, small states tend to be big supporters of international organizations because they provide collective security and a reliable environment for the security challenges that they are facing. In other words, small states prefer to place negotiations and conflicts within a multilateral framework.

Qatar relies on public diplomacy as a tool for its foreign policy in order to build its regional and international profile, especially through media, culture, and sport. This type of diplomacy targets "resources in specific areas able to generate returns worth having."[30] In this regard, Qatar's most impressive diplomatic achievement has been the initiation of the Al Jazeera media network in 1996—a first in uncensored media in the Arab world. Since the creation of this world-class news, Al Jazeera competes with the BBC and CNN. It has become a voice of the people and an open platform and is still the Arab world's most widely watched regional news channel. It is used to highlight Qatar's mediation initiatives and to enhance the image of Qatar in the world and public opinion. Al Jazeera news channel—as a pillar of soft power strategy—is now increasingly seen as an organ of Qatari foreign policy.

In parallel, Qatar invests in cultural diplomacy, which is a type of public diplomacy and soft power that includes the exchange of ideas, information, art, and other aspects of culture among nations and their peoples in order to foster mutual understanding and to build broad support for economic and political goals. In this context, Qatar has invested billions of dollars to host campuses of prominent US universities such as Georgetown, Cornell, Texas A&M, Virginia Commonwealth, and Carnegie Mellon of Pittsburgh in Qatar. Qatar is also very active in the cultural field through its Cultural Village (KATARA) and the creation of a number of world-class museums. According to Eggeling, Qatar's cultural projects can be seen as part of Doha's insurance policy to make sure that the world knows about Qatar.[31] In the sports scene, Qatar invests massively in sporting projects by seeking and successfully hosting major sporting events on its territory, especially winning the bid to host the FIFA World Cup games in 2022, the first Middle Eastern country to host this event. But there is also its sponsorship of many European football clubs such FC Barcelona and Paris Saint-German. In addition, BelN, a global sports broadcasting network, provides Qatar with a large regional and international audience. Qatar has become a global sports hub through this soft power strategy.

[30]Ungerer (2007), p. 548.

[31]Eggeling (2017), p. 5.

15.5 Conclusion

The analysis of Qatar's military power and diplomacy brings to light a good number of important points. The main line of argumentation is that Qatar cannot ensure its security on its own due to its limited military power. It has to find political and military shelter with Turkey and the USA to maintain a regional balance with its Gulf neighbors, which is a major cause for concern for its security. In parallel with this strategy of sheltering, Qatar continues to expand and deepen its self-defense capacity and institutional military expertise. In a region of great geostrategic value and the site of numerous intrastate and interstate conflicts, the Qatari balancing act and the attitude of "pragmatism" with regard to other regional and global powers prove the ability of small states to meet their domestic interests and security challenges. In general, small states seek their security through self-defense and alliances, but they remain heavily dependent upon the shelter or hegemon.

In terms of diplomatic strength, the strategy of soft power allowed Qatar to virtually enlarge its presence abroad and spread a unifying national identity. This is evident in its policies and mechanism of mediation, multilateralism, and public diplomacy. In this regard, Qatari experience could be a rich source of knowledge and insights for small states that can also have diplomatic power and a number of resources to be deployed for diplomatic purposes. The Qatari experience demonstrates that international relations theory needs to adapt to the changing realities of the international system, which is increasingly influenced by the role of the small states. The traditional idea that small states are weak actors in the international system due to their lack of resources of power in terms of population, territory, economy, and military is now much contested. The Qatari case shows that small states have the potential to improve their importance and presence in the international relations by getting alternative power resources, such as military shelter, diplomatic engagements, mediation, public diplomacy, and an active role in international organizations. Contrary to the ideas defended by Sheila Harden in her edited book *Small Is Dangerous*,[32] the small states in the globalized world and contemporary international system are no longer outside the corridors of power.

References

Akpınar P (2015) Mediation as a foreign policy tool in the Arab Spring: Turkey, Qatar and Iran. J Balkan Near East Stud 17(3):253. https://doi.org/10.1080/19448953.2015.1063270

Antwi-Boateng O (2013) The rise of Qatar as a soft power and the challenges. Eur Sci J 9(31):357

Aras B, Akpınar P (2017) Turkish foreign policy and the Qatar Crisis. Istanbul Policy Center, Sabancı University, August, p 4

[32]Harden (1985).

Bailes AJK (2015) Small states and security: does size still matter. In: Baldersheim H, Keating M (eds) Small states in the modern world: vulnerabilities and opportunities. Edward Elgar Publishing, Inc., Cheltenham and Northampton, MA, p 23
Bailes AJK, Thayer BA, Thorhallsson B (2006) Alliance theory and alliance 'shelter': the complexities of small state alliance behaviour. Third World Thematics: TWQ J 1(1):14
Browning C (2006) Small, smart and salient? Rethinking identity in the small states literature. Camb Rev Int Aff 19(4):669
Cohen SA (1995) Small states and their armies: restructuring the Militia Framework of the Israeli Defense Force. J Strateg Stud 18(4):89
Cooper AF, Momani B (2011) Qatar and expanded contours of small state diplomacy. Int Spectator 46(3):117
Dorsey JM (2015) How Qatar is its own worst enemy. Int J Hist Sport 32(3):422–439
Eggeling KA (2017) Cultural diplomacy in Qatar: between 'virtual enlargement', national identity construction and elite legitimation. Int J Cult Policy:5. https://doi.org/10.1080/10286632.2017.1308505
Fox AB (1969) The small states in the international system, 1919–1969. Int J 24(4):751–752
Harden S (ed) (1985) Small is dangerous. Micro states in a macro world. Palgrave Macmillan, London
Kamrava M (2011) Mediation and Qatari foreign policy. Middle East J 65(4):540
Maass M (2009) The elusive definition of the small state. Int Polit 46(1):65
Nuruzzaman M (2015) Gulf Cooperation Council (GCC), Qatar and dispute mediations: a critical investigation. Contemp Arab Aff:8. https://doi.org/10.1080/17550912.2015.1078073
Nye JS Jr (2004) Soft power: the means to success in world politics. Public Affairs, New York, p 5
Ólafsson B (1998) Small states in the global system. Analysis and illustrations from the case of Iceland. Ashgate, Aldershot
Rothstein R (1968) Alliances and small powers. Columbia University Press, New York, p 29
Saidy B (2017) Qatari-US military relations: context, evolution and prospects. Contemp Arab Aff 10:286–299
Szalai M (2015) The inapplicability of traditional small state theory in Central Europe – the case of Hungary. Research Paper, International Visegrad, p 2
Ungerer C (2007) The 'middle power' concept in Australian foreign policy. J Polit Hist 53:548

Brahim Saidy is currently an Associate Professor of Diplomacy, Security and Defense Studies at Qatar University. Founder of the study plan of the master's degree in defense studies at the same university. Prior to this, he served as a Lecturer in International Relations in Canada. His research interests are in NATO, military strategy, civil-military relations, and GCC's defense cooperation. In 2010, he was a researcher in residence at the NATO Defence College in Rome. He has also been a visiting scholar at the Foreign Policy Research Institute (Philadelphia, USA) and the Korea Research Institute for Military Affairs (Seoul, South Korea). He is a visiting professor at Ahmed Bin Mohamed Military College and Joaan bin Jassim Joint Command and Staff College (Doha, Qatar). He is the founder of the study plan of the master's program in defense studies at Qatar University.